Sex
lives
of the FAMOUS GAYS

Sex lives
of the FAMOUS GAYS

Nigel Cawthorne

PRION

First published in Great Britain in 2005 by

Prion
an imprint of the
Carlton Publishing Group
20 Mortimer Street
London W1T 3JW

A catalogue record for this book is available from the British Library.

ISBN 1 85375 554 0

The publishers would like to thank the following sources for their
kind permission to reproduce the pictures in this book:

Corbis Images: Bettmann: 1, 2, 7 (top); /S.I.N. 7 (bottom)
Getty Images: American Stock: 4 (bottom); /Hulton Archive: 3
Topfoto.co.uk: 4 (top), 5, 6, 8

Every effort has been made to acknowledge correctly and contact
the source and/or copyright holder of each picture and Carlton
Books Limited apologises for any unintentional errors or omissions
that will be corrected in future editions of this book.

Typeset by e-type, Liverpool
Printed in Great Britain by Mackays

Contents

Golden Gays of Olden Days

According to the *Oxford English Dictionary* the word "homosexual" did not come into the English language until 1892. It arrived with the translation of *Psychopathia Sexualis* by the pioneering German neuropsychiatrist Richard von Krafft-Ebing, which was first published in Germany in 1886. It seems that the term was originally coined in 1869 by a Hungarian doctor. "Gay", by the way, only came to be used in the current sense in 1935, originally as American prison slang.

Of course, men did have sex with each other before the word homosexual came into use, but it was only in the late nineteenth century that people began to become defined – and define themselves – by their sexual identity. That, at least, is my excuse for excluding chapters on the famous gays from earlier eras. If that is what you are after, you will find chapters on the great sodomites – a term in use since the fourteenth century – such as Richard the Lionheart*, Edward II* and James I of England* (VI of Scotland) in *Sex Lives of the Kings and Queens of England*. Pope Leo X's* proclivities are discussed in *Sex Lives of the Popes*. America's famously gay president, James Buchanan*, appears in *Sex Lives of the US Presidents*, along with my speculation about the coyly discreet Martin Van Buren*. Gay artists Michelangelo*, Caravaggio*, Andy Warhol* and the painter Francis Bacon* are in *Sex Lives of the Great Artists*. Gay composers Tchaikovsky*, Camille Saint-Saëns* and Benjamin Britten* are in *Sex Lives of the Great Composers*. And thespians Rock Hudson*, Cary Grant* and James Dean* are in *Sex Lives of the Hollywood Idols*. There are no "out" gay men in *Sex Lives of the Great Dictators*, though Hitler's* possible gay experiences are discussed.

Of course, the golden age for gay men was back in Ancient Greece. Before they married, most young Greek men had gay lovers and after they wed it was common to keep a catamite. The Spartans thought that gay lovers banding together in their army built *esprit de corps* and the Theban army was famously led by the elite Sacred Band, which was exclusively gay. Both Achilles and Alexander the Great had boyfriends who fought alongside them, though you won't see that in the latest Hollywood blockbusters. Socrates was a lover of young boys and Plato's love was far from Platonic, but I am saving them all for *Sex Lives of Ancient Greece*. Meanwhile, the gay experiences of Julius Caesar* and Augustus*, along with the orgies of the emperor Elagabalus* are covered in *Sex Lives of the Roman Emperors*.

This book covers modern homosexual love, which begins essentially with Oscar Wilde and Bosie – who had such raving sex lives that they fill two chapters here. Since then there have been more famous gays than could possibly fit into one book, so watch out for *Sex Lives of the Famous Gays 2, 3, 4...* If you want me to write these sequels, or if you have any other ideas for new titles you would like in my *Sex Lives...* series, then email them to me via my website at www.nigelcawthorne.com.

Sex Lives of the Famous Gays contains a richly diverse collection of gay lives – from the noble and heroic, through the comically camp to the compellingly creepy. Its cast includes poets, playwrights, novelists, soldiers, dancers, film directors, actors, entertainers and models. Like the other books in the *Sex Lives...* series, *Sex Lives of the Famous Gays* contains a mixture of the erotic, the exotic, the pathetic, the excessive, the absurd, the crazy, the tragic and the downright comic. It aims to excite and amuse, while giving a genuine insight into the characters of people who have shaped our history and culture, and, hopefully, shedding some light on the human condition.

You will, by now, have noticed the annoying little asterisks that are dotted through the text above. This is part of a new feature that I trust we have now perfected in the *Sex Lives...* series. It is the "daisy chain". The asterisk indicates that the figure mentioned appears in another of the *Sex Lives...* books, or in another chapter of this book. At the back of this volume you will find the "Daisy

Chain" section which lists, in alphabetical order, all the people starred and giving all the other *Sex Lives...* books that they have appeared in. In the 1960s, Truman Capote* – who, sadly, does not appear here, but who may well turn up in *Sex Lives of the Famous Gays 2* – developed a game called "International Daisy Chain". The idea was to link any two prominent figures via an interlocking chain of lovers. The player who comes up with the least lovers wins (unlike in real life). This list is designed to help you play the game at home.

Chapter One

Wilde Oats

Oscar Wilde would not have called himself a homosexual or gay – a word often associated with female prostitution in nineteenth-century England. He would have called himself a uranist, which gave Wilde the delightful pun in the title of his most famous play, *The Importance of Being Earnest*. The word comes from a reference made by Plato in his *Symposiums* to the Greek goddess of love Aphrodite – also known as Urania. A uranian is another nineteenth century word for homosexual. Sadly, it also means an inhabitant of Uranus – though there is no evidence that Oscar was a science-fiction fan.

He was born Oscar Fingal O'Flahertie Wills Wilde in Dublin with rather too many names. On October 16, 1854, he slipped from his mother's womb; a thing he never wanted to look back on. His father, the doctor Sir William Wilde, was a womaniser and had several illegitimate children, some of whom took his surname. He had personal hygiene problems that would have repelled the fastidious Oscar. A popular conundrum in Dublin at the time was – Question: "Why are Sir William Wilde's nails black?" Answer: "Because he scratches himself." This did not go down too well with some of his prey. One woman, Miss Mary Josephine Travers, claimed that he gave her a whiff of chloroform so that he could have his way with her and she sued him for criminal assault. The trial was the sensation of the 1860s. Sir William lost, but Miss Travers was awarded just one farthing, the smallest coin of the realm. Her chastity, it seems, was deemed to be worth just over 0.1p.

Sir William's dirty and dishevelled appearance did not dampen the ardour of his wife, Lady Jane, who turned a blind eye to his other amorous exploits, and shared his passion for archaeology.

They went on many digs together and she gave him three children. Though Sir William was Orange as well as black, Lady Jane wrote republican poetry under the pseudonym "Speranza" – the Italian for hope. Coincidentally, the colour of hope in Italian is green. In Ireland it is the colour of republicanism. In England it is the colour of nausea and sexual jealousy. Lady Jane even had her children baptised as Catholics behind their father's back. When the priest told Sir William, he said that it did not matter "so long as they became as good as their mother".

Oscar was named after King Oscar I of Sweden, who had once been one of Sir William's patients. He had an older brother, Willie, named after … oh, never mind. It is said that, after having Willie, Lady Jane longed for a girl and when Oscar came along she insisted on dressing him in girl's clothing. He was four when his mother finally got her wish and gave birth to a daughter, but the respite did not last long. His younger sister Isola Francesca died when she was eight and a bizarre accident would have put the family off any further transvestism. Two of Oscar's half-sisters were burnt to death when one of them danced too close to an open fire in a long dress and the other came to her assistance. However, Oscar did wear his hair long, like a girl's, when he and Willie went to boarding school in Enniskillen. At school, he read a lot and avoided football, saying later: "I never like to kick or be kicked."

Nor was there any other physical outlet.

"No one appeared interest in sex," he said with evident disappointment. "We were healthy young barbarians and that was all."

But Oscar was anything but a barbarian.

"Knowledge came to me through pleasure," he said. "I was nearly 16 when the wonder and beauty of the old Greek life began to dawn upon me … I began to read Greek eagerly, and the more I read the more I was enthralled."

He already knew he was on dangerous ground. One winter night, when he was talking with friends about what they wanted to do when they grew up, Oscar said that he "would like nothing better in life than to be the hero of such a *cause célèbre* and to go down to posterity as the first defendant in such a case as *Regina* versus *Wilde*".

He was to get his wish.

Certainly Oscar was given some inkling of his true nature at that time. He later told the celebrated – or rather, self-celebrated – womaniser, Frank Harris, that he was "great friends" with a boy a year or so younger than himself. They used to talk interminably and take long walks together. The day Oscar left school, this boy came with him to the station to say goodbye. The Dublin train was about to depart, when the boy turned to him cried out: "Oh, Oscar."

"Before I knew what he was doing, he had caught my face in his hot hands and kissed me on the lips," Wilde told Harris. "The next moment he had slipped out of the door and was gone."

Oscar then became aware of "cold, sticky drops" trickling down his face ... no, they were the boy's *tears*. Oscar had had his first gay kiss.

"For a long while I sat, unable to think," he told Harris, "all shaken with wonder and remorse."

And no wonder. In the uptight Victorian era, uranists were universally condemned as "sodomites". God had punished them with fire and brimstone. In 1828 – within his parent's lifetime – the penalty for sodomy had been increased from imprisonment to death. Then it was reduced to penal servitude for life in 1861, when Oscar was seven. However, Oscar was already familiar with the idea of "Greek love", which is defined in his commonplace book to be "the romantic medium of impassioned friendship" between men and boys which took place in Ancient Greece. What's more, the young Oscar had an older man to straighten him out on the finer points. His name was John Pentland Mahaffy. A noted classics scholar at Trinity College Dublin, he was a close friend of the Archbishop. At the time, Mahaffy was writing a book called *Social Life in Greece* and he encouraged Oscar to lend a hand. Some literary detectives say that they can scent Oscar's youthful fumblings in this tome.

Social Life in Greece is said to be the first book to contain a frank discussion of "Greek love" – well, frank for the time. The book had to be prefaced with a sturdy condemnation of that sort of thing. Mahaffy calls Hellenic hanky-panky "that strange and to us revolting perversion, which reaches it climax in later times, actually centred upon beautiful boys all the romantic affections we naturally feel between opposite sexes, and opposite sexes alone".

Got that Oscar?

"These things are so repugnant and disgusting that all mention of them is usually omitted in treating of Greek culture," Mahaffy's book says. Nevertheless, he thought it worthwhile to examine the social context of the "peculiar delight and excitement felt by the Greeks in the society of handsome youths ... which gave to almost every feast the same sort of agreeable zest which young men of our own time feel in the company of young ladies, while such an entertainment as the modern ball would have appeared to the old Greeks profoundly immoral and shocking". This usually led to friendships of "purity and refinement", though there could be "strange and odious consequences".

Wasn't this love between two men unnatural? the Victorian reader would ask. Mahaffy had an answer for them: "As to the epithet *unnatural*, the Greeks would answer probably that all civilisation was unnatural."

Whether their collaboration on the book was pure and refined or strange and odious, or a bit of both, is not known, but when the book came out, its author warmly and publicly thanked one Oscar Wilde for his "improvements and corrections all through the book". Oscar later reciprocated, calling Mahaffy "my first and best teacher ... the scholar who showed me how to love Greek things". And, in 1877, they sampled the pleasures of Greece together, taking a holiday there that summer.

When Oscar went up to Oxford, "Greek" was seldom off his tongue and he wrote poetry to celebrated male lovers in Greek history. Soon he was practising what he preached. In October 1875, his friend John Bodley wrote in his diary that people were saying that "Wilde is a damned compromising acquaintance". He had a habit of leaving "foolish letters from people who were 'hungry' for him ... for his friends to read". While condemned by friends, Oscar implied that his parents approved of his antics.

"Come home with me," he asked a college friend. "My mother and I have formed a society for the suppression of virtue."

With the coining of the word "homosexual" on the Continent,

in intellectual circles, the sexual love between two men began to be thought of as a psychological problem that required the attention of a doctor, rather than a crime that belonged in the courts. Oscar picked up on this. He said that fellow Magdalen undergraduate Cresswell Augustus "Gussy" Cresswell "is charming though not educated well: however he is 'psychological' and" – again – "we have long chats and walks". Oscar uses another word "spooning" to describe another undergraduate's activities with a choirboy. According to the *OED*, by that time spooning already meant "to lie close together, to fit into each other, in the manner of spoons". Surely, that's forking?

Oscar fancied a bit of cutlery work with a chorister too. Around 1876, he wrote a poem called "Choir Boy" spelling out what he wanted to do in the stalls. It opens with a quote from Elizabeth Barrett Browning: "Ah God, it is a dreary thing to sit at home with unkissed lips." It then describes how he "went out into the night" and waited like Lilli Marlene* "under a lamp's light" for his intended to appear. Then the boy "with eyes of fire" turned up:

> And he looked on me with desire,
> And I know his name was Love ...
> O he is lovely, this boy of mine.

Oscar never published this poem. Which was lucky. Otherwise he would have spent rather longer in Reading Jail. Besides, Oscar was trying to go straight at the time. He was in correspondence with the poet John Addington Symonds, who had fallen in love with a choirboy called Alfred Brooke 15 years before when he was 22 years old. Symonds wrote that "the sort of love I felt from Alfred Brooke was wicked" and that "it was regarded with reprobation by modern society. At the same time I knew it to be constitutional, and felt it to be ineradicable. What I attempted to do in these circumstances was to stifle it so far as outward action went. I could not repress it internally any more than I could stop the recurrence of dreams in sleep or annihilate any native instinct for the beauty of the world."

But, after a little handholding and a few stolen kisses it all went badly wrong. So Symonds set about trying to "divert my passions from the burning channel in which they flowed for Alfred Brooke, and lead them gently to follow a normal course".

But Oscar began to believe that he could have both a burning channel and his normal course. After all, the Greeks did. Once they reached marriageable age, most Greek men in classical times gave up homosexual love and took a wife and a couple of mistresses and paid regular visits to the *hetaerae* – female prostitutes – though he might keep a catamite for special occasions.

Oscar also considered that what occurred between men was materially different from what you did with women. Sex with women involved full coitus. For Oscar at this time, sex with men rarely, if ever, involved penetration. He was not interested in fellatio or buggery – indeed, he was not interested in what has come to be known on cards in phone boxes as "Greek". For him, it was kissing, caressing and mutual masturbation. Pass the hanky.

John Addington Symonds eventually gave up the struggle and was dubbed "Mr Soddington Symonds" by the poet Algernon Swinburne*. In response, Oscar denounced Swinburne for posing as a sodomite and a pederast, when, in reality, he was no such thing. Get real, Algy.

Like a lot of public school pederasts, Oscar thought that he would go straight when the right woman came along. And he made an effort in this direction. In 1875, the mother of a young woman wrote to him, saying: "Dear Oscar, I was very much pained the last time I was at your house when I went into the drawing room and saw Fidelia sitting upon your knee. Young as she is, she ought to have had (and I told her) the instinctive delicacy that would have shrunk from it – but oh! Oscar, the thing was neither right, nor manly, nor gentlemanlike in you."

Oscar had gone further, however. The concerned mother's letter went on to reproach him for "kissing Fidelia ... out of sight as it were". Does she mean where the sun don't shine? "For instance ... you left me, a lady, to open the hall door for myself, you staying behind at the same time in the hall to kiss Fidelia. Did you think for a moment that I was so supremely stupid as not to know that you always kissed F. when you met her, if you had the opportunity." Phew, that's a relief.

However, Oscar was two-timing Fidelia. In October 1875,

another mother wrote to him saying that "dear Eva" would accept him if his proposal of marriage was "truly in earnest" – which seems a little ironic in hindsight. And, when visiting Dublin the following summer, he wrote to his friend Reginald "Kitten" Harding: "I am just going out to bring an exquisitely pretty girl to afternoon service at the Cathedral. She is just 17 with the most perfectly beautiful face I ever saw and not a sixpence of money. I will show you her photograph when I see you next."

This was Florence Balcombe. He made a pencil sketch of her and gave her a watercolour he had painted. Then, at Christmas, he gave her a small gold cross with their names inscribed on it. They were in love. There was talk of marriage and Oscar gave up panting after choirboys to write:

> She is too fair for any man
> To see or hold his heart's delight
> Fairer than any Queen or courtesan
> Or moonlit water in the night …

This time the poem was published. However, Florrie went on to meet and fall in love with Bram Stoker, then a young Irish civil servant, but later the author of *Dracula*. Wilde was devastated. Stoker was seven years his senior and it is said that Wilde only delayed his own proposal because he had been diagnosed with syphilis. He wrote more poems lamenting "unkissed kisses and songs never sung". Then he wrote and asked for his gold cross back, for "it serves as a memory of two sweet years – the sweetest of all the years of my youth – and I should like to have it always with me". And when Florrie made her debut on the London stage three years later, Oscar got Ellen Terry to give her a crown of flowers, pretending they were from her.

"I should like to think that she was wearing something of mine the first night she comes to the stage," he wrote, "that something of mine should touch her … She thinks I never loved her, thinks I forgot. My God, how could I!"

In the meantime, Oscar was having an affair with a portrait painter called Frank Miles, who he slept with while still at Oxford. Through Miles he met the sculptor Lord Ronald Gower, who introduced him to London society, the city's sexual underworld and the delights of "rough trade" with soldiers, sailors and labourers. Gower was the model for Lord Henry Wotton, the corrupting influence in *The Picture of Dorian Gray*.

The three of them went to visit Miles' father, the rector of Bingham in Nottinghamshire, where Oscar flirted with Frank's four sisters – "all very pretty indeed," he wrote. "My heart is torn in sunder with admiration for them all." Walking in the rectory's garden, Oscar remarked "only that there are no serpents or apples it would be quite paradise". And it was serpents and apples that Oscar was after. He wrote later: "Life's aim, if it has one, is simply to be always looking for temptations. There are not nearly enough of them. I sometimes pass a whole day without coming across a single one." But he seems to have found some in Nottinghamshire as he wrote of "dallying in the enchanted isle of Bingham Rectory, and eating the lotus flowers of Love".

Oscar and Frank then took off for a holiday in Ireland – hunting, shooting and f***ing. But there was one thing that Oscar did not like about Frank. He wore a moustache. Oscar preferred his boyfriends clean-shaven. Soon he turned up at Lord Ronald Gower's place in Windsor with the young artist Arthur May. "I have taken a great fancy to May," he wrote. There were many others.

In 1877, Oscar reviewed an exhibition at the Grosvenor Gallery that drooled over the images of beautiful young boys and the "bloom and vitality and the radiance of this adolescent beauty". It is stuffed full of references to Greek boys, St Sebastian and Ganymede – the beautiful shepherd boy kidnapped and anally raped by Zeus in the shape of an eagle. This put him in contact with the art critic Walter Pater, leader of the Aesthetic movement who advocated "art for art's sake" and who had already courted scandal through his relationship with the "Balliol Bugger" William Money Hardinge. It was said that Oscar's "intimacy" with Pater turned him into an "extreme aesthete". Pater preached the doctrine of squeezing every sensation out of life.

Asked what his ambition was, Oscar said: "Somehow or other I'll be famous, and if not famous, I'll be notorious."

Following that, Oscar now published some openly homoerotic poetry. One called "Wasted Day" reads:

A fair slim boy not made for this world's pain,
With hair of gold thick clustering round his ears ...
Pale cheeks whereon no kiss hath left its stain,
Red under-lip drawn in for fear of Love.

Oscar's confessor, Father Sebastian Bowden at Brompton Oratory, was disturbed by this development.

"You have, like everyone else, an evil nature," he wrote to Oscar in 1878, "and this in your case has become more corrupt by bad influences, mental and moral, and by positive sin."

Bowden urged Oscar to "find yourself a new man" in Catholicism, an injunction he was all too eager to follow and, when the time came for his next confession, he sent a bunch of lilies instead. Lilies had become the emblem of the Aesthetic movement.

When Oscar came down from Oxford, he set up home with Frank Miles in Salisbury Street, off the Strand. A young woman visiting for tea found "lots of 'intense' young men, such duffers, who amused us awfully. The room is a mass of white lilies, photos of Mrs Langtry, peacock-feather screens and coloured pots, pictures of various merit."

Lillie Langtry* came to tea one afternoon and Oscar was smitten. It was said that he was deeply in love with her and sent a single lily to her everyday. He said: "I would rather have discovered Mrs Langtry than have discovered America." He eulogised her beauty in his poem "The New Helen", sending her a copy inscribed: "To Helen, formerly of Troy, now of London." The passion was not reciprocated. Lillie found Oscar "rather ugly" and went on to become the mistress of the Prince of Wales.

Oscar reacted by growing his hair long and wearing outfits that were altogether more *outré*. It was said that he had walked down Piccadilly, dressed in a flowing velvet jacket and knee breeches, holding a single lily, but he was dismissive.

"Anyone could have done that," he said "The great and difficult thing was what I achieved – to make the whole world believe that I had done it."

Oscar greeted Sarah Bernhardt's* arrival in England by throwing armfuls of lilies at her feet. She came to dinner at Salisbury Street.

His publicity seeking did not go unnoticed. From 1880, *Punch* lampooned him as the limp-wristed poet Jellaby Postlethwaite. And this poem appeared about him:

> The haunt of the very aesthetic,
> Here comes the supremely intense,
> The long-haired and hyper-poetic,
> Whose sound is mistaken for sense.
>
> And many a maiden will mutter,
> When Oscar looms large on her sight,
> "He's quite too consummately utter,
> As well as too utterly quite."

The editor of *Punch*, Frank Burnand, also wrote a play called *The Colonel* with a character called Lambert Streyke clearly based on Oscar. He was already famous for being famous. When he actually did something and published a slim volume of poetry, simply called *Poems*, he got slammed. "The poet is Wilde, but his poetry's tame," said *Punch*. Even the Oxford Union refused his gift of a signed copy on the grounds that his poems were immoral. This was terrific publicity and *Poems* was reprinted five times in as many months.

But things at home were not going smoothly. Frank had syphilis and was being blackmailed over an affair with a young man. Then Frank's father, who had read Oscar's *Poems*, advised the two to separate as Oscar's poetry was "licentious and may do great harm to any soul that reads it". Frank agreed with his father and Oscar moved to rooms in Charles Street, Mayfair.

Then there was the young poet James Rennell Rodd, who accompanied him on a walking tour of France in 1880. Rennell dropped the Rodd for the occasion and styled himself Sir Smith. Oscar was Lord Robinson. There were lots of fervid kisses, as well as handholding in this "richly empassioned friendship" and, when they returned to London, they fancied they were in love.

Living up to her *nom de plume*, Oscar's mother still hoped he would marry. Oscar proposed to Charlotte Montefiore, the sister of a male friend at Oxford. She turned him down. He then met the beautiful 17-year-old Violet Hunt, daughter of the Pre-Raphaelite landscape painter Alfred Hunt. They met at a party in 1879.

"In ten minutes, I was the fashion, wrapt into sudden glory by the fact that Mr Oscar Wilde allowed me to monopolise him for a couple of hours," she said.

Ever the aesthete, he complimented her on her beauty.

"We will rule the world, you and I," he told her. "You with your looks and I with my wits."

He told her mother that Miss Hunt, if you'll excuse the expression, was the "sweetest Violet in England". Violet said that he was "really in love with me – for the moment and perhaps more than the moment". He proposed by sending "a single white Eucharist lily without a stalk, reposing on cotton wool in a box". This was ridiculed by Violet's younger sisters. The Hunts, though, were poor. There would be no marriage settlement and Violet "as nearly as possible escaped the honour of being Mrs Wilde".

In the summer of 1881, Oscar met 23-year-old Constance Mary Lloyd, the sister of another friend at Oxford. She was instantly dazzled and when he visited her he found her trembling with excitement – or fright. Like a lot of young women, she fell instantly in love with the charming young Oscar, who told his mother: "I am thinking of marrying that girl."

Oscar's courtship of Constance was not helped by Gilbert* and Sullivan, who satirised him in their comic opera *Patience* as the effeminate "fleshly poet" Bunthorne. But, Oscar was to gain from the notoriety this parody gave him. When the New York production received rave reviews, the producer Richard D'Oyly Carte and his business partner Colonel Morse arranged for Oscar to go to the United States. He dressed the part. The *New York World* reported: "He wore patent-leather shoes, a smoking-cap or turban, and his shirt might be termed ultra-Byronic, or perhaps *décolleté*. A sky-blue cravat of the sailor style hung well down upon his chest. His hair flowed over his shoulders in dark-brown waves, curling slightly upwards at the ends."

Not everyone was impressed. The captain of the *Arizona*, which took him across the Atlantic, said: "I wish I had that man lashed to the bowsprit on the windward side."

But Oscar was an immediate sensation. When he declared that the Atlantic was neither as big nor majestic as he expected, the newspaper headlines blared: "Mr Wilde disappointed by Atlantic." And his famous comment to the New York customs official – "I have nothing to declare but my genius" – was the talk of the town. Naturally he went to see *Patience* wearing velvet knee breeches and a silk cravat; an identical outfit to the one Bunthorne wore on stage. He revelled in the comparison.

"Caricature is the tribute which mediocrity pays to genius," he said.

His lectures were a sell-out. However, the newspapers were soon calling him "girlish". The *New York Times* commented on his "affected effeminacy" and called him a "mama's boy". His eyebrows, the *Newark Daily Advertiser* said, were "neat, delicate and arched, and of the sort coveted by women", while the *Boston Evening Transcript* confined its jibs to doggerel:

> She looks as much like a man
> As ever she can;
> He looks more like a woman
> Than any feminine human.

Friends from England joined in. John Bodley told the *New York Times* that Oscar was "epicene". Henry James called him an "unclean beast"; while James' friend, Mrs Henry Adams, said that his sex was "undecided".

When invited to a function Oscar was attending, people refused to meet "her" socially and it was widely said that he was a "Charlotte-Ann" – the then-current US slang for an effeminate sodomite.

The *New York Tribune* noted that his lectures were attended by "pallid and aesthetic young men in dress suits and banged hair" – only women wore their hair in bangs – "in medieval attitudes against the wall". The butch *Brooklyn Daily Eagle* predicted that on Fifth Avenue in Manhattan "the pallid and lank young man" – Oscar – would find "a school of gilded youths eager to embrace his peculiar tenets". The *Washington Post* swore that his male followers "painted their faces" and wore "rouge on their cheeks".

If anything, Oscar encouraged this speculation about his sexual preferences. When the socialite and politician Robert Barnwell Roosevelt sent him a note delivered by a handsome young man, Oscar wrote back indiscreetly: "What a little Ganymede you have sent me as your herald! The prettiest thing I have yet seen in America." And he was keen to meet Walt Whitman*, whose poems were openly homoerotic – or "Greek" as Oscar told the *Philadelphia Press*. The two men hit it off instantly. Whitman told a reporter: "One of the first things I said was that I should call him 'Oscar'. 'I like that so much,' he answered, laying his hand on my knee. He seemed to me like a great big, splendid boy." Whitman never concealed his liking for splendid boys. "He is so frank, and outspoken, and manly. I don't see why such mocking things are written of him."

According to the Philadelphia publisher Joseph Stoddart, who was there, things proceeded much further.

"After embracing, greeting each other as 'Oscar' and 'Walt', the two talked of nothing but pretty boys, of how insipid was the love of women," he said.

After downing a bottle of elderberry wine, Whitman suggested that they go upstairs where, he told Oscar, "we could be on 'thee and thou' terms." Afterwards, Oscar boasted to his friend George Ives, "I have the kiss of Walt Whitman still on my lips."

Stoddart was later to commission and publish Oscar's only novel, *The Picture of Dorian Gray*. For now, though, Oscar persuaded him to publish Rennell Rodd's first volume of poetry, adding the dedication "To Oscar Wilde – 'Heart's Brother'" and a lengthy introduction which says of Rodd: "There is none whose love of art is more flawless, none indeed who is dearer to me."

Rodd was appalled by this public declaration of love and tried to have the book stopped. It was too late. Copies got back to London and Rodd was mocked as 'the Hephaestion of that all-conquering Alexander" – Hephaestion being the gay lover of the youthful Alexander the Great. To save his career in the diplomatic service, Rodd broke off the affair with Oscar, who would describe him as "the true poet and the false friend".

In Chicago, Oscar visited the studio of the sculptor John Donoghue who produced rough-hewn bas-reliefs in the style of the Ancient Greeks. Oscar praised him as an "athlete" – of course, Greek athletes performed nude. Later he bought a bas-relief from Donoghue showing the nude figure of a boy playing a harp.

After ten months on the road, Oscar returned to New York in time to greet Lillie Langtry*, who had arrived for her Broadway debut, with a bunch of lilies. Oscar was heading back to London, but beforehand he was picked up on Fifth Avenue by a "thin-faced" young man, taken to a house and relieved of $1,200. Afterwards, Oscar went to the bank and stopped the cheque, then jumped on the *SS Bothnia* bound for England.

Back in London, the newspapers had reported the rumour that Oscar was engaged to the daughter of his millionaire backer Julia Ward Howe. Oscar denied this, but his mother wrote immediately: "Are you in love? Why don't you take a bride? Miss Howe was given to you by all the papers here."

The long-suffering Constance Lloyd was also concerned. She sent her uncle round to see Oscar's mother.

"I had nearly in mind to say I would like her for a daughter-in-law," Lady Jane told Oscar.

When Oscar arrived back in London, he did visit Constance, but immediately headed off for Paris, where he stayed for three months. He met the famous diarist Edmond Goncourt, who described him as an "individual of doubtful sex, with the language of a third-rate actor, full of tall stories". Hardly a ringing endorsement.

He had no better luck with the poet Robert Sherard, who was the great grandson of William Wordsworth. Though Oscar was immediately taken by his honey-blonde hair, Sherard was no uranist and had a taste for young female prostitutes. The writer, Pierre Louÿs, recalled a night with him that ended at dawn with a breakfast of bacon and oysters, accompanied by two 16-year-old prostitutes with "suppurating syphilitic sores the size of walnuts".

Sherard disliked the way Oscar kissed him on the lips and used his Christian name. Although they spent a great deal of time together, Sherard remained convinced that Oscar was straight. Even during Oscar's trial, he refused to believe the charges that were laid against him. And he had good reason. During his stay in

Paris, Oscar visited a demi-mondaine. Announcing one evening that "Priapus was calling", Oscar headed for the notorious Eden music hall where he met the cocotte Marie Aguétant, who achieved posthumous fame when her paramour slashed her throat as she rode him during sex. Telling Sherard of his indulgence with Aguétant, Oscar rued: "What animals we are, Robert."

The episode puzzled Sherard for an entirely different reason than it puzzles us. He was left wondering "how a well-fed, well-wined, full-blooded man as Oscar was at 29 could so control himself as to restrict his sexual contacts to once in 42 days."

In fact, this was not a unique event for Oscar. He had also visited female prostitutes in Oxford, London and in the United States. In Victorian times, gay men frequently went with prostitutes in the hope that they might "cure" themselves by instilling the habit of straight sex. It did not work. In fact, it usually made things worse. After one particularly unappetising encounter, he said: "It was like cold mutton."

When he returned to London, he had his long hair shorn. He now sported curls "in the style of Nero*". His friend Laura Troubridge said: "He is grown enormously fat, with a huge face and tight curls all over his head – not at all the aesthetic he used to look." She dismissed him as "vulgar" and said that he lolled about in "poetic attitudes with crumpled shirt cuffs turned back over his coat sleeves".

Wannabe poet Richard Le Gallienne said that his "unashamedly curled" hair looked like a wig. He was even more scathing about Oscar's new-found flab: "His large figure, with his big loose face, grossly jawed with thick, sensuous lips, and a certain fat effeminacy about him, suggested a sort of caricature Dionysius disguised as a rather heavy dandy of the Regency period."

Constance was not put off though. When they met, at his mother's salon, he was in sparkling form. Showing off his celebrated wit, Oscar described Switzerland as "that dreadful place, so vulgar with its ugly big mountains, all black and white, like an enormous photograph". That must have cracked everyone up. They met again at Lady Wilde's and, in a gathering of 60 people, Oscar spent his entire time in conversation with

Constance. She later revealed that they had not agreed on a single subject.

The courtship was interrupted again when Oscar went back to New York for the production of his play *Vera, or the Nihilists* – an everyday tale of love among Russian revolutionaries. It flopped, closing after a week. He sent a copy of the script to Constance, who criticised it for its lack of "morality".

Oscar headed for Dublin. Constance found she had some business there, too. With her cousins, she dropped a note at his hotel asking him to visit that evening. Three days later, they announced they were going to marry.

"I am engaged to Oscar Wilde and perfectly and insanely happy," the poor insane Constance wrote to her brother.

She was certainly in love with him and had turned down "three good proposals" since she had met him, much to the annoyance of her family. They were hardly overjoyed that Constance had finally got her man. Five days after hearing the news, they sent a note saying that they had "no objection to you personally as a husband for Constance". However, Speranza was delighted. It was a case of hope over experience.

For Oscar, marriage was a matter of hard cash. He had blown all the money he had earned in the United States while he was in Paris and was now deeply in debt. Constance brought with her £5,000 – enough for them to be able to set up home – and an income of £250 a year, rising to £800 a year on the death of her grandfather. Not a fortune, but enough to live comfortably on. Violet Hunt said spitefully: "I hear that Oscar's fiancée only has £400 a year instead of £800. I expect to hear of that engagement being broken off." Constance's family were also worried about the couple's financial prospects. Questioned by the family solicitor about his ability to pay off his debts, Oscar said that he could not promise "but I would write you a sonnet, if you think that would be of any help".

There is no doubt that Oscar was in love with Constance when they got engaged. Even Oscar's subsequent lover Lord Alfred Douglas – "Bosie" – admitted that. Oscar had often told him that the marriage was "purely a love match".

"I'm going to be married to a beautiful young girl called Constance Lloyd," he wrote to Lillie Langtry*. "A grave, violet-eyed little Artemis, with great coils of heavy brown hair which make her flower-like head droop like a flower, and wonderful ivory hands which draw music from the piano so sweet that the birds stop singing to listen to her." Now that's real *lurve*.

The choice of describing her as Artemis is telling. Artemis was the goddess of chastity and childbirth. The rest of the description is interesting, too. Wilde's biographer, Neil McKenna, said that it bore a remarkable similarity to his poem "Madonna Mia", which was a reworking of his homoerotic "Wasted Days" with the "fair slim boy" with "hair of gold" replaced by a "lily-girl" with "brown, soft hair". The rest is the same.

McKenna insists this reworking was done before Wilde met Constance. Had he fallen in love with the woman that inhabited his imagination, rather than the real Constance? And was that woman secretly a beautiful boy? Indeed, Constance was said to be boyish by some observers.

Some thought that Oscar was marrying in an attempt rid himself of his homosexual feelings, as John Addington Symonds had tried to do. Most gay men were advised to marry in those times. Even doctors and other so-called experts recommended it as a "cure". There is little evidence it did any good. In fact, Symonds found, to his disappointment, that "the tyranny of the male genital organs on his fancy increased". Oscar still corresponded with Symonds, so that might have increased the thrill. The other advantage was that, by marrying, he fancied he would no longer have to suffer the barbs of the press about his sexuality.

And he may even have been marrying for the sex. Having a wife would give him a ready outlet for his sexual energy. He disliked going to prostitutes and was constantly afraid of catching venereal diseases.

Between their engagement in November 1883 and their marriage in May 1884, Oscar and Constance hardly spent any time together. Oscar was constantly away on lecture tours and he certainly did not confide any of his sexual history to her. However, she knew that he had proposed to other women and forgave him.

"When I have you for my husband," she wrote, "I will hold you fast with the chains of love and devotion so that you shall never leave me, or love anyone else."

Fat chance.

Sometimes he let his mask slip. In an unguarded moment, he once said to Aimée Lowther, the 15-year-old daughter of a friend: "If only you were a boy, how I would adore you."

Before they married, Oscar paid a visit to the doctor. It is rumoured that he was checking to see that he had been completely cured of the syphilis he is said to have contracted from the prostitute in Oxford. It is also possible that he was seeking professional encouragement to go ahead with the marriage, while his interests remained so firmly in another direction.

Having got the medical all clear, the wedding went ahead at St James's Church, Paddington. Oscar stage-managed the whole thing and even designed the bridesmaid's dresses. The result was too stagy and showy. Robert Sherard wrote: "No woman who was not blindly convinced of the superiority of her bridegroom's taste would have consented to such a masquerade." He felt foreboding, saying: "Where a woman is entirely hypnotised and subjugated, her marriage is not often a happy one."

The couple honeymooned in Paris. The sex was good – as Oscar told Robert Sherard the morning after. Oscar was going into detail about his activities with his virgin bride, until an embarrassed Sherard shut him up.

"You mustn't talk about that to me," he said. "It is sacred."

Instead Oscar sent a huge bunch of flowers and a love note to the bride he had left only minutes before.

Oscar also wrote to a friend in the United States, saying that he had "not been disappointed in married life". The friend promptly sent the letter to the *New York Times*, while another gay friend, André Raffalovich, who later wrote a uranist manifesto, satirised Oscar's nuptials in his novel *A Willing Exile*. Oscar responded by calling Raffalovich, a former lover, "as ugly as a foetus in a bottle".

Oscar talked to others of his pride in deflowering his virgin bride. The problem was that she was no longer a virgin afterwards.

Constance seems to have enjoyed the experience too. She wrote to her brother telling him that she was very happy. She also mentioned that there was another person in Paris during their honeymoon – "the young sculptor Donoghue who I have seen several times, very handsome Roman face but with Irish blue eyes." And she remarked that Oscar was "out" a lot, no doubt delving into Greek matters with Donoghue.

Oscar left Constance to visit the bars and brothels with Robert Sherard. At the Château Rouge they spent time with "the saddest *filles de joie*".

While in Paris, Oscar read Joris-Karl Huysmans' *A Rebours – The Wrong Way* – which was the literary sensation of the time. It tells the story of a man who thinks he is straight but, after a series of ambiguous sexual encounters, ends up going with a male prostitute. To Oscar it was a revelation. Now he had found safety in marriage and sex with Constance, he realised that what he craved was danger. He wrote that married love was "more of a sedative than an aphrodisiac", but that did not prevent him performing his conjugal duties. Four months after the wedding, Constance was pregnant.

Oscar was delighted by the birth of his first son, Cyril, in July 1885 and his second, Vyvyan, in 1886. Constance embraced the duties of motherhood, but she might have been harbouring some doubts about her marriage. At a dinner party, at their new home in Tite Street, she caused a sensation by saying that she supported the idea of a trial marriage and that either party should be free to go off at the end of the first year. Oscar said that the marriage contract should last for seven years only, then it would be "renewed or not as either party saw fit".

As Oscar's fame grew, Constance found herself increasingly out of her depth, though she was still bedazzled. "How passionately I worship and adore you," she wrote. By this time Oscar said he was "fond" of Constance – well, "really very fond", which does not make it any better.

"There is one thing infinitely more pathetic than to have lost the woman one is in love with," he said, "and that is to have won her and found out how shallow she is."

With his legendary originality he also said: "She could not understand me and I was bored to death with married life."

It was not just Constance he was bored with, however, it was women generally, because they were "always on the side of morality, public and private" – though he also castigated women for being "prompted by sexual urge and devoid of what the bourgeois call morality". And he urged a male friend to "act dishonourably" by dumping a women he had eloped with – "it's what sooner or later she will do to you."

The whole business of pregnancy and childbirth repelled him because he could no longer kid himself that he was having sex with a virgin, or a boy.

"When I married, my wife was a beautiful girl, white and slim as a lily, with dancing eyes and rippling laughter like music," he told Frank Harris. "Within a year or so the flower-like grace had all vanished; she became heavy, shapeless, deformed. She dragged herself about the house in uncouth misery with drawn blotched face and hideous body, sick at heart because of our love. It was dreadful. I tried to be kind to her, forced myself to touch and kiss her, but she was sick always and – oh! I cannot recall it, it is all loathsome. I used to wash my mouth and open the window to cleanse my lips in the pure air."

Oscar hated ugliness and detested suffering. To him, pregnancy was a form of deformity. Harris asked Oscar if he did not feel any pity for Constance when she was pregnant.

"Pity!" cried Oscar. "Pity has nothing to do with love. How can one desire what is shapeless, deformed, ugly? Desire is killed by maternity. Passion buried in conception."

He was a straightforward gynophobe. And he was no better when it came to menstruation, saying that a husband must love his wife very much indeed "not to feel an inward sinking feeling when a few days after the wedding he finds his bride's middle parts tightly tied up in foul and bloody rags". You just could not beat a boy.

"There is no comparison between a boy and a girl," he told Harris. "Think of the enormous, fat hips which every sculptor has to tone down and make lighter, and the great udder breasts which the artist has to make small and round and firm." And when it came to sex: "A woman's passion is degrading. She is continually tempting you. She wants your desire as a satisfaction for her vanity more than anything else, and her vanity is insatiable if her desire is weak, and so she continually tempts you to excess, and then blames you for the physical satiety and disgust which she herself created." And women only stopped shagging when they had "glutted their lust".

So how's the marriage going, Oscar?

He expressed his feelings about women, in the bedroom department at least, in his poem "The Sphinx".

Get hence, you loathsome mystery! Hideous animal, get hence!
You wake in me each bestial sense, you make me what I would
  not be.
You make my creed a barren sham, you wake foul dreams of
  sensual life.

Secretly, Oscar began writing a homoerotic novel call *Teleny*. In it, a man struggled against his sexual attraction to the pianist René Teleny – being "musical" was code for being gay – by raping a chambermaid who had "the slender lithesomeness of a young boy, and might well have been taken for one, had it not been for the budding, round and firm breasts, that swelled under her dress". It did no good. He still fancied Teleny.

In the book, Wilde expressed his physical loathing of women in a scene where a man and a woman had just had sex:

Her thighs were bare, and the thick curly hair that covered her middle parts, as black as jet, was sprinkled over with pearly drops of milky dew … yet Teleny, leaning on his elbow, was gazing at her with all the loathsomeness we feel when we look at a kitchen table covered with offal of the meat, the hashed scraps, the dregs of the wines which have supplied the banquet that has just glutted us. He looked at her with the scorn which a man has for the woman who has just ministered to his pleasure, and who degraded herself and him.

Fortunately, Oscar was away from home a lot giving lectures about the aesthetic movement. Judging from his bulging postbag, these attracted a lot of young men who shared his tastes. He would respond by sending them a signed photograph, or by passing a few "golden hours" with them in his hotel when he was giving a talk in their home town.

Things got more intense when 20-year-old student, Harry Mariller, whom Oscar had known as a 15-year-old schoolboy and who was now a student at Cambridge, turned up in London. He agreed to "talk of poets and drink Keats' health" with him, but could only spare an hour before he caught a train. That hour, he said later, was "intensely psychological".

Afterwards Oscar wrote to Harry, praising his youth and begging to see him again.

"I find the earth as beautiful as the sky, and the body as beautiful as the soul," he said.

He also said that if he was born again he would like to be a flower – "no soul but perfectly beautiful". And as if to say "Come off it, Oscar" to himself, he pricks the bubble by adding: "Perhaps for my sins I shall be made a red geranium."

A week later, he wrote again, telling Harry "you have the power of making others love you". He asked for a photograph and asked after Charles Sayle, the author of a book of homoerotic poems called *Bertha: A Story of Love*, who had just been sent down for having an affair with another man. Two days later, Oscar wrote again. Then he went up to Cambridge to spend two or three days with him.

Plainly he had had a good time with Harry and when he returned to London he wrote: "Does it all seem a dream, Harry? Ah! What is not a dream? … I remember bright young faces, and grey misty quadrangles, Greek forms passing through Gothic cloisters." And he warned Harry about "playing with fire". Oscar himself rejected the idea of fidelity, saying: "How much more poetic it is to marry one and love many," and: "I wanted to eat of the fruit of all the trees in the garden of the world."

He started calling the love between two men *"l'amour de l'impossible"* – "the love of the impossible" and he rejected romance.

"Someday you will find, even as I have found, that there is no such thing as a romantic experience," he wrote in another letter to Harry. "There are romantic memories, and there is the desire of romance – that is all. Our most fiery moments of ecstasy are merely shadows of what somewhere else we have felt, or of what we long some day to feel."

For now, though, there was always the fiery moments of ecstasy.

He wrote Harry a "suitcase-full" of love letters and Harry invited him to spend a night or two with him at a house near Hampton

Court. Oscar replied, saying: "Let us live like Spartans, but let us talk like Athenians." It was all Greek again then.

Oscar invited Harry to Tite Street for lunch. Constance's suspicions were allayed because Oscar had already gone off Harry, fancying his friend Douglas Ainslie instead. The two of them then came to lunch at Tite Street. Later, Oscar invited Douglas to "drink yellow wine from green glasses in Keats' honour". He also fancied Ainslie's roommate at Oxford, Lord Osborne.

He continued having sex with Constance, but nothing could compare with the excitement of illicit sex with men.

"In mad and coloured love," he wrote, "there is much danger. There is the danger of losing them no less than the danger of keeping them."

Oscar was now supplementing his lectures by writing for the *Pall Mall Gazette*, whose campaigning editor, W.T. Stead, had caused a scandal with a series of articles called "The Maiden Tribute of Modern Babylon" about how easy it was for dirty old men to buy the sexual services of underaged girls. The Tory government reacted by passing "An Act to make further provisions for the Protection of Women and Girls, the suppression of brothels, and other purposes" in 1885.

Stead also sent evidence of widespread male prostitution in London and other big cities to maverick Liberal MP and editor of the weekly *Truth* Henry Labouchère. Oscar admired "Labby" as he was known, calling him "the best writer in Europe". Labby did not reciprocate. He called Oscar an "epicene youth" and "an effeminate phrasemaker ... lecturing to empty benches". Reviewing Oscar's lecture "Impressions of America", *Truth* pointed out that he had used the word "charming" 17 times, "beautiful" 26 times and "lovely" 43 times. Touché.

Although sodomy was against the law, sexual practices that stopped short of actual penetration were not. Indeed, to prove sodomy there had to be evidence of the "emission of seed" up the rectum. Armed with Stead's evidence on male prostitution, Labby lobbied to get the law tightened up and succeeded in getting an amendment added to the Protection of Women bill, which read:

"Any male person who, in public or private, commits, or is party to the commission of, or procures or attempts to procure the commission by any male person of, any act of gross indecency with another male person, shall be guilty of a misdemeanour, and being convicted thereof, shall be liable at the discretion of the court to be imprisoned for any term not exceeding two years, with or without hard labour."

This was the provision that Oscar Wilde would fall foul of ten years later.

Symonds – now seen as leader of the uranian movement – called the clause a blackmailer's charter. Terms like "gross indecency" and "procure" were undefined and there was no indication of what sort of evidence was required. Was one man claiming that another had propositioned him good enough? Labouchère was also unhappy with the bill. He thought that the punishment should be a lot longer than two years' hard labour.

While the bill was going through parliament, Oscar had been picked up in a public lavatory by 17-year-old Robbie Ross, who he said had "the face of Puck and the heart of an angel".

Robbie liked anal sex and he liked it both ways. He offered himself as the passive partner to older men like Oscar, while taking the active part with younger men or boys, particularly if they were from the working classes. He was also dangerously "out" – having told his mother and his older brothers of his proclivities. Oscar, who was never avowedly gay, was fascinated.

Their intense romance turned into a lasting friendship, with both regularly taking other partners. In fact, Robbie made a speciality of bedding the literary men of the day.

Robbie was a regular visitor to the Moorish smoking room in Tite Street. Constance found him charming. In 1887, when Robbie's mother was on holiday on the Continent, he came to stay as a paying guest. He and Oscar were up long into the night while Constance was asleep or away.

Oscar had now given up lecturing for writing. He became editor of the *Lady's World*, which he promptly retitled *Woman's World*, and published the poem "*Un Amant de Nos Jours*" – "A Lover of Our Time" – which seemed to rue his marriage to Constance. By that time, they had stopped having sex altogether. It is said that this was because the syphilis he had caught in Oxford had recurred. They did not even sleep together and, when they were invited to stay at a country house, Oscar insisted on separate bedrooms. Constance found this no great sacrifice as she did not want any more children, though she became depressed because he showed no interest in her and was out all the time. Even when he was in he was surrounded by adoring young men. And "*Un Amant de Nos Jours*" made it clear that Oscar's real interests now lay with innocent young boys.

Poetry was the means of communication for late-Victorian uranians and Oscar considered himself, first and foremost, a poet. He went to bed with several other poets, including Richard Le Gallienne, who sent him his privately printed *My Ladies' Sonnets* after seeing Oscar lecture when he was 17. He later wrote a poem which he called a "love token ... in secret memory of a summer day in June '88". It includes the lines. "With Oscar Wilde, a summer day/Passed like a yearning kiss away." While Oscar gave him a copy of his *Poems* inscribed: "To Richard Le Gallienne, poet and lover ..." Their affair was short-lived, however, and Le Gallienne later married. Another poet he had bedded was Robbie's friend Arthur Clifton; there had also been Rennell Rodd.

Oscar went to Oxford to see the unveiling of his old friend Lord Ronald Gower's statue of Shakespeare. He wrote to Robbie that the band had "played God Save the Queen in my honour". He gathered around him an "admiring cohort" of young men who he had sex with once or twice before moving on. He called them "the exquisite Aeolian harps in the breeze of my matchless talk". And he introduced them to Constance, who surely must have known what was going one by this time.

His taste now turned to actors and dancers. He wrote a flirtatious letters to 26-year-old Henry Dixey, who he had seen dancing in a musical called *Adonis*. He sent a tie to the actor Roland Atwood, with a note saying that it would make him look "Greek".

Other lovers were culled from those who sent fan letters to him. Aubrey Richardson was told that he had a pretty name and was invited to tea. So was 23-year-old aspiring poet Graham Hill. W. Graham Robertson, reputed to be one of the handsomest men in London, was invited to illustrate some of Oscar's fairy stories. He boasted of their affair later.

When the good-looking young American art historian Bernard

Berenson turned up at Tite Street, Oscar invited him to stay, but, though he flirted, he would not succumb, prompting Oscar to tell him that he was "completely without feeling; you are made of stone".

Robbie Ross introduced Oscar to the Crown in Charing Cross, described by the writer Rupert Croft-Cooke as a "queer pub ... used by those who wanted to find a young sailor or an out-of-work stable boy", while Max Beerbohm called it "a literary tavern full of young nameless poets and cocottes and old men who have been ministers of the Church of England and are not longer". It was there that Oscar met Fred Althaus. A lowly City clerk, he was not the sort of person Oscar could take home to Constance. They spent two nights together in Barnes.

Once the affair had been consummated, Oscar's interest flagged. Fred bombarded him with letters and telegrams, begging Oscar to spend a weekend with him in Eastbourne. He even threatened to turn up at Tite Street. This led Oscar to put a brutal end to the affair.

Oscar then astonished the literary world with *The Portrait of Mr WH*, which fleshed out the theory that Shakespeare had an affair with the Elizabethan boy actor, Willie Hughes. Although many feared that the story would harm his reputation, it impressed 23-year-old American playwright Clyde Fitch, who was described as having "many of the more charming qualities that we used to called feminine, without being effeminate".

Clyde told Oscar that he was a genius – "and, oh, such a sweet one. Never was a genius so sweet so adorable ... And I – wee I – am allowed to loose the latchet of your shoe ... Am bidden tie it up – and I do, in a lover's knot."

While Oscar loved compliant young male lovers, he found this cloying. Fortunately, Robbie sent him a "honey-coloured and charming" boyfriend from Cambridge called Frederic Wisden who he claimed was the reincarnation of Willie Hughes. Then Oscar gave Clyde the slip by going to the Continent, where he met up with an old lover in Ostend. Clyde returned to New York heartbroken. With him he took a copy of Oscar's *The Happy Prince and Other Tales*, inscribed in the flyleaf: "Clyde Fitch from his friend Oscar Wilde. Faëry-Stories for one who lives in Faëry-

Land." Fairy was already New York slang for an effeminate gay man.

Oscar began to spend much of his time in the house of two like-minded souls, Charles Shannon and Charles de Sousy Ricketts – who he christened "Marigold" and "Orchild" – in The Vale off Kings Road. Max Beerbohm called them "the ladies of the Vale". However, it was a welcome change from Tite Street. However, it was the handsome young poet John Gray that Oscar truly fell for. He worshiped his beauty and fell deeply in love with him. He plied him with compliments and expensive gifts and, after several months, Gray succumbed.

Gray was a self-made man who had been sent to work as a metal-turner in Woolwich arsenal when he was 13. He taught himself German, French, Latin and mathematics. He got a job in the Civil Service, rose quickly through the ranks and at the age of 22 was appointed to the Foreign Office. It is clear that a number of important men must have taken an interest along the way. Determined on a literary career, Oscar was the next rung up the ladder for Gray. He stuck with him for three years, then moved on to André Raffalovich, who was considerably richer. By that time, Oscar had immortalised him in *The Picture of Dorian Gray*. The Dorians, of course, were an Ancient Greek tribe and Dorian was Oscar's pet name for John Gray. Gray even signed his letters to Oscar "Dorian".

Oscar's one and only novel, *The Picture of Dorian Gray* is positively throbbing with homosexual innuendo and many fellow uranists felt he had gone too far. The reviewers thought so, too. It was called "poisonous", "unmanly, sicking, vicious", "heavy with the mephitic odours of moral and spiritual putrefaction", "a tale spawned from the literature of the French Décadents" and "a gloating study of the mental and physical corruption of a fresh, fair and golden youth". They were hardly notices that you would want to put on the cover of the paperback. The homosexual undertones were not lost on the Press either. Dorian was compared to Ganymede, but, like all bad publicity, it didn't half help sales.

Soon after the publication of *Dorian Gray*, Oscar was invited to join the Crabbet Park Club, an exclusive literary club run by a cousin of Lord Alfred Douglas. On their summer outing to Crabbet Park, Oscar was seen to play tennis like "a great wobbly blancmange trying to serve underhand". Afterwards, George

Curzon, the future viceroy of India, rounded on him for his "reputation of sodomy and for the treatment of the subject in *Dorian Gray*". Oscar's only response was to smile helplessly, but when Curzon had finished, Oscar made a spirited defence of pederasty.

This was a courageous thing do as the Cleveland Street Scandal was just breaking. In 1889, the police raided a homosexual brothel at 19 Cleveland Street. When the owners of the brothel were arrested, they dropped the names of their aristocratic clients. These included Lord Arthur Somerset, the Earl of Euston and Prince Eddy*, the oldest son of Bertie, Prince of Wales* and grandson of Queen Victoria*. The names of these highborn gentlemen were kept out of the subsequent trial, which éarned the lowborn brothel keepers nine months' hard labour. However, Ernest Parke, the crusading editor of the *North London Press*, published the names of Somerset and Euston.

Somerset fled to France, where he stayed until his death in 1926, but Euston sued Parke for libel. He claimed that he had been given a flier advertising "*poses plastiques*" – that is, nude girls posing as classical Greek statues – at 19 Cleveland Street. Naturally, when he went there and discovered what was really going on, he was appalled and fled, he said.

That was not what one of the young boys, called John Saul, who worked at the brothel, claimed. He said that Lord Euston had picked him up on the street and had taken him back to Cleveland Street for sex. Euston was "not an actual sodomite," however. "He likes to play with you and then 'spend' on your belly," said Saul.

The judge dismissed Saul was a "loathsome object". He later wrote *Recollections of a Mary-Ann* – the British equivalent of a Charlotte-Ann. Parke went down for a year with hard labour. Lord Euston was fully rehabilitated and was appointed aide-de-camp to Edward VII at his coronation in 1901.

Even so, in 1889, the public – and Henry Labouchère – were baying for the blood of "sodomites"; at the same time, *Dorian Gray* had made Oscar the standard bearer for uranian love. A young lover of Walter Pater called Lionel Johnson wrote a poem in Latin "in honour of Dorian and his creator". In it, he offers Oscar the "apples of Sodom". Naturally, Oscar was keen to meet the young man and caught him one Saturday morning half-asleep in bed. Johnson found Wilde "delightful" and wrote to a friend after that first meeting saying: "I am in love with him."

Although Johnson was a 23-year-old undergraduate, Oscar said that he looked "more like the head boy of a preparatory school". He gloried in Johnson's child-like looks and, when Johnson needed a cab, Oscar joked about him going out and "hailing the first perambulator".

Chapter Two

Enter Bosie

There was a distinct pecking order in Wilde's circle of gay friends. While John Gray was still the "official beloved", Lionel Johnson entered as "new boy". But Johnson was anything but new when it came to gay love. One of his lovers at Oxford was an old school-friend, Lord Alfred Douglas.

Douglas was the son of the ninth Marquis of Queensberry, though everyone knew him as Bosie. This arose because his doting mother was from the West Country and had called her little boy "boysie". He was three years younger than Johnson, who had dedicated a daringly homoerotic poet with clear references to anal penetration to him. In the spring of 1891, Johnson lent his copy of *Dorian Gray* to Bosie, who said that it had a terrific "intoxicating" effect on him. He claimed to have read it 14 times running and was eager to meet the author.

In June, Johnson brought Bosie to tea at Tite Street. Oscar was immediately captivated by the 20-year-old's golden hair, blue eyes, peaches-and-cream complexion and slim and elegant figure. Bosie was a typical product of the public school system. He had first been involved in a sex scandal at his prep school at the age of 11. Sent to another school, he became "passionately fond" of another boy there. Then he went to Winchester, where he reckoned that "at least 90 per cent" of boys were having sex.

"The practice of Greek love is so general that it is only those who are physically unattractive that are reduced to living without it," he said.

A school-friend recalled having sex with him: "He was usually the ascendant and I the pathic, although positions were sometimes reversed."

"Pathic" means being the passive partner, a term now only used in medicine. Many tangled love affairs followed. Although most public schoolboys gave up same-sex love when they left school and started having sex with women, Bosie went to Magdalen, which, thanks to Oscar, had become the centre of the fashionable cult of boy-love. He became its undisputed leader, considering himself a pagan of the Greek school for whom sex is no sin at all and the sex between two men is, not just equal to sex between men and women, but actually a higher form of love.

This was also Oscar's philosophy. He admired Bosie's youthful poetry, took a snobbish delight in his title and was spellbound by his beauty, which even crusty old George Bernard Shaw said inspired "passionate admiration in men and women indiscriminately" – though he could not make up his mind whether this was a blessing or a curse. In contrast, Oscar was, by this time, an elephantine figure with bad teeth, a large pasty face and red cheeks who "never stopped smoking opium-tainted Egyptian cigarettes".

Oscar was instantly infatuated and introduced Bosie to his wife. But Oscar was not his type. With the exception of Lionel Johnson, who looked like a schoolboy, Bosie had never been to bed with anyone older than himself. He went for "youth and beauty and softness" – Oscar had only the softness. Nevertheless, Bosie was flattered by the attention of such a distinguished figure and consented to have lunch with him three days later. Presents and overtures began right away.

Undaunted by Bosie's refusal to have sex with him, Oscar bombarded the young man with letters, telegrams and invitations. He even wrote a sonnet to him and gave it to him one night in a restaurant. But while Bosie continued to resist, Oscar was captivated by his conversion. Bosie talked of nothing but boys and buggery. He lived dangerously, picking up working-class boys and male prostitutes while slumming it in pubs and music halls. Oscar was fascinated.

The seduction had to be put on hold while Oscar made a trip to Paris where he wrote, in French, his play *Salomé*. In his hands, the biblical story became a rich condemnation of female and heterosexual lust. Only the homosexual characters were pure. Oscar would have been familiar with that word now. Bosie said that

Oscar had read Richard von Krafft-Ebing's *Psychopathia Sexualis*, in preparation for *Salomé*. In Paris, where homosexuality was legal under the Napoleonic Code, Oscar could be "out" and he spent time with young men who would become the Gallic gay glitterati – André Gide*, Pierre Louÿs and Marcel Schwob. What they got up to, no one knows. The tortured soul, André Gide, who had a *marriage blanc* – a sexless marriage – with his cousin Madeleine Rondeaux, tore out the pages of his journal that covered the three weeks he and Oscar had spent together and destroyed them.

In Paris, homosexual men had taken to wearing green cravats. Green was the colour favoured by effeminate men in classical Rome. However, in 1891, a new fashion had started in Paris. Committed uranists began to sport, as a badge of honour, green carnations in their buttonholes.

A few minutes before the curtain rose at the St James's Theatre for the premiere of *Lady Windermere's Fan* in February 1892, a dozen young men, some in make-up, took to their seats in the stalls wearing green carnations. Another young man wore one on stage. Oscar had supplied them. He had a flower shop in the Royal Arcade dye white ones. At the end of the play, Oscar took a curtain call wearing a metallic blue carnation.

If this display of arrogance was not shocking enough, Oscar had a lighted cigarette between his daintily gloved fingers! At that time gentlemen never smoked in the presence of ladies. Oscar was puffing in two senses of the word, and "puff" was just coming into slang used for an effeminate man. The cartoonists had a field day.

Poor Constance had to sit through all of this. She had been escorted to the premiere by Oscar's former lover Arthur Clifton. The play mocked her mercilessly and, at the first night, Oscar ignored her. He shared his box with Bosie. Constance went home alone, while Oscar entertained his friends in the Albermarle Hotel. Then he took 17-year-old publisher's clerk Edward Shelley to his suite, undressed him and took him to bed.

Shelley later claimed to have been traumatised when Oscar had first seduced him a few days before. He had plied him with whisky and soda, and champagne. When Oscar – a writer he greatly admired – kissed him, he fainted. He was in a stupor as Oscar touched his private parts and awoke in his bed. He returned to

Oscar's bed several times – because he was "weak", he said – and was seen out with him in restaurants and at the theatre. However, it was widely rumoured that he had already been having sex with his employer John Lane, who was Oscar's publisher, and dressed in clothes he could ill-afford on a clerk's wage. Shelley also had sex with Bosie and John Gray. At work, however, he was taunted as "Miss Oscar" and "Mrs Wilde" and, in a fit of jealousy, Lane sacked him. By this time, Oscar had also dropped him. As a comfort in his new-found poverty, he turned to religion and bombarded Oscar with letters, which he tore up. Later, Oscar was to regret how he used to pick a boy up, love him "passionately" and then cast him aside when he grew bored. He was, he admitted, "utterly reckless with young lives" – and was to be so to the end of his days.

Green carnations were to make another public appearance two weeks later at the opening of John Gray's translation of Théodore de Banville's play *The Kiss*. While the *Lady's Pictorial* condemned them as "unmanly", the *Artist and Journal of Home Culture* taught readers how to make their own.

By this time, John Gray was on the verge of suicide – not because of Shelley, who was no threat, but because Bosie had now become the "official beloved". Up at Oxford, Bosie had become the victim of blackmail. He turned to Oscar as the only person he knew who could handle the situation. Oscar had been blackmailed on numerous occasions, usually by the male prostitutes who held a particular fascination for him. He admired their "infamous war against life" and told Robert Cliburn, who had blackmailed the Earl of Euston, that he deserved the Victoria Cross. One of his favourite bedmates was Fred Atkins, a female impersonator, male prostitute and professional blackmailer who had been interviewed in Rochester Row police station about his activities.

Oscar got lawyer George Lewis and private detective Edwin Levy to handle Bosie's blackmailer and stumped up £100 in a full and final payment. Whatever Bosie was being blackmailed over was so shocking that it lost Oscar Lewis's friendship and Levy urged Oscar to have nothing more to do with Douglas.

But Bosie was grateful to his rescuer – and showed it. In June 1892, Constance was away and he let Oscar take him back to Tite Street after a night on the town.

"After about two hours' discussion, he induced me to stay the night in the spare bedroom," Bosie told Frank Harris. "In the end he succeeded in doing what he had wanted to do ever since the first moment he saw me." And he was explicit. "Wilde treated me as an older boy treats a younger one at school ... what was new to me and was not (as far as I know) known or practised among my contemporaries: he 'sucked' me."

It was well known that Oscar liked sucking cocks. It gave him "inspiration", he said. He would pay delivery boys to let him suck them off.

"Love is a sacrament that should be taken kneeling," he said on numerous occasions.

The Marquis of Queensberry was right on the button when he later accused Oscar of being a "cock-sucker".

Bosie denied being sodomised by Oscar. However, we already know that he preferred being the "ascendant," rather than the "pathic".

Two months after being bedded by Oscar, Bosie wrote his poem "Two Loves" which contains the line. "I am the love that dare not speak its name." And he readily admitted that that he "adored" Oscar and "was crazy about him". It was reciprocal. For Oscar, Bosie was an ideal and having him was the culmination of a lifelong quest. Bosie told his mother, Sybil Queensberry, that no one could ever love him as "faithfully, loyally, devotedly, unselfishly and purely as Oscar loves me". It was a "perfect love, more spiritual than sensual, a truly Platonic love, the love of an artist for a beautiful mind and a beautiful body".

And this was true love, not just sex. They both continued having sex with other people, procuring each other new lovers, sharing lovers, swapping lovers. It was "spiritual fidelity" they were after, they said.

In July, Oscar told Constance that he was going to take the cure at Bad Homburg, a fashionable spa town near Frankfurt. Bosie was there visiting his grandfather, who was also rumoured to have uranist tendencies. And he wanted to make a gesture of leaving the country after the Lord Chamberlain – who then censored plays – refused him a licence for *Salomé*, on the grounds that it was "half Biblical, half pornographic". He announced that he was going to take French citizenship. Max Beerbohm saw through this, pointing out that Oscar would first have to serve in the French army – and could not really see any possibility of that.

Returning to England, Oscar took the family on a holiday, renting a farm in Norfolk. While there he began work on *A Woman of No Importance*, another comedy replete with homoerotic subplots. He soon craved a sexual outlet. He telegrammed Shelley, inviting him to stay, but he had his hands full with John Gray. Then Bosie turned up for a three-week stay.

Back in London, Bosie introduced Oscar and Constance to his mother at her house in Cadogan Square. Although slightly alarmed by the relationship between Oscar and Bosie, Lady Queensberry tried to solicit Oscar's help, getting him to take on the role of surrogate father as she had divorced Bosie's real father, a drunken womaniser, five years before.

Oscar was happy to take Bosie under his wing and the two of them took a short holiday in Bournemouth. Lunching in the Café Royal on their return, Oscar spotted Lord Queensberry. Bosie invited him to their table, where Oscar proceeded to charm him. They continued their conversation long after Bosie had left, and both got the impression that the other was not as bad as had been made out.

In Oxford, Bosie took over the magazine *Spirit Lamp* and it took a distinctly uranian turn. He even published a poem that described the joys of oral sex – in a suitably veiled Victorian way, of course. The magazine announced that it was for those who were interested in the "new culture". Culture here was another code word. The "new culture", the "new individualism" and the "new Hellenism" became political rallying cries for the uranists. There was even a "democratic" tendency in the uranist movement for those who wanted sex with working men. For Oscar is was just "rough trade".

George Ives set up a vanguard for the movement called the Order of Chaeronea, after the battle where the Theban Sacred Band of gay warriors were slaughtered in 338 BC. Oscar was an early recruit. Ives wanted to take Oscar's "Love is a sacrament that should be taken kneeling" as the order's motto, but the outfit was not to Oscar's taste. Ives wanted it to be a serious organisation, not a pick-up place for men. Besides, Ives had a moustache and Oscar loathed facial hair.

Oscar and Constance passed the winter of 1892 in Torquay. Robbie Ross came down for a few days to relieve the monotony. Bosie sent letters and love poems. In January 1893, Oscar left Constance in Torquay and scuttled back to London where he had a new friend, Alfred Taylor. Taylor had, in full drag, gone through a marriage service with 25-year-old male prostitute Charles Mason, as his husband. With his colleague Maurice Schwabe, Taylor ran a lively trade, procuring boys for other men. The first one they supplied to Oscar was Edward Harrington, but Oscar found him rather too butch. The next one was the slim and feminine Sidney Mavor, who was known as Jenny. Taylor took him to meet Oscar in Kettner's restaurant. Oscar took him back to the Albemarle Hotel. The next morning an expensive silver cigarette case was delivered to Mavor's parent's house. Oscar gave out scores of cigarette cases. Bosie's was solid gold.

Then Taylor and Schwabe picked up 16-year-old cockney crook Fred Atkins. They took him to meet Bosie and Oscar at a restaurant in Rupert Street where "Mr Wilde kissed the waiter", as Atkins later testified. Oscar did not have Fred that night – one of the others had first go – but, over lunch the next day, Oscar invited him to go to Paris with him as his "secretary". In a discreet hotel in the Boulevard de Capucines, they took adjoining rooms. That night, Oscar gave Fred the money to go to the Moulin Rouge but warned him to stay away from the women there, who were "the ruin of young fellows". When he got back to the hotel, Oscar asked if he could "perform certain operations with the mouth". When Schwabe arrived the next morning, he found them in bed together. Fred got his cigarette case two days later. Back in London, they had sex at Tite Street. Oscar also visited the rooming house where Fred Atkin's lived with his partner in the blackmail business and they had anal sex there. The housekeeper noticed that "sheets were stained in a peculiar way". The judge at Oscar's trial said primly that he did "not wish to enlarge upon this most unpleasant part of this most unpleasant case".

Oscar received a telegram from Bosie, who had been having sex with an unemployed clerk called Alfred Wood. Bosie begged

Oscar to "share love's burden" with him and meet Wood at the Café Royal. Oscar liked what he saw – a blonde 17-year-old who was obviously willing. He took him off for supper in a private room where, Wood said; Oscar "put his hand inside my trousers beneath the table and compelled me to do the same". They went back to Tite Street. Oscar put his "person" between Wood's thighs and thrust it back and forth until he came. Then he gave Wood £2. The same touching scene was replayed every night for the next week, but Wood began putting the price up and demanded expensive gifts, so Oscar high-tailed it back to Constance in Torquay.

When Oscar returned to London, Wood began doing the rounds with him, Bosie and Schwabe. He even visited Bosie in Oxford, where they had sex in the Mitre Hotel. During the trip, Wood stole a handful of compromising letters from a morocco box Oscar had thoughtfully provided Bosie.

Bosie then visited Oscar, who had returned to Torquay. There was a scene. Bosie flounced out and Oscar determined never to see him again, but after a tearful telegram they were reconciled. At Bosie's request, Oscar took adjoining rooms for them at the Savoy, but wrote to him begging not to make any more scenes – "I'd rather be rented by the day," he said.

Oscar and Bosie ran up a huge bill at the Savoy, dining on the best food and wine with a succession of rough trade, calling the boys that sucked their cocks "gourmets". On March 10, Oscar dined in a private room at Kettner's with Alfred Taylor, who brought with him two teenage brothers he had been sleeping with called William and Charles Parker. Oscar immediately took a fancy to the younger one, Charles, and fed him morsels with his own fork. He even fed him preserved cherries from his own mouth. Oscar was not one for preserving cherries, though. Mouths were another matter.

Charles was whisked back to the Savoy, where he and Oscar stripped off completely.

"I was asked by Wilde to imagine that I was a woman and that he was my lover," said Parker. "I had to keep up this illusion. I used to sit on his knees and he used to play with my privates as a man might amuse himself with a girl."

Oscar also sucked Charles' cock, but Charles refused to be a gourmet, even though Oscar suggested it several times. He asked the boy to toss him off and had anal sex with him. Then Oscar gave him £2. Charles returned the following week when he was given a cigarette case, a cheap one. He considered this no different from a girl taking a present from a man who liked her. There is no doubt that the Savoy knew what was going on. Chambermaids and other hotel staff saw young "rough-looking" boys in Mr Wilde's bed – some as young as 14 – though he always had an innocent explanation. However, the sheets and his nightshirt were stained with Vaseline, semen and human excrement. Oscar's defence counsel later claimed he had had diarrhoea. I hope he tipped well – and not just the pageboys who got a whacking half-a-crown a time and, usually, a kiss.

Alfred Wood, Edward Shelley and others – at least five – were given the same Savoy treatment, with similar consequences for the linen. From the description of the staining, it is clear that Oscar liked to be the pathic as well as the ascendant – just as he liked to suck and be sucked – which was stretching the current bounds of pederasty. One can only pity the laundry staff.

Charles Parker also visited Oscar when he had moved back to the Albermarle Hotel, where both Oscar and Bosie had him. And it seems that Bosie was slipping though the adjoining door to join in the action at the Savoy, too. In fact, Oscar later told Frank Harris that it was really Bosie who was the bad boy at the Savoy.

"I was never bold enough," he said.

Indeed, Bosie wanted to come clean and take the rap for some of the sodomy. But there was no doubt that Oscar was also going at it.

"I was not in prison an innocent man," he said.

Constance turned up at the Savoy, on the pretext of bringing the post, and begged him to come home, to see the children at least. Oscar said he could not. It had been so long since he had been in Tite Street he had forgotten the number of the house. It was plain that the bed had been slept in by more than one person. And Pierre Louÿs, who was visiting, noticed that there were tears in her eyes.

There was nothing secret about what Oscar was up to. His behaviour was the talk of literary Paris. Henri de Régnier told

Edmond de Goncourt: "He admits to being a pederast. He told me that he has been married three times: once to a woman and twice to men."

Following the success of his play in London, he left his wife and three children and moved into a hotel where he lived "conjugally with a young British lord".

The succession of rent boys and the soaring laundry bill finally forced Oscar and Bosie to leave the Savoy where they were now unwelcome. Lord Queensberry heard rumours that Constance was going to divorce Oscar on the grounds of sodomy and questioned Bosie about them. And both Bosie and Oscar were being blackmailed by Alfred Wood over the letters he had stolen. Wood was now involved with a couple of professional blackmailers, William Allen and Robert Cliburn, who Oscar admired so much. Oscar paid for a ticket for Wood to go to the United States, but the blackmail was not over. Cliburn delivered a copy of a love letter from Oscar to Bosie to Herbert Beerbohm Tree, the actor-manager who was putting on *A Woman of No Importance*. Oscar decided on a bold strategy. The letter was wrapped up in the classical illusions, so he had Pierre Louÿs translate it into French and Bosie published it in *Spirit Lamp* as a prose poem. When Allen turned up demanding money, Oscar laughed at him – Allen could hardly blackmail him over something that had already been published. Cliburn returned the original and Oscar gave him half a sovereign. It is thought that Oscar and Cliburn later became lovers and he certainly watched as Cliburn and George Ives had sex.

Even this new attempt at blackmail failed to make Oscar more discreet. Frank Harris saw him in the Café Royal with two rent boys, talking about how Greek athletes in the Olympic Games performed naked. Oscar loved sex with rough trade, as it was "all body and no soul". Ugly stories circulated about him. He was considered dangerously out of control and other uranists began to give him a wide berth. Even the New York newspapers were printing vague rumours about Oscar's sex life.

He was, however, committed to the cause. He had a limited edition of his homoerotic novel *Teleny* published anonymously, by the pornographer Leonard Smithers. Friends backed away, but Oscar did not care. He went to Paris with Bosie, actor Harry Barford and Oxford undergraduate Trelawny Backhouse. Everyone was sleeping with everyone else. Oscar was also having his fill of rough trade. And at the Hotel Bristol, he underwent a mock marriage "with a catamite in female attire from the gutter and the results of their union were concrete and visible on the drapery of the nuptial couch". Too much detail there, I think.

When they returned to England, Bosie went back to Oxford. Oscar visited every weekend and their sodomitical activities were satirised in a student magazine. In Oxford, Bosie and Oscar shared 16-year-old Walter Grainger. Oscar, he said, unbuttoned his trousers and played with his private parts. He later had intercrural sex with him, satisfying himself between Grainger's thighs. Oscar told Grainger that he would be in "very serious trouble" if he told anyone about it.

Bosie quit Oxford and he and Oscar set up home together in a house called, appropriately enough, the Cottage, in Goring, which was big enough to have Constance and the boys to stay. Walter Grainger was employed as assistant butler. He was given a room next to Oscar's. Each night Oscar would have intercrural sex with him.

Although Oscar continued to warn Grainger not to tell anyone, it was an impossible secret to keep. The head butler caught Grainger naked in Oscar's room and gossip circulated among the servants.

Oscar and Bosie took to stripping off in the gardens. One day the vicar came around and caught them naked. "You have come just in time to enjoy a perfectly Greek scene," he was told. Embarrassed, the vicar fled. What Constance and the boys made of these scenes when they visited, one cannot begin to imagine. Constance could not bear to spend more than a short time there and would leave the boys in the care of the nanny, Gertrude Simmonds, who was soon privy to the secrets of the Cottage.

A group of undergraduates from Oxford came to stay. Bosie got upset when Oscar flirted rather too ardently with one of them and flounced out, leaving an offensive letter. Four days later he telegrammed, begging to be allowed to return. Meanwhile, he was having an affair with Robbie Ross. They shared lovers and spent time together at Bosie's mother's house in Cadogan Place.

In Oscar's next play *An Ideal Husband*, the husband in question makes several references to his "shame" – a code word Bosie introduced in his homoerotic poem "In Praise of Shame". The protagonist, Sir Robert Chiltern, was said to have been based on the then foreign secretary Lord Rosebery. Rosebery certainly embraced his own. A man with a large, thickset penis, he was said to be an expert in the art of anal intercourse. When the Marquis of Queensberry discovered that Rosebery had sodomised his son, Bosie's elder brother Viscount Drumlanrig, he set out for Bad Homburg, where Rosebery was at the time, and was only prevented from beating him up – no mean threat from the Marquis of Queensberry – by the personal intervention of the Prince of Wales, who was also taking the waters in Bad Homburg.

The domestic idyll of the Cottage could not last. Oscar had already proved that he was not the marrying kind and Bosie was always throwing tantrums. There were frequent trips to London for rough trade – what Oscar called "feasting with panthers". His new friend Aubrey Beardsley said he boasted of "having five love affairs and resultant copulations with telegraph and district messenger boys in one night". Oscar had told him: "I kissed them each one of them in every part of their bodies. They were all dirty and appealed to me for just that reason."

Beardsley – who, despite his appearance, was straight – was appalled when Oscar then proceeded to describe in mouth-watering detail the delights of rimming.

Robbie Ross was sleeping with a schoolboy called Claude Dansey, who was supposed to be back in school the following day. When Bosie heard about it, he promptly went round, stole Dansey off Ross and slept with the boy himself. The following day he passed him on to Oscar, and then the next night Bosie paid for him to have sex with a female prostitute. Dansey arrived back at school three days late. The school authorities then kept a close watch on his correspondence and quickly found out who the culprits were. The boy's father was only dissuaded from going to the police when George Lewis told him that his son would almost certainly go down for six months as well.

Terrified that this might not be the end of the matter, Robbie went to Switzerland. At Oscar's urging, Bosie also left the country.

He went to Egypt where he could indulge himself to his heart's content with Arab boys, while Oscar kept his head down in Paris. But Oscar could not stay long. He was needed back in London to work on *An Ideal Husband*, but precious little got done. There was a constant stream of young male visitors to the rooms he had taken at 10 St James's Place. Meanwhile, Bosie was cruising the Nile with a party of louche expats, including Robert Hichens, who was later to write the *roman à clef, The Green Carnation*.

Bosie boasted that he had had a "romantic meeting" with Lord Kitchener in Cairo and was eventually flung out of Egypt for his behaviour. He headed for Athens, where he began to fear that Oscar was falling out of love with him. He contacted both his mother and Constance, begging them to get Oscar to make contact. When Oscar telegrammed him in Athens saying that he would not write to him or see him for many months, Bosie threatened suicide. Oscar relented and agreed to meet him in Paris. There was a passionate reunion and they returned to London together.

A few days after they returned, they were having lunch again in the Café Royal when the Marquis of Queensberry turned up and joined them. Everything was perfectly cordial, but soon after, Queensberry was standing by a window in Carter's Hotel, when a hansom cab drew up. Oscar and Bosie were in it and Queensberry watched as Oscar "caressed" his son in "an effeminate and indecent fashion".

Queensberry wrote to his son saying he would cut him off without a penny if he did not break with Oscar. He wrote to Oscar in a similar vein. Bosie impetuously answered his father with a telegram that said simply: "What a funny little man you are." A solicitor's letter followed declining any further financial support from his father.

Enraged, Queensberry threatened him with a thrashing for his impertinence and to make a public scandal if he caught him with Oscar again. To add insult to injury, Lord Rosebery had just been made prime minister. Worse still, Queensberry had doubts about his own sexual prowess. He had recently married a young woman who, after a disastrous wedding night, asked for an annulment on the grounds of "impotence" and "malformation of the parts of generation". Meanwhile Bosie set off in search of "beauty" – code for sex with young men – in Florence, a city known for its tolerance of such thing. Soon after, Oscar and André Gide joined him.

Back in London, Oscar was packing for a weekend in the country with another young man when Queensberry turned up at Tite Street, threatened him and accused him of "posing as a sodomite". Oscar's response was that he could charge him with criminal libel for the accusations he was making and asked him to leave. He told his manservant that, if the Marquis of Queensberry ever came to the door again, he should call the police.

Despite the bravura performance, Oscar knew that he was in deep do-do – though judging by the sheets in the Savoy and the Hotel Bristol, he may not have minded that. During the altercation, Queensberry mentioned Oscar's flight from the Savoy and Wood's blackmail attempt over the love letter Oscar had written to his son. It is quite possible he had learnt about these things from George Lewis, who had acted for him in his dispute with Rosebery and in the matter of his annulment.

Bosie urged Oscar to sue for criminal libel, but the rest of his family urged caution. His older brother, Viscount Drumlanrig, was now a junior minister in Rosebery's administration. Any scandal would damage his career and, given his relationship with the prime minister, possibly bring down the government, but something had to be done. Queensberry was bandying the word "sodomy" about and, if that got to the ears of Scotland Yard, the consequences could be very severe indeed. So, on July 11, 1894, Oscar sent a solicitor's letter asking the Marquis to retract his accusations and make an apology. Queensberry refused.

By this time, Queenberry was stalking the Café Royal and other haunts in the hope of catching Oscar with Bosie and making a public scene. As Queensberry was returning Bosie's letters unopened, Bosie goaded him further with a postcard, saying that Oscar had the power to put him in prison. He also said he was carrying a gun and would be happy to shoot his father if the situation came to that. Indeed he did carry a loaded revolver. It went off one afternoon in the Berkeley, smashing a window. Fortunately, no one was hurt.

Queensberry responded by writing to Oscar's solicitors, telling them that, if Bosie did not stop carrying a gun, or stop making a show of himself in public places with Oscar, he would go to the police. Meanwhile, he set about investigating what had gone on at the Savoy. In the face of Queensberry's onslaught, Oscar and Bosie found themselves more deeply in love than ever. They wrote passionate letters to each other and fancied themselves as martyrs, persecuted for their superior love, which they continued to indulge promiscuously with others, including underage boys. And they sought protection in the occult, which was fashionable at that time. Many uranians believed that anal intercourse was, somehow, magical.

While Bosie had refused any financial help from his father, Oscar found himself strapped for cash. That summer he, Constance and the boys holidayed in Worthing, where prices were rock bottom due to an outbreak of typhoid the previous season. Constance did not want Bosie to visit and Oscar begged him not to. He came anyway, on one occasion with a rent boy. Together Oscar and Bosie picked up local boys. Oscar jerked 15-year-old Alfonso Conway off on the road to Lancing and the Borough Council noted that "indecent bathing" was going on in front of the house that Oscar was renting, with naked men disporting themselves on the beach. There was nudity in the house as well, with Oscar undressing Conway and taking him to bed. He also took Conway on a trip to Brighton, when they checked into a hotel. This time "he used his mouth", Conway said, and he received an engraved cigarette case from Oscar in the morning.

Meanwhile, Constance was conducting a passionate affair – by letter at least – with one of Oscar's editors, Arthur Humphrey. Though they probably did not do anything physical, their correspondence reads like a Victorian version of txt sex. Back in London, a number of prominent uranians – including Alfred Taylor and Charles Parker – were arrested at a club in Fitzroy Street, where some of the other denizens were in full drag. The net was tightening.

Earlier that year, Bosie had introduced Robert Hichens who, in September, published, anonymously, *The Green Carnation*. This was clearly based on the love affair between Oscar and Bosie and, by the end of the year, it had gone through four editions. The book confirmed everyone's worst suspicions. It even portrays Bosie as lusting after a nine-year-old boy – indeed, Bosie had expressed a desire for Oscar's nine-year-old son, Cyril. The book was read for libel by George Lewis. Aware of the danger, Oscar made plans to leave the country at a moment's notice.

Bosie persuaded Oscar to take him to Brighton to stay in the Hotel Metropole, which Oscar could scarcely afford. When Oscar came down with the flu, Bosie abandoned him. There was a series of terrible fights. Oscar determined to end his relationship with Bosie and even planned to get George Lewis to send a letter conveying that fact to Queensberry. To pay his bills, Oscar secured an advance on *The Importance of Being Earnest*, which he dashed off for much-needed cash. It is chockfull of uranian references. The device used by the two young protagonists to escape female company is called "Bunburying". Quite.

The publication of *The Green Carnation* had rattled the Marquis of Queensberry's cage again. Not only did it make it clear what was going on between his younger son and Oscar – and people were soon asking what he proposed to do about it – it also painted a vicious portrait of him, even relating word-for-word Bosie's "What a funny little man you are" telegram.

In October, Viscount Drumlanrig put a shotgun in his mouth, pulled the trigger and killed himself. Drumlanrig had been planning to marry to save Rosebery from scandal, but Queensberry had evidence – in the form of soiled sheets – that the affair between his son and the prime minister was still active. To save Rosebery, Drumlanrig could see only one way out. Of course, his suicide, though recorded as "accidental death", only led to more speculation.

Drumlanrig's death drove Oscar and Bosie back together again. It also removed any restraint on Queensberry – who now had the dirt on a number of leading Liberals – as he could no longer damage his older son. Meanwhile, Bosie published two explicit poems in the new and even more daring uranian magazine *Chameleon*. A copy soon fell into Queensberry's hands. Already mad with grief, he determined to bring down what he saw as the "house of sodomy" by attacking its principal architect – Oscar.

At the beginning of 1895, Oscar had two hit plays running in the West End. He entertained his upper-class uranian friends lavishly in the best restaurants, while entertaining himself with lower-class rent boys back at the Albemarle Hotel. Then Oscar and Bosie took a holiday in Algiers, where they indulged themselves with hashish and 13-year-old Arab boys, who "fluted on our reeds for us". In Bilda, they met André Gide who, with the help of Oscar and a young boy called Mohammed, finally fully embraced his uranism. After a row with Bosie, Oscar headed back to London, leaving Bosie and Gide to enjoy ever-younger Arab boys. Bosie fell in love with one young boy called Ali, but was devastated when his beloved had sex with a female prostitute. Bosie lamented to Gide: "Boys, yes boys, as much as he likes. But I will not stand for him going with women."

On his return to London, Oscar moved into the Avondale Hotel in Piccadilly, as he had an outstanding bill at the Albermarle – indeed his bill at the Savoy also remained unsettled. He also discovered he had gonorrhoea. In the days before penicillin this had to be treated with a sickening mixture of heavy metals and peppers, all washed down with turpentine. Strong doses of opium were needed to dull the pain of the treatment. Nevertheless, Oscar managed to find the energy for a fling with a 19-year-old undergraduate called Tom.

The Marquis of Queensberry intended to disrupt the opening night of *The Importance of Being Earnest* by standing up in the stalls, denouncing Oscar as a sodomite then pelting the stage, and possibly Oscar himself, with rotting vegetables. Oscar got wind of it, however. Queensberry's ticket was returned with a refund. When he turned up at the theatre he was turned away by a cordon of 20 policemen, though he was allowed to leave his bouquet of over-ripe turnips at the box office.

When Bosie turned up the Avondale Hotel and heard about this, he ranted about putting his father in prison. Then he made things worse by bringing the roughest rent boys he could find back to the hotel. When Oscar begged him not to, he denounced Oscar for being a moral coward by being worried about what people might think.

After a couple of weeks, Oscar finally dared to show his face at the Albermarle. The hall porter handed him a card that had been left six days before by Queensberry. It was in an unsealed envelope addressed in Queensberry's hand: "For Oscar Wilde ponce and somdomite (sic)" – or do I mean (sick). Oscar now felt he had no alternative but to sue. He could not even flee. He did not have the money.

Oscar informed Robbie Ross, then he went to see Constance to tell her to brace herself. As George Lewis had been retained by Queensberry, Oscar, Bosie and Robbie went to see another solicitor, Charles Humphreys, but neglected to tell him that Queensberry's allegations were by-and-large true. Not only that, but when Humphreys asked him to swear that there was no truth to the libel, Oscar assured him that the accusation was a lie.

Then Humphreys enquired about money. Oscar admitted that he could not afford to mount an action, but Bosie promptly stepped forward saying that his family – that is, his mother – would pay. They then went to Marlborough Street police court to swear out a warrant for Queensberry's arrest.

When Queensberry was arrested and charged, Bosie sent a press release to the newspapers. Everyone then gathered at the police court. Bosie beamed to see his father squirming in the dock. He claimed not to have called Oscar a "ponce and a sodomite", but had accused him of "posing as a sodomite" – words that he had used before in the row at Tite Street. Bail was set at £1,500 and Queensberry smiled as he left court. Robbie and Bosie were happy too, certain that Oscar was going to win. Queensberry had admitted addressing the envelope and leaving it for Oscar. There was no doubt that what he had written was libellous and, under the Libel Act of 1843, Queensberry faced two years in jail and a heavy fine.

To escape jail, Queensberry would have to prove that Oscar had done what he had accused him of. Robbie and Bosie did not believe that he could come up with enough evidence to justify the enormity of the libel. However, Oscar saw something in court that disturbed him. George Lewis was defending Queensberry and he knew rather too much about those damaging blackmails. Embarrassed by his position, Lewis told Queensberry he would no longer act for him, but by telling Queensberry about the blackmail the damage had already been done.

Queensberry was cock-a-hoop. He told the press that he had

sent the card to bring things to a head – and that Oscar had walked into his trap. Max Beerbohm and others ruefully agreed. Oscar's foreboding only increased when Queensberry took Edward Carson as his barrister, a childhood friend of Oscar's who had been up at Oxford with him.

Although Queensberry already had a copy of the love letter Wood had tried to blackmail Oscar with, Carson did not think that his case was strong enough, so Queensberry hired a private investigator and two ex-Scotland Yard detectives. Together with Queensberry's new solicitor, Charles Russell, and vengeful actor Charles Brookfield, who had once been snubbed by Oscar for wearing the wrong type of suit, they scoured the West End for evidence. It has to be said that these men would now be considered committed homophobes who believed that sodomy was a disease and that its carrier was Oscar.

The name of Alfred Taylor soon came up in their investigation. In their effort to track him down, they found that he had skipped from his lodgings, owing his landlady money. She had found a box full of papers. It contained compromising letters and cheques which indicated that Taylor was pimping young men to Oscar and others. When the boys concerned were found, they were told that they faced prosecution unless they made incriminating statements about Mr Wilde.

Detectives interviewed the staff at the Savoy, the Albemarle Hotel, St James's Place, Goring, Worthing and other places that Oscar had stayed. Queensberry was a wealthy man and informants were paid handsomely. The defence team soon had statements from Edward Shelley, Walter Grainger, Alfred Wood, Charles Parker and Alfonso Conway.

Oscar had no idea how thorough these investigations had been. He tried to bluff it out by taking Constance and Bosie out to dinner and appearing with them in a box to watch *The Importance of Being Earnest*. This was a public statement that, if his wife saw nothing wrong with Wilde's friendship with Lord Alfred Douglas, how could anyone else condemn it?

He turned up for the committal proceedings at Marlborough Street Police Court on March 9, 1895 with Bosie in a coach with a liveried coachman and a footman wearing a cockade. Dressed in a blue velvet overcoat with a huge buttonhole, Oscar quipped: "Have no fear. The working classes are with me, to a boy."

The hearing caused even more of a sensation because it had to be adjourned. Evidence to be presented included letters that mentioned the names of "exalted persons" – perhaps the prime minister, Lord Rosebery – and the prosecution did not want them read out in open court. More rumours that Rosebery might be mixed up in the case leaked from the Grand Jury.

By this time Bosie had got wind of the kind of evidence his father had been amassing. Nevertheless, after the hearing, he beguiled Oscar into taking him to Monte Carlo, at the very time he should have been working on the case with his lawyers. In Monaco, they were asked to leave their hotel after other guests complained.

Back in London, Oscar's barrister, Sir Edward Clarke, said he would only take the case if Oscar swore on his honour "as an English gentleman" that Queensberry's accusations were groundless. Oscar was happy to do this, although, of course, he was Irish. Meanwhile, he had to borrow heavily to pay his legal expenses.

A fortune-teller assured him that victory would be his but, at the Café Royal, Frank Harris – who had been following Queensberry's investigation – and George Bernard Shaw urged him to drop the suit and to go abroad. Oscar repudiated them, saying that they were no friends of his.

The love between Oscar and Bosie had always thrived in adversity and Bosie urged him on. Uranians were iniquitously persecuted and it was his duty to stand up for all men of their sexual persuasion.

Three days before the trial started, Queensberry filed a "Plea of Justification". It cited *The Picture of Dorian Gray* as a book that encouraged "sodomitical" practices, along with an issue of *Chameleon*, which Oscar had contributed to as well. Oscar had already seen off the critics and felt confident that he could defend his art in a courtroom. What he was not expecting in the Plea, however, were the names of nine of his lovers – including Maurice Schwabe, Sidney Mavor, Fred Atkins and Herbert Tankard, a pageboy from the Savoy – plus a list of others not named, along with times, dates, places and details of the "indecent liberties" that had taken place. The libel suit now seemed certain to be lost.

By now, he was facing the horrible truth: Queensberry was not just alleging "gross indecency" under the Labouchère amendment to the 1885 Act. He was accusing Oscar of attempted sodomy in every single case. If just one count of it were proved, Oscar would go to jail, possibly for life. Even Oscar's palm readers told him that fate was now about to deal him a terrible blow. All he could do was keep on lying.

Although immaculately dressed, he wore no buttonhole on the day of trial. He still turned up with Bosie in the carriage he had hired for the early hearing, even stopping on the way at shop in St James's to buy "a gayer tie". When they arrived at the Old Bailey, the courtroom was full and someone made a remark about "The Importance of Being Early".

Sir Edward Clarke outlined the case against Queensberry – how the peer had hounded Oscar over his relationship with Bosie, which was entirely innocent. Lord Alfred Douglas had frequently dined with Mrs Wilde at Tite Street. Oscar had visited Lady Queensberry in Cadogan Square. He had even dined with the Marquis of Queensberry on two occasions in the Café Royal to try to mend the "strained feelings" between father and son. His literary work was easily defended. Oscar was a loving husband and a good father. And, of course, Sir Edward would not trouble the jury with a blow-by-blow repost to those monstrous sexual allegations.

Oscar then took the stand and discharged himself well under Sir Edward's questioning. The jury seemed to warm to him. Then Edward Carson rose. First, he asked Oscar how old he was. Oscar replied: "Thirty-nine." Carson flourished a copy of Oscar's birth certificate. He was 41. He had lied under oath.

He was asked that, if he lied about that, would he not lie about bigger things? If he posed as being younger than he was, might he not also pose as a sodomite? He was then asked if he had read any of Bosie's more explicit poems. Did he approve of them? What about the other things that appeared in *Chameleon*? Was he happy to associate himself with them or did he disavow them? These questions put him in an impossible position.

Questioned about *The Picture of Dorian Gray*, he was forced to concede that it could be read as a work about sodomy. Had he ever adored a younger man, as Dorian had? He was forced to admit that there was one man he loved, but it was a sacred love, in no way base or sordid.

Carson's cross-examination lasted for a day and a half. On the witness stand, Oscar was denied his opium-tainted cigarettes. He found it difficult to concentrate without them. Carson went through the allegations of the young men who had made statements saying that they had had sex with him. Every detail was put to him. He denied everything over and over again, but the mass of material began to have an effect on the jury.

He could not deny that he knew the boys concerned though – they had often been seen in public together. He had entertained them innocently and sometimes helped them out with a little money. But why had he paid Alfred Wood to go to the United States? The cigarette cases and other gifts he had given to young men were brought up. And while the jury might have been able to accept that he found the company of Oxford undergraduates stimulating, what did he get out of the company of a 15-year-old boy he had picked up on the beach at Worthing, or a cockney scamp introduced to him by Alfred Taylor?

There was to have been a dinner party to celebrate after the first day of the trial. Oscar cried off, spawning rumours that he had fled the country. Instead he was closeted with his lawyers who, by now, realised he was lying. They told him that the only sensible course was to drop the prosecution, pay Queensberry's cost, swallow the scandal and hope that it would end there. Bosie, however, determined to revenge himself on his father, urged him to fight on.

The next day, Carson asked about Alfred Taylor and the tea parties he had had. What did he think Taylor did for a living? Had Oscar ever seen him in women's clothing? How many young men had he introduced him to? How many had he become "intimate" with? Oscar admitted five. And every one of them had received money and presents from him.

Oscar was forced to admit that he was attracted to youth, that he recognised no class distinction in those he shared his company with and that he would happily take a street Arab to his rooms if he was interesting. The incident of feeding Charles Parker preserved cherries from his mouth upstairs at Kettner's was brought up. Why had he taken female impersonator Fred Atkins to Paris? Oscar managed to fend off these questions. However, when he was asked about Walter Grainger, he made a terrible slip.

"Did you ever kiss him?" asked Carson.

"Oh no," said Oscar with his usual hauteur. "He was a peculiarly plain boy."

Carson pressed home the point. Why had he said that? Would he have kissed him if he had not been so ugly? Did he kiss other boys who were not so ugly? Oscar was lost.

Opening the case for the defence, Carson promised to produce a roster of witness who would say, in court, that they had had sex with Mr Wilde. The next day there was a queue to get into the courtroom. Sir Edward Clarke conceded that Oscar had "posed as a sodomite" in his literary work and would drop the case. That was not good enough for the judge, though. Queensberry was either guilty or not guilty and his Plea of Justification must be found to be true or false. And if it was true, it would have to be published for the benefit of the public. The jury returned a verdict of not guilty in minutes and Queensberry was discharged to cheers that the judge made no effort to quell. That night, Carson told his wife: "I have ruined the most brilliant man in London."

When Oscar and Bosie left the court they were followed by Queensberry's detectives. They went to see George Lewis to see what could be done. He said that if they had brought Queensberry's card to him in the first place, he would have torn it up and no harm would have been done. As it was, there was nothing further he could do. Resigned to his fate, Oscar went to the Cadogan Hotel where he sat in an armchair and drank hock and seltzer. Meanwhile, Queensberry sent a note to the government. Either they arrest and imprison Wilde or he would name a number of senior Liberal politicians as sodomites. At a hasty meeting in the Treasury building, it was decided to charge Oscar with gross indecency, despite Queensberry's allegations of sodomy. It was the least they could get away with.

Five hours after the collapse of the criminal libel case, warrants were drawn up for Oscar and Alfred Taylor. A sympathetic journalist brought the news to Oscar, who was now a little drunk. At 6.20 p.m., two policemen arrived at the Cadogan Hotel to arrest him. He was taken to Bow Street, where he was charged with several counts of indecency with men. Bosie turned up at 8 p.m. and offered to stand surety, but he was told there was no possibility of bail.

The following morning, Wilde and Taylor appeared in the dock at Bow Street Magistrates' court and heard Charles Parker and Alfred Wood testify against them. Sidney Mavor retracted his sworn statement after meeting Bosie in the corridor outside. It did not make any difference. More arrests were expected and there was a discreet exodus of known uranians. Robbie Ross left, but Bosie stayed on to campaign vigorously for a change in public attitudes to sex between men. As usual, he made things worse, but Oscar lived only for his visits.

At the committal proceedings a number of chambermaids, housekeepers and landladies testified about what they had seen, and the state of the bed linen. The decision was made at the highest levels not to prosecute Bosie – on the grounds that he could maintain that he was one of Wilde's victims. It is likely, though, that a political decision was made not to cross Queensberry with the reputations of so many in the government at stake. Nevertheless, Bosie was eventually persuaded to leave the country, as his presence was more likely to hurt Oscar than to help him.

At the trial at the Old Bailey, Wilde and Taylor were charged with 25 counts of gross indecency and conspiracy to commit gross indecency – so, even if they had not succeeded in being grossly indecent, but had intended to, they would have been found guilty.

Despite the damning evidence against them, Oscar made a stout defence. When asked what was "the love that dare not speak its name", he talked of the love between an older, intellectual man and a joyful youth as a beautiful and noble thing. No one said that it dared not speak its name because it had is mouth full. Anyway, the jury was gobsmacked and could not reach a verdict.

Oscar was released, but the newspapers insisted on a new trial. If there was not one, they said, it would be because the government was trying to hush something up. Meanwhile, hotels refused to take Oscar and he sought shelter with his brother. Everyone urged him to jump bail and flee abroad. Frank Harris even hired a steam yacht to take him to France. To run away, Oscar thought, would be to admit that uranian love was ignoble.

At a second trial, Oscar Wilde was found guilty on seven counts of gross indecency and sentenced to two years hard labour. In passing sentence, the judge said that it was the worst case he had ever tried and thought that two years – the maximum he could give – was totally inadequate.

In jail Oscar had to strip in front of the warder and bathe in disinfectant. His head was shaved. The food turned his stomach and he suffered constant bouts of diarrhoea. Rosebery and other sympathetic members of the Liberal government tried to organise a special soft regime for him, but they were voted out of office less than a month after Oscar was sent down.

Even Labouchère was sympathetic, urging the authorities to leave Oscar to meditate on his crimes in Pentonville and a petition was sent to Queen Victoria. "Friends" in New York offered the governor of Pentonville £100,000 in gold to free him. This secured him a transfer to Wandsworth, where conditions were worse. There he was found masturbating compulsively in his cell. This continued throughout his incarceration and is celebrated in "The Ballad of Reading Gaol". In Victorian times, it was thought this would drive you mad and he risked being sent to Broadmoor, but the doctors who examined him decided that he was not mad, just bad. However, they recommended that he should not be in the company of other males without supervision.

Still owing a bill at the Savoy, he was declared bankrupt in October. Constance wanted a divorce on the grounds of sodomy with Walter Grainger, but Oscar fought it. He claimed that he had been suffering from erotic madness and Bosie was to blame. Fearing that evidence of sodomy presented in the divorce courts might invite new criminal charges, he agreed to a separation, relinquished the children and agreed to live abroad when he was released. He also agreed to eschew "any moral misconduct or notoriously consort with evil or disreputable companions" – Bosie – in return for a small financial consideration.

It is easy to see why he renounced Bosie. While Oscar was in jail, Bosie was having a high old time, shagging his way around the Mediterranean with other exiled uranians. At one point he was warned that, if he was not a little more discreet about cock-sucking young boys, then the French authorities would deport him back to England. He moved on to Italy, where he and Robbie swapped their gourmet delights.

After a year in jail, Oscar no longer saw himself as a uranian martyr. Instead, he petitioned the home secretary for his release on the grounds that he was suffering from "sexual madness". His lust for young men, he said, was a "strange disease". Those who visited him at the time became convinced that he really meant this.

Bosie did not believe it, though. He lived for the moment when they would be reunited and, ever tactful, sent Oscar uranian poems. How that must have helped.

At Reading Gaol, the stern disciplinarian of a governor was replaced with a kinder one, who allowed Oscar paper, pen and ink, and any books he liked. He spent three months writing the 50,000-word *De Profundis*, which began as a bitter repudiation of Bosie and ended up as a kind of love letter. He stopped protesting that he was suffering from erotomania and began to indulge it by having sex with other prisoners. The warder even helped him pass notes to "the one I liked best", 20-year-old soldier, Harry Elvin. After he was released he sent money to nine fellow prisoners in Reading Gaol.

The verdict of a heterosexual friend on his incarceration was: "Two years' hard labour had not been able to cure him of his urge to fondle and caress males who appealed to the woman he fancied himself to be when the homosexual craze got hold of him."

He was released a day early to avoid the press and left for France. He took the name Sebastian Melmoth – Sebastian, because of the saint who is said to have been gang-banged by the Praetorian Guard while he bled to death, and Melmoth from the gothic tale of an man who sells his soul for 150 years of perpetual youth.

Oscar momentarily considered entering a Jesuit seminary. Then he begged Constance to take him back, but Robbie was on hand to induce him to have sex with men again.

At Berneval-le-Grand, a seaside town just outside Dieppe, a series of young male artists and poets came to see him. One of them was the poet Ernest Dowson, who really preferred young girls. He induced Oscar to visit the local brothel in an effort to help him acquire "a more wholesome taste in sex". They pooled their resources and went, Dowson said, "accompanied by a cheering crowd".

When Oscar emerged after a dalliance with a woman, he said: "The first these ten years, and it will be the last."

Then, addressing the crowd, he said: "But tell it in England, for it will entirely restore my character."

Despite the fact that Bosie was giving interviews that made Oscar even more notorious, Oscar began writing to him every day. Just four weeks after Oscar's release from jail, they arranged to meet. Bosie was to come to Berneval under a false name. Oscar received a letter from his solicitor warning that this contravened the agreement he had signed with Constance. Besides, the Marquis of Queensberry was threatening to shoot Oscar if he ever went near his son again.

The meeting was cancelled. Bosie blamed Robbie who, like many of Oscar's friends, blamed Bosie for Oscar's downfall and believed that any further contact would do Oscar irreparable harm. Oscar gave them the slip, however, and met Bosie in Rouen, where they slept together. Bosie was still his "darling boy" and Oscar begged him to "remake my ruined life for me".

Oscar borrowed the train fare and they eloped to Naples, a haven for uranians at the time. They ran up a huge hotel bill, then set up home together in the nearby village of Posilippo - where Lord Rosebery had a villa - with a maid and two boys to serve them. They went on trips to Capri where the Emperor Tiberius* used to enjoy orgies with little boys. And with tempting young boys all around, it was business as usual. According to Robbie, in Naples, Oscar began drinking too much and "reverted to homosexual excess, both of which continued until he died".

Constance got wind of Oscar's domestic arrangements and threatened to cut him off without a penny. She was backed by Robbie who was determined that, if he could not have Oscar, Bosie would not have him either. Even the British consul put pressure on them to leave. So Oscar and Bosie pretended to have a row and split.

They moved to Paris. Soon after, Constance died in Genoa - "of a broken heart" her son said - without reinstating Oscar's allowance. Robbie kept him in funds that he spent on drink and boys. He fell for ex-soldier Maurice Gilbert, who was happy to have sex with Oscar, Robbie, Bosie and other friends. He also shared other interests. Maurice, Oscar said, was "devoted to a dreadful little ruffian aged 14, whom he loves at night ... every time he goes home with Bosie he tries to rent him. This, of course, adds to his terrible fascination. We'll call him the 'Florifer', a lovely name. He also keeps another boy, aged 12! whom Bosie wishes to know, but the wise 'Florifer' declines."

Oscar and Bosie met up twice a week and other friends visited, but Oscar spent most of his time with boys he picked up on the boulevards. There was a Russian youth called Maltchek Peervinsiki; Georges, "a beautiful boy of bad character", a boy known as "Le Premier Consul", Léon, who he used to smoke and sleep with, Casquette, who wore a blue suit, Eugene, "the harvest moon", so called because he was uncircumcised, a "passionate faun" called Giorgio, Walter, "a snub-nosed little horror" who walked the streets day and night, a blackmailer called Alphonse; "a little Dionysiac" called Joseph who went to jail for attempted murder and a boy Oscar sarcastically called "Edmond de Goncourt", who also went to jail and, when he came out, went straight back into business again.

Robbie begged Oscar to stop consorting with these "gutter perverts", but Oscar said that it was the only thing that consoled him. He spent three months on the Riviera with two fisher boys. In Nice there was bronzed boulevard boy, Georges. He shared a "very pretty Italian boy" Eolo with Harold Mellor in Gland, Switzerland. Visiting Constance's grave he picked up a "beautiful young actor" and considered staying in Genoa "for ten francs a day (boy *compris*)". In Sicily, he had Manuele, Salvatore, Francesco and the 15-year-old seminarist Giuseppe, who he "kissed behind the high altar" in Palermo cathedral. In Naples, he fell for "a sea-god". In Rome, there was "dark and gloomy" Pietro; talkative Homer; Robbie's ex Omero; Arnaldo and his friend Armando, and student Dario who tried to kiss him at the door of the Vatican.

Back in Paris, in the Hotel d'Alsace, Oscar uttered his famous last words: "My wallpaper and I are fighting a duel to the death; one or other of us has to go." On November 30, 1900, he died.

Chapter Three

Rumbled by Rimbaud

Paul Verlaine was the outstanding French lyric poet of the 19th century. Born in Metz in 1844, he had a troubled upbringing. His mother kept three of her miscarried foetuses, pickled in jars in a locked cabinet in her bedroom. It was only when Verlaine broke in and smashed the jars that she was forced to bury them. No wonder his first known poem – which he sent to Victor Hugo when he was 14 – was called "*La Mort*".

As a youth he fell in love with his male cousin, Dujardin. A friend said that he spoke of him "as a lover praises his mistress". His boyfriend at school, the "exquisitely proportioned" Lucien Viotti, is praised in "Memoirs of a Widower". In the cafés of Paris he hung out with the Parnassian group of poets and became addicted to absinthe. He took as his lovers Lucien Létinois, Germain Nouveau and a farm boy, whose death sparked "a violent frenzy of homosexual sensuality".

He had his straight side, too. He fell in love with another cousin, who married another and died in 1867, leaving money for him to publish the poems he had written for her in the book *Poèmes saturiens*. That same year, he published a collection of libertine verses called *Les Amies – The Women Friends –* which was banned by a French court in 1868.

In 1869, he began writing *Le Bonne Chanson* for 16-year-old Mathilde Mauté, who he married the following year. On hearing of the engagement, Viotti promptly joined the army and died soon after. Then, three days before the wedding, a young man turned up at Verlaine's office clutching a revolver and a copy of his will. The next day, he blew his own brains out as a wedding present. This was handy for Verlaine, who was trying to put that sort of thing behind him, as it were. He was 26 and already a well-known poet. Together with Mathilde he settled down to a bourgeois marriage, indulging his gay side only with the odd homoerotic poem. Everything was going swimmingly until, in 1871, 16-year-old poet Arthur Rimbaud wrote to him from the Ardennes.

As a child, Rimbaud had played with country girls who, in rural France back then, wore no underwear. He recalled biting one girl on the buttocks. At school, masturbation was widespread, with boys doing it in class under the desk or when the teacher's back was turned. One sympathetic teacher took a hand and lent Rimbaud some homoerotic books. Rimbaud soon developed a passionate interest in the poet François Villon, who was condemned to death by Louis XI, probably for sodomy.

In 1870, he began writing seductive letters to the Parnassians, claiming to be older than he was. Their journal *La Charge* published his poem "Three Kisses", but they could not publish "Nina's Replies" which compares heterosexual love to a stable full of warm dung heaps and "*Vénus anadyomène*" which portrays Aphrodite as a fat old lady rising from a bath tub "her wide crotch hideously embellished with an anal ulcer".

In "The Sly Women" and "At the Cabaret Vert" he described waitresses with huge tits who invited him to suckle. His poems are full of ugly women and reek of misogyny. They are also peppered with naked buttocks and *renifleur* – "sniffers" – who hung around urinals in the hope of sex.

Rimbaud's adolescent work shows a good grasp of female anatomy and it is thought that he had some early sexual experiences with a farm girl or a prostitute – though he claimed to have lost his virginity with a dog. There was also an early heterosexual humiliation when he had arranged to meet what he thought was an ordinary girl for a date and she turned up dressed to the nines with her maid.

On an earlier trip to Paris – as he had come from an area of France occupied by the Prussian army without a ticket – he was arrested at the Gare du Nord. In jail, he seems to have been raped. His subsequent poems are full of pain, disgust, erect penises and ejaculation. Authority figures are depicted as pederasts and paedophiles. In "*Un Coeur sous une soutane*" – "A Heart Beneath a Cassock" – a young seminarist is somehow "sullied" by his masturbating superior. His letter to Verlaine made his sexual proclivities clear. He enclosed poems that were full of references to buttocks and acts of pederasty. A second letter enclosed "*Les Premières communions*", "*Mes Petites amoureuses*" and "*L'Orgie parisienne*".

By the spring of 1871, it was clear that he hated women. He wrote:

> One night, you hailed me as a poet,
> You blonde eyesore,
> Come down and let me whip you
> In my lap.

He is no more fond of a "black-haired eyesore" or a "red-haired eyesore", the gullies of whose breasts are still filled with his dried-up sputum. Delightful. He concludes:

> Oh my little lovers,
> How I hate you!
> Cover up your ugly udders
> With painful rags.

Verlaine was impressed and invited Rimbaud to visit him in Paris. With his friend, the poet Charles Clos, Verlaine went to the railway station to meet Rimbaud but, thinking he was older, failed to recognise him. However, Rimbaud managed to find Verlaine's house, where he was greeted by Mathilde and her mother. Mathilde took to him, at first.

"His eyes were blue, rather handsome," she said, "but they had a sullen expression that, in our indulgence, we took for timidity." One can only imagine what he thought of her.

Other friends spotted the danger signs though.

"Big hands and feet," wrote one. "An absolutely childish face that could have belonged to a boy of 13, deep blue eyes, character more savage than shy, that is the kid whose imagination, full of power and unbelievable corruption, fascinated and terrified our friends."

Rimbaud and Verlaine seem to have started having sex almost right away. They were frequently absent from the house and Mathilde did not know where they were. Rimbaud stole her favourite ivory crucifix and took it to the Latin Quarter when he consorted with whores. People were also concerned about his casual acts of cruelty. He blew hot ashes from his pipe up a horse's nose and forced Mathilde to take down a picture of a relative because it "upset and worried" him.

The following year, he wrote "Young Couple", a vicious description of Verlaine's marriage. Outside the couple's bedroom walls "gums of imps vibrate", a clear reference to acts of fellatio going on elsewhere. Rimbaud's presence seems to have re-awakened Verlaine's interest in promiscuous gay sex elsewhere as well, causing one friend to boast that he was the only one in their circle who "had never been fucked in the arse by Verlaine". What disturbed Verlaine's friends more, however, were Rimbaud's mood swings, his boasts of having fought in the Franco-Prussian war – which was plainly untrue – and his casual knife play.

Verlaine made no attempt to keep is relationship with Rimbaud secret. His friend, Edmond Lepelletier, wrote of seeing Verlaine at the first night of a play with "a Mademoiselle Rimbaud on his arm". Rimbaud was definitely the girl. Stéphane Mallarmé likened him to a laundress with big red hands. Rémy de Gourmont compared him to "one of those women about whom you are not surprised to hear it said that they converted to religion in a whorehouse". He added: "But what was even more revolting is that he seems to have been a jealous and passionate mistress."

In verse, Verlaine celebrated these early nights together as "*nuit d'Hercules*". He was not just alluding to the night when Hercules deflowered the 50 daughters of Thespius. He also alludes to the period of captivity where Hercules dressed as a woman.

Mathilde could no longer tolerate Rimbaud in the house and he moved in with Charles Clos, but alienated him by cutting his poems out of literary reviews and using them as lavatory paper. He then moved in with the pianist and composer Ernest Cabaner, who liked to drink a glass of milk every day for his failing health – Verlaine described him as "Jesus Christ* after ten years of absinthe". When he was out, Rimbaud would find the milk and piss or ejaculate into it. Rimbaud also drew a caricature of Cabaner, showing his host as a contortionist sucking his own penis. Cabaner asked Rimbaud to leave and Verlaine rented a room for him in Montparnasse. By this time, he was also paying for Rimbaud to eat, though he was soon sharing his room and his bed with the painter Jean-Louis Forain. To Forain, Rimbaud was a "large dog". To Rimbaud, Forain was a "little blonde girl cat" – though he was also a "young dog" who ran after women and eventually got married, telling Rimbaud after they parted: "Your type of love disgusts me."

At a meeting of Parnassian poets called the "Naughty Chaps", Rimbaud punctuated the readings of others by exclaiming "Shit!" at the end of every line. When one of the readers complained, Rimbaud grabbed Verlaine's sword-cane and lunged at him, cutting his hand, then waited outside and stabbed him in the stomach. He was only calmed when the handsome young blond painter, Michel de l'Hay, took him back to his studio for the night.

By this time Verlaine's marriage was on the rocks. He punched Mathilde, splitting her lip, and put a lighted match to her hair. During a fight, he picked up their three-month-old son George and threw him against the wall. Fortunately he hit it with his feet and fell back into his cot unhurt. Mathilde picked up the child and fled. Without his wife, Verlaine's condition deteriorated quickly. Soon he was as dirty and dishevelled as Rimbaud, who considered body lice as a joke.

The sexual relationship between Rimbaud and Verlaine was complex. In a letter to Rimbaud, Verlaine says: "I am your old cunt, ever open or opened." In the poem "The Good Disciple" he invites the reader to "Climb on my backside and throb". And one friend began calling Verlaine "Verulanus".

On the other hand, Rimbaud said of Verlaine loudly in a café: "He can satisfy himself on me as much as he likes. But he wanted me to work out on top of him? Not on your life. He's far too filthy and his skin is disgusting."

According to Edmond Goncourt, Rimbaud frequently boasted of being the recipient of anal sex.

"Rimbaud, Verlaine's lover, that glorious one of abomination and disgust," Goncourt wrote in his journal, "arrived at a café and, laying his head on the marble of the table, began to describe his latest doings in a loud voice: 'I am killed, I am dead. Jean fucked my arse all night long, and now I can't keep my shit in.'" I hope no one was eating at the time.

In his poem "Young Guzzler" Rimbaud writes: "Cap/of silk/prick/of ivory/Grab/very black/Paul spies/the tall wardrobe/projects/little tongue/over a peach/readies/his baguette/ and diarrhoea."

After his death, Rimbaud's poems *La Stupra - The Defilement* – were published. They talk of animals having sex while they are running and ancestors who "showed off their members proudly by the fold of the sheath and the grain of the scrotum". The poet himself talked constantly about the size of men's penises, speculating on the proportion of various historical figures, while Verlaine mused on finding his ideal – "a boy, hung like a man."

Rimbaud enjoyed showing off his erections. Chambermaids in the house across the street would complain about his antics. He said that he had merely taken off his lice-ridden clothes, but it would take more than the sight of a naked man at a window to shock a Parisian chambermaid.

In *La Stupra*, Rimbaud compared men and women, making it clear where his preference lay.

"Our buttocks are not like theirs," he wrote. "Oh to be just naked, seeking joy and rest/Forehead turned to his glorious portion/both free to murmur and to sob?" This last line is thought to refer to oral-anal sex.

Verlaine responded to this with his own poem, *Hombres, Femmes*, comparing male and female arses and together they wrote "Sonnet to the Arsehole", which is a reply to a poem by Albert Mérat, where he praises the various parts of his lady's body – her nose, her lips and her vagina. Their version begins: "Dark and wrinkled like a violet *oeillet* ..." *Oeillet* means both a carnation and an eyelet or hole and was gay slang for the anus at the time.

Then we get "filament like tears of milk" that weep "through little clots of russet earth", before disappearing "where inclination led them". That was Verlaine's contribution. Rimbaud added:

Oft did my dream suck at its vent …
The tub from which the celestial browned almond drops

Now wash your mouth out.

According to Goncourt, Rimbaud did not mind "a little shit and cheese" on the body of an unwashed partner, because he loved so much to "*gamahuche*" – a Victorian word that means both to fellate and perform cunilingus, though I guess we are talking about rimming here. And, in his letters to Verlaine, Rimbaud begs him to "shit on me".

In *Hombres, Femmes*, Verlaine also describes the penis as the "nectar and remedy of my soul" and says, ambiguously, "climbed on me like a woman I fuck like a boy". He also drew pictures of small men with swollen, dripping penises.

There was an S&M aspect to their relationship, too. One day in a café, Rimbaud told Verlaine to put his hand on the table, then he pulled a knife from his pocket and slashed Verlaine's wrist. An eyewitness said that Verlaine then "went out with his sinister companion and received another two knife wounds in the thigh".

They frequently had knife-fights in bars and "if a little blood flowed, they soon ran to make it up over pints of bitter ale or brandy".

With Forain, Raoul Ponchon, Jean Richepin and Maurice Bouchor, they formed a group called the Zutistes, who produced the *Zutiste Album*, which is full of poems and drawings of penises, anuses, buttocks and bums.

In February 1872, Verlaine persuaded Rimbaud to return to the Ardennes and, soon after, Mathilde moved back in with him. Verlaine could not live without his soul mate, however, and begged him to return.

"As soon as you get back, take me in your fist right away," he wrote.

When Rimbaud returned to Paris in May, violence erupted between Verlaine and his wife again. Soon the two men had to flee the city. On the train, they were overheard boasting about imaginary crimes they had committed and the police were called.

They made it to Brussels, where Matilde caught up with them. She persuaded Verlaine to take the train with her back to Paris, but on the way he jumped off and returned to Rimbaud. Later, he wrote to her, inviting her to come and live with them. When she refused, they moved on to England. Along the way they had plenty of sex – "Long live happiness each day when in the morning the Gallic cock sings" – and guzzled copious amounts of alcohol and smoked as much hash as they could get their hands on. They found the English cuisine was not to their taste though. Verlaine wrote of oxtail soup with "a man's sock and a rotten clitoris floating in it", coffee that "evidently comes from Father Mauté's [his father-in-law's] teat … and then gin – its anisette drawn from a vulture's single bollock". So no Michelin star there then.

However, he did approve of the service. When you leave the loos, he said, "you fall right into the hands of young boys in tight-fitting suits who for two sous, brush you from head to foot. For a little more, I don't know what they must do for those in the know, but they have a mightily suspicious appearance with their clinging little suits and their generally charming faces."

If they had moved in more vaunted circles they could have asked Oscar*. As it was, Verlaine seems to have found out pretty quickly for himself. He wrote to a colleague that he had a new boyfriend: "I believe I have found something very sweet, almost childish, young, very candid, with amusing and charming brutalities and gaieties. To find that, you must dig arterial wells."

Digging arterial wells sound very painful indeed.

Rimbaud also drooled over the tiny grooms with their great coats and whips – the French assumed that English grooms were sex-toys for aristocrats. He, too, pursued them. The purpose of their visit to London seems to have been sex tourism.

By this time, Mathilde was seeking a legal separation and possibly a divorce on the grounds of adultery. In a letter to an old friend, Verlaine boasted that he and Rimbaud were willing to undergo an anal examination to "prove" that they were not lovers.

"If necessary we are ready, Rimbaud and me, to show our cunts (virgin) to the whole group," he wrote. It really does not bear thinking about, given their lamentable lack of attention to personal hygiene.

In fact, Verlaine later had to submit to a mandatory proctological examination, which revealed that he was a seasoned dirt-track rider. For the moment, though, he was trying to bluster it out. He tried to put a respectable face on things by having his mother come to stay with him and sending Rimbaud back to France. Once he had gone, though, Verlaine admitted to feeling a "terrible emptiness".

"The rest does not matter to me," he said. "It's all smut."

He did not understand the British and their heterosexual ways.

"As for love here," he said, "it seems that ladies' ten fingers play a great role around insular penises than the *barbatum antrum* [bearded cave]."

In a letter dated November 14, he made it clear where his interests lay: "Did you know, I just learnt from a 'canny French fellow' that our *membrum sacro sanctum* [sacred limb], apart from names like prick, cock, wang, creator, sub-prefect, dick, weewee – the later two used by children – bone, member, thing, tail etc. is also called turtle – the head of a cock. Hence these drawings."

And he enclosed an obscene triptych, entitled: "Triple Demonstration Way of Fine Arts". A turtle?

He wrote of the prostitutes at work in the Haymarket.

"The grenadiers, splendid men in red, curled and pomaded, 'give their Alms' on Sundays to ladies for an average of sixpence, but the Horseguards, breast-plated, booted and in helmets with white tassels – a shilling."

Again, all these men were getting from their money was a wank.

"The Widow Fist reigns at these orgies," he said.

This was not doing the business for Verlaine, however, who soon complained that he was dying. His mother took pity on him and paid Rimbaud's fare to return. The two men then headed off on a tour of Belgium. Verlaine got drunk all the time, while Rimbaud wrote his famous *A Season in Hell*. In the book, Rimbaud pictured himself as a "foolish virgin", which shows just how powerful his imagination was. Verlaine also had a great imagination, claiming to have been "chaste … since leaving Paris" although they never stopped having sex.

There were lovers' tiffs, break-ups and reconciliations. Verlaine threatened suicide, said he was going to join the Spanish militia, then bought a gun and shot Rimbaud, who ended up in hospital with a bullet in his wrist. Verlaine was arrested. Rimbaud asked for the charges to be dropped, but the judge insisted that Verlaine be examined for "any traces of pederastic habits". The report by Doctors Semal and Vleminckx read:

> 1. The penis is short and not voluminous, the glans is especially little and it narrows, tapering off toward the end, starting with the crown. The latter protrudes little and does not have a marked relief.
> 2. The anus can be dilated rather significantly by a moderate separation of the buttocks, to the depth of about one thumb. The movement displays a tunnel-shaped flaring, a sort of shortened cone, with its top portion below. The folds of the sphincter have no lesions and bear no marks ... The contractibility remains more or less normal.

> Conclusion: The examination shows that P. Verlaine bears on his person the signs of active and passive pederastic habits. One and another of these two signs are not strong enough to create the suspicion of inveterate, old habits but more or less recent habits.

> Brussels July 16, 1873

Thank you, gentlemen. That was more than I really wanted to know.

The Belgian police also wrote to their French counterparts seeking information about the "Parnassian poet" who had shot "his girlfriend Rambaud" in a fight "about money". The Sûreté replied that Verlaine's "head had long been unhinged before misfortune brought to Paris a kid named Rambaud ... In terms of morals and talent this Rambaud, aged 15 or 16, was and is a monstrosity. He possesses the mechanics of verse like no one else, only his works are absolutely unintelligible and repugnant. Verlaine fell in love with Rambaud who shared his passion and they went to Brussels ... practising their love openly. Verlaine told his wife: 'We, we have the loves of tigers.' And saying this he showed his wife his chest tattooed and wounded with knife cuts which his friend Rambard applied. These two beings fought and tore each other apart like ferocious animals in order to have the pleasure of making up again."

Mathilde did not speak to the police, but plenty of other witnesses came forward to testify to Verlaine's depravity. When a Belgian priest came to hear his confession and Verlaine started to list his sins, the padre interrupted with the question: "You've never been with animals?"

Verlaine was sentenced to two years. In prison, he wrote "*Crimen Amoris*". Set in Ecbatana, the capital of Ancient Media, it talks of beautiful 16-year-old boy, an angel of evil, who burns down the palace where orgies are held during the Festival of Seven Sins. It can be read as plea that he and Rimbaud are guilty only of "crimes of love".

Rimbaud finished *A Season in Hell* and it was printed privately in Brussels at his mother's expense. She had remained remarkably loyal, despite the scandal and receiving an anonymous letter explaining the exact manner of her son's relationship with Verlaine. She even visited Mathilde to beg her to stop her divorce proceedings as they would undoubtedly reflect badly on her Arthur. Meanwhile, Rimbaud visited Verlaine's jail to deliver an inscribed copy of *A Season in Hell*, which must have been a comfort.

The two lovers continued writing of their love for one another – Rimbaud's, particularly, are dripping with "spunk". But then the young poet Germain Nouveau joined the Zutistes and Rimbaud whisked him off to London. According to Richepin, Rimbaud "had begun to visibly dominate Nouveau, who had a weak nature and exalted character, and the nervousness of a sensual woman abandoning herself to someone strong". And their flight to London "looked very much like an abduction". Nouveau did not seem to object. He was soon writing: "I am a pederast in my soul/I say it alone and standing erect/But lying in your bed ..." He also began making explicit drawings of Rimbaud nude.

They got tickets to the Reading Room of the British Museum, even though Rimbaud was not yet 21. However, he was not allowed to see the works of the Marquis de Sade, or other pornographic material from the closed case.

In March 1875, Verlaine – now dismissively dubbed "Loyola" after the founder of the Jesuits for the revival of his faith in prison – was released. He was reunited with Rimbaud in Stuttgart with "a rosary in his paw".

"Three hours later we had denied his god and made the 98 wounds of Our Saviour bleed," wrote Rimbaud. They were back to the S&M – which is ironic as St Ignatius of Loyola got the idea for the Jesuits while convalescing after being wounded in battle.

Rimbaud did not come out unscathed from this encounter. Verlaine wrote a description of him sleeping with his "feet still painful from the road/the breast, marked by a double punch/and the mouth, still a red wound/and the quivering flesh ... Sad body! How weak and how punished".

However, the affair was over. Rimbaud was now 20. He gave up his writing career and began to travel further afield. In Vienna he was robbed by a coachman, though according to his account of the episode there was a sexual element to the crime. After a series of odd jobs and journeys to the Far East, where he even considered becoming a missionary, he settled in Africa where he ran guns to fuel a local war. He was not, as is alleged, a slave trader, though he did own a couple of slaves for his personal use. He kept a number of African women and had a long relationship with an Abyssinian lady, who liked to wear European clothes. For over two years, he kept her in an arrangement called *da damouss*, where he paid her a small retainer so she had no claim on his property when he abandoned her and moved on. At one point, he even expressed a desire to get married and have children.

One of his employees, a young Greek called Righas, told a particularly unpleasant story about Rimbaud's sex life in Africa. When he was living in Harer in Ethiopia, a young infibulated girl entered his home – in that part of the world it was common for young women to be circumcised and infibulated by having the remains of the labia sewed together leaving only a tiny opening. The vagina was re-opened before marriage. For Rimbaud, such difficulties proved no discouragement.

"Rimbaud set about things a little too bluntly," said Righas, "and, coming up against this obstacle, tried to perform the operation of opening her up with a knife. He inflicted a nasty wound on the girl who started screaming."

Fortunately, local people heard her and came running.

Rimbaud did not, as some biographers had maintained, go all

macho in Africa. He stayed very much in touch with his feminine side, dressing in flowing robes like Lawrence of Arabia* and squatting to pee. He also seems to have maintained a relationship with a young African serving boy called Djami Wadaï, who would be his heir. Returning to France with a tumour on his knee, Rimbaud died of cancer in 1891

Verlaine continued to write. In 1890, he was working on a "series of masturbatory poems". One of them was given the English title "Auburn" – in French "*aux burnes*" means "to my bollocks". Addicted to absinthe, Verlaine became a sexual vagabond, staggering from lover to lover. In his last year, he lived in the company of two ageing prostitutes, though he also frequented a gay lover called André Salis, whose nickname was Bibi-le-Purée – which means "Yours truly, the sperm". However, publicly, Verlaine denied that he was gay and that there was any sexual dimension in his relationship with Rimbaud.

He also met up with Oscar Wilde* during Oscar's exile in Paris. Oscar was put off by his shabbiness, but praised him from afar saying that his life was "one of the most perfect lives I have come across in my own experience" and that he was "the one Christian poet since Dante". When he died in 1896, thousand of Parisians turned out to follow the coffin.

Verlaine and Rimbaud's fame as poets has grown steadily ever since. So has their fame as gays. In France, they are considered the Adam and Eve of modern homosexuality, but who did what with the apple and where the snake fits in remains unclear.

Chapter Four

A Little Bit of Madeleine (Or Was It Fruit Cake?)

The French novelist Marcel Proust famously begins the seven volumes of *À la recherche du temps perdu* – known, strangely, in English as *Remembrance of Things Past* – with the consumption of a little bit of Madeleine, a small French cake, dissolved in tea. From this he evokes a whole world of memory of, on the surface of it at least, largely heterosexual goings-on during *la belle époque*. However, Marcel himself was a bit of a fruit cake.

Not that he did not like the opposite sex. From an early age he discovered that he found girls as attractive as boys. One day while playing in the garden, he saw Marie de Benardaky, an "elegant, tall and beautiful" blonde. He fell in love with her and spent every free minute pursuing her. However, his parents discouraged the match.

In fictional accounts of Marcel's youthful romps, Marie becomes Gilberte and they tickled and fought.

"I held her gripped between my legs like a young tree which I was trying to climb," he wrote. "In the middle of my gymnastics, when I was already out of breath with the muscular exercise and the heat of the game, I felt, like a few drops of sweat rung from me by the effort, my pleasure expressed itself in a form which I could not even pause for a moment to analyse ..." I think we catch the drift. "... Whereupon Gilberte said good-naturedly: 'You know, if you like, we might go on wrestling a little bit longer.'"

Typical woman, always wanting more.

Although these heterosexual feelings had been stirred up in him, he refused older classmates' invitations to accompany them to the brothel and he had a lifelong distaste for prostitutes. He was, however, able to appreciate beauty in both sexes. While

79

being drawn to the handsomest boys in the class, he was eager to go with a friend called Daniel Halévy to see a woman that he had discovered in a cheese shop in Montmartre. Her name was Mme Chirade and Marcel was quite taken with her black hair, fair skin and fine features. He compared her to Flaubert's Salammbô and said to Daniel: "Do you think we can sleep with her?"

Daniel was shocked, as he had always considered Proust to be a sissy. But a few days later they returned to Montmartre. This time Proust was carrying a huge bunch of roses. Shy, Daniel hung back but Proust walked right up to Mme Chirade and started talking to her. Daniel could see her shaking her head and saying *"Non"*, but Proust did not give up until she had thrown both him and his flowers out onto the sidewalk.

Equally, the young Proust was not afraid to express his homosexual desires to his own classmates and, in 1887, even wrote a love letter to a younger boy called Jacques Bizet. When a specific offer of sex was turned down, he did not give up, but wrote back saying: "I always find it sad not to pluck the delicious flower that we shall soon be unable to pluck. For then it would be fruit ... and forbidden."

Proust wrote again begging Bizet to help him out. His parents had discovered the nature of his sexuality.

"This morning, dearest," he wrote, "when my father saw me ... he begged me to stop wanking for at least four days."

Indeed, his parents were so worried about his excessive masturbation that his father gave him ten francs to visit a brothel. But everything went disastrously wrong and he lost his money without getting a shag. In desperation he wrote to his grandfather, explaining what went wrong the first time and asking for the money to have another go: "Here's why. I so desperately needed to see a woman in order to put an end to my bad habit of masturbating that Papa gave me ten francs to go to the brothel. But in my agitation I broke a chamber pot costing three francs and in this same agitated state was unable to screw." So he asked for 13 francs to cover the damage and another bunk up, explaining: "I dare not ask Papa for money again so soon and I hope you will be able to come to my assistance in this instance, which, as you know, is not only exceptional but unique; it can't happen twice in one lifetime that a person is too upset to screw."

One can only hope that granddad was sympathetic.

Daniel was also worried that Proust was over-exerting himself with his five-fingered friend – "Weak, young, he fornicates, he masturbates, he engages, perhaps, in pederasty," he wrote.

Proust wrote reassuring him: "If this interests you and you promise me absolute secrecy – not even to tell Bizet – I will give you documents of very great interest, belonging to me, addressed to me, from young men and especially ones in the age from eight to 17 who love other guys, eager always to see them (as I do Bizet), who cry and suffer far from them, and who desire only one thing to embrace them and sit on their lap, who love them for their flesh, who devour them with their eyes, who call them darling, my angel, very seriously, who write them passionate letters, and who would not for anything in the world practise pederasty."

The boy's going to be a writer.

Now he has explained what he and his friends don't do, he tells Daniel what they do do.

"Generally love wins out and they masturbate together. But don't mock them and the friend of whom you speak, if he is like this. They are simply in love. And I do not understand why their love is any more unclean than normal love."

Well, Marcel, in other forms of love you dump your wad in the receptacle provided.

But Proust would not be told. He was about to celebrate the whole messy business in one of his first short stories *"Avant la nuit"* – "Before Nightfall".

There were other boys he fancied at school beside Bizet. Raoul Versini promised to cure Proust of his homosexual tendencies by explaining the dangers. Proust was all ears and, when his parents went away, he seized the opportunity to spend the night at Raoul's. It is not known what transpired that night, but plainly the cure did not work.

Proust also engaged in what he called "a very filthy act" with an older boy. It seems he had agreed to a certain amount of fondling and caressing, when the older boy over-powered him and, in a "moment of madness", he consented to anal sex. Proust even told his father about this, who was not too cross, though he considered Marcel's "error a surprise".

But maybe it was not such an error. By the autumn of 1888, he had written a sonnet entitled "Pederasty", celebrating the joy of the love of young boys, which he sent to Daniel Halévy. Daniel was shocked, but Proust continued writing to him, assuring him that he was not "jade and effete" and that the love between men and boys need not be corrupt. Indeed, he tried to seduce him.

"I cannot separate your keen mind from your agile body," Proust wrote, and he yearned to "refine and enhance 'the sweet joy of love'" with him. He said he did not deserve Halévy's "contemptuous words, which would have been more fittingly addressed to someone surfeited with women and seeking new pleasures in pederasty".

And he sought to reassure Daniel that a quick one behind the velocipede sheds would be okay.

"I am glad to say that I have some highly intelligent friends, distinguished by great moral delicacy, who have amused themselves at one time with a boy," he wrote. "That was at the beginning of their youth. Later on they went back to women."

In England, we called them public school boys.

Proust flourished the names of Socrates and Montaigne – though later the confessed that he had got it wrong about Montaigne in justification. These were men, he said, who permitted "men in their earliest youth to 'amuse themselves' so as to know something of all pleasures". After all, "sensual and intellectual friendships are better for a young man with a keen sense of beauty … than affairs with stupid, corrupt women."

His professor at the lycee intercepted a letter which mentioned that Proust had "impure hands" and questioned him about it. He had also noticed that Proust, who had frequent crushes on other boys, now had a new friend.

"What number did you give him when he passed through the door of your heart?" asked the elderly teacher.

Everyone was surprised when Proust's youthful beauty came to the attention of the famous courtesan, Laure Hayman, who had been celebrated as *Gladys Harvey* in the novel by Paul Bourget.

She gave Proust a copy of the book bound in the silk of her petticoat. In it she wrote:"To Marcel Proust, Do not fall in love with a Gladys Harvey." Well, you never know.

The boys who he had sent love letters to were now deeply confused. Could he really be having an affair with a woman whose sexual accomplishments were so well known? She called him "my little psychologist in porcelain". His schoolmates quickly picked up on this and teased him mercilessly.

Nevertheless Proust went walking with her every morning and obviously doted on her. Daniel Halévy recorded in his diary that when he, Proust and Bizet had been out for a walk, they had passed Laure Hayman's house and Proust could not resist dropping in. When he returned a quarter of an hour later, he told them an amusing anecdote. Over dinner Bourget had asked Barbery d'Aurevilly whether it was true he was a pederast and Barbery replied: "My tastes, my age, my whole life inclines me in that direction, but the ugliness of the sex in question has always prevented me from entirely becoming one."

While Proust was away doing his military service, he kept falling in love with the wives and girlfriends of the other men. He found he could love a woman from a safe distance and spend hours mooning over photographs of sweethearts comrades had brought with them, but he could not deal with women up close and personal.

Until her death, Proust's mother still believed that he would marry and he fuelled her hopes. Even to friends he admitted that he had some feelings in that the direction. There were problems though.

"As for me, I feel love only for young girls, as though my life were not complicated enough as it is," he said. "You will tell me that marriage was invented to cope with such eventualities, but young girls don't remain young girls when they are married. One can have a young girl only once. I do so understand Bluebeard: he was a man with a weakness for young girls ..."

From time to time he even made some genuine effort to marry. Anatole France offered his 18-year-old daughter. Proust was tempted, but he hesitated, and then found that he was relieved when she married someone else.

Thanks to Laure Hayman's salon, he had entry into literary and artistic circles, where he moved at ease. There he met the handsome young Venezuelan composer Reynaldo Hahn, who, it was rumoured, had been a lover of his mentor, Camille Saint-Saëns*. He was also a friend of the ballerina Cléo de Mérode, whose circle attracted a lot of gay men. Reynaldo denied being gay and spoke out against homosexuality. However, he and Proust spoke "*moschant*" – the French equivalent of polari – together. He also offered to teach it to Prince Antoine Bibesco.

Prince Antoine, Reynaldo and Proust talked of homosexuality, but called it Salaïsme, after the young nobleman Antoine Sala, who took little trouble to hide his sexual preferences. Later they learned that Sala was distressed by such a public airing of his sex life.

When Prince Antoine suggested that Proust's interest in Salaïsme stretched beyond the academic, he denied it. He was interested in Salaïsme only in the way that he was interested in Gothic architecture, he said. He was a complete virgin in that department. What about admiring all those Gothic spires, Marcel?

Later, Proust "professed his friendship" for the prince. They had a secret pact to tell one another what other people were saying about them behind their backs. The prince also lavished expensive gifts on him. Writing to thank him for one, Proust said that he had had some "profound thoughts about Salaïsme" and would share them at their next "metaphysical conversation".

On the less meta and more physical level, there was Bertrand de Fénelon, who Proust called his "Nonelef" or "Blue Eyes". They swapped adolescent letters marked "top secret", most of them are still in the hands of private collectors. Those that are not, used silly anagrams and other codes and can be characterised as "affectionate".

Meanwhile Antoine got into trouble talking about Salaïsme and Proust had to draft a letter of apology to Sala. To Antoine he wrote: "We must absolutely stop this horrible business of being the public denouncers of Salaïsme." However Proust himself went on using the words Salaïsme and Salaïst – denying that he was one, of course. However, there is a good deal of jealousy between Antoine and Bertrand over who was the prime object of Proust's affection.

Proust's name was linked with other men, but he also showed

an interest in the beautiful young actress Louisa de Mornand. He gave her a copy of his French translation of John Ruskin's* Gothic guidebook, the *Bible of Amiens*, with a dedication in the cover which read: "He who Louisa cannot win/Must be content with Onan's sin." Proust had already proved himself deft at this.

She invited him to her apartment, where he watched her read in bed before she fell asleep. Well, you can't keep a girl waiting all night. She sent him an autographed photograph inscribed with the message: "The original who is so fond of little Marcel, Louisa."

He wrote back saying that he was mad about her and enclosed a 33-line poem describing her in bed. In her memoir, Louisa hinted that their relationship took a step beyond the bounds of friendship, but even though he was attracted to her, it seems plain that he could only get it up for men.

In 1907, like other French gays, he greatly enjoyed the details of a sex scandal at the highest levels of Kaiser Wilhelm II's court. He found the subsequent trial "comic". Berlin was nicknamed *Sodome-sur-Spree* and "parlez-vous allemand?" became the latest pick-up line for Frenchmen seeking partners in what came to be known as the "German vice". He also joined in the fervid speculation about the homosexuality of Lord Kitchener.

Although Proust continued to feign interest in girls – for the sake of his mother – he found it hard to keep his true feelings hidden. One evening, he met Marcel Plantevignes, the 19-year-old son of a necktie manufacturer, and went on a long walk with him. A woman, perhaps concerned about the young man's reputation, hinted strongly that Proust was a homosexual. Instead of leaping to Proust's defence, Plantevignes remained silent. When he heard of this, Proust wrote to Plantevignes, accusing him of having "stabbed him in the back".

"You have carelessly spoiled what could have been a very beautiful friendship," he said.

Concerned, Plantevignes' father visited Proust, who promptly challenged him to a duel. They went through the motions of selecting weapons and, seconds before, the whole thing was dropped amicably.

While concealing his instincts socially, Proust continued to write openly about homosexuality and found it difficult to find publishers, as most considered his work "obscene". He also paid Albert Nahmias handsomely to work as his part-time secretary, though the young man had no training or aptitude for the position. There was bound to be gossip.

He also hired an athletic young chauffeur called Alfred Agostinelli, who was devoted to his ugly wife. This made Proust immensely jealous, especially when Agostinelli began fooling around with other women, while his love remained unrequited. Agostinelli's death in a plane crash left Proust devastated.

Later he hired a handsome, young, blond Swiss valet called Ernest Forssgen, but denied that he was keeping him for the same purposes as Prince Constantin Radziwill kept his 12 handsome butlers to each of whom, it is said, he gave a pearl necklace. However, he asked the duchess de Clermont-Tonnerre to destroy a letter in which he had praised a blond footman.

Friends were concerned about the homosexual undertones in *Swann's Way*, the first volume of *À la recherche du temps perdu*, but Proust was adamant. If he could write about pederasty without ever mentioning it, "I should then have all the pederasts on my side, because I should be offering them what they like to hear. Precisely because I dissect their vice (I use the world vice without any suggestion of blame), I demonstrate their sickness, I say precisely what they most abhor, namely that this dream of masculine beauty is the result of a neurotic defect."

It was precisely for this reason that Proust was later attacked by André Gide*.

Research for *À la recherche du temps perdu* took Proust to Turkish baths and male brothels run by Albert Le Cuziat, but funded by Proust himself. A male prostitute at the house on the rue de l'Arcade gave a unique insight into Proust's sexual needs. The house had a window into a room where the prostitutes play cards. Clients looked through it and made their selection.

"He picked his partner and went upstairs," said a young man frequently selected by Proust. "A quarter of an hour later, I knocked on the door, went in and found Marcel already in bed with the sheet pulled up to his chin. He smiled at me. My instructions were to strip off all my clothes and remain standing by the door while I satisfied myself under anxious gaze of Marcel, who was doing the same. If he reached the desired conclusion, I smiled at him and left without seeing any more than his face or touching him. If he didn't reach the desired conclusion, he would gesture for me to go and Albert would bring two cages."

This is where it gets a bit nasty.

Each cage contained a famished rat. Albert would set the cages together and open the doors. The two starving animals would than attack each other, making piercing screams as they torn each other to bits. This brought Proust to orgasm.

Even Richard Gere's putative gerbil pales into insignificance beside that.

It is true that, as Proust got older, he became terrified of germs, so the idea of touch-free sex rings true. His housekeeper and sometime confidante, Céleste Albaret, doubted the bit about the rats though. However, Proust confessed that it was true to Gide.

"During a memorable night of conversation (of which there were so few that I remember each of them well) Proust explained his pre-occupation with combining the most diverse sensations and emotions in order to achieve orgasm," Gide wrote. "That was the justification for his interest in rats, among other things." Other things? There's worse? "In any case Proust wanted me to see it as such. Above all I saw it as an admission of some type of psychological inadequacy." Well, you'd know André.

It is thought that maybe Proust's intake of drugs and caffeine had left him otherwise impotent.

Proust also confided to Gide that he had "never liked women except platonically and had only known love with men". This surprised Gide who had never thought that Proust was entirely homosexual.

It was also said that Proust liked to take photographs of his distinguished lady friends and get male prostitutes to spit on them, crying "Who is that whore?" over a picture of "the princesse de C***". Some say that the same treatment was meted out to photographs of his mother.

Outside the brothel, Proust still developed strong crushes on handsome young men. He encouraged the young writer Paul Morand and visited the young man in the middle of the night. Morand concluded that the reason for these furtive nocturnal visits could only be sexual. They became close friends, but Proust was furious when Morand wrote his "Ode to Marcel Proust". If people started writing about his private life, could revelations about rats be far behind?

Proust invited the valet Paul Goldschmidt around to his own apartment – if not to his cork-lined bedroom, who, according to the housekeeper Céleste "belonged to the 'Sodom party'". And, despite the cork, he was plagued by noisy neighbours.

"The neighbours in the adjoining room make love … every day with a frenzy that makes me jealous," he wrote.

He must have had a glass to the wall as, in a letter to a friend, he concluded that as soon as the couple had finished making love, they jumped from the bed into a sitz-bath before taking care of the children and getting on with the household chores. Then he made the most astonishing admission: "The total absence of a transition makes me tired for them, for if there is anything I detest afterwards, at least immediately afterwards, it's moving, no matter how much egotism there is in keeping in the same place the warmth of a mouth that no longer has anything to receive."

Plainly, he is talking about fellatio. He had not been so frank in his correspondence since he was a schoolboy.

As more volumes of *À la recherche du temps perdu* came out the work was condemned in gay Parisian circles because of its anti-Salaïst attitudes. While Proust could talk openly about his sex life with Gide, he could not own up to anyone else. However his homosexuality is the guiding principle of his masterpiece, which continued to be published after his death. Marcel Proust's great achievement was to weave the gay lifestyle into some of the longest sentences ever written. *Remembrance of Things Past* is not, it has to be said, recommended reading for asthmatics.

Chapter Five

Tights of Spring

Ballet dancers are expected to be gay. Classical dancing by its very nature is camp and then there are those tights. In fact, in the 19th century, the ballet was the perfect showcase for a young dancer – male or female – who wanted to solicit the interest and protection of, shall we say, a wealthy patron.

When the young dancer Vaslav Nijinsky* joined the Mariinsky Theatre in St Petersburg in 1907, he was 17 and sexually naïve, but he was about to suffer a baptism of fire. There was a man in the ballet called Alexandrov who was employed as a pimp by the elite of St Petersburg society. His main function was to introduce them to young ballerinas, who often returned to the chorus line wearing expensive jewellery. However, he was happy to cater for all tastes.

He and an accomplice invited Nijinsky to dinner in a private room at Cubat, one of the best restaurants in St Petersburg. Their host was to be Prince Dmitrievitch Lvov, who was then about 30 years of age; tall, handsome with a shock of white hair and big blue eyes – one of which glinted behind a monocle, he had seen Nijinsky dance and was fascinated by him and determined to seduce him. And he had a plan. Over dinner, he showed the young dancer an exquisite miniature depicting a beautiful young woman. This, Lvov said, was his sister. She was in love with Nijinsky and wanted to buy him a ring. Any young man would have been flattered. The next day, they went to Fabergé. Then they had dinner again and went to a nightclub. There were more presents and more parties, during which "Vaslev and the Prince would retire to discuss the merits of the unseen princess".

Nijinsky now appeared around town in hand-tailored clothes.

He ate in expensive restaurants and dined in the homes of the wealthy. As a dancer, he knew instinctively how to pose and move and all his actions became provocative and feminine. He became vain and spent an inordinate amount of time trying out new hairstyles.

However, it seems that Lvov was a little let down by the affair. According to Nijinsky's sister, the dancer was small in a place when size is normally admired – though, to be fair, she probably only saw it when he was a child, unless there was something else going on that we should be told about. Lvov even arranged for Nijinsky to have his first sexual experience with a woman. He brought a prostitute to his house for Nijinsky to sample, but the dancer was frightened and it seems he could not perform.

Lvov then tried to palm Nijinsky off on Count Tishkievitch, a rich Pole who bought Nijinsky a piano.

"I did not love him," Nijinsky lamented in his diary. "I loved the prince not the count."

But Nijinsky had already attracted another admirer, the rapacious impresario Sergei Diaghilev*. At the interval at the Mariinsky, Diaghilev found Lvov and Nijinsky walking up and down the big mirror hall at the back of the house. Lvov introduced them and afterwards the three of them had dinner together at Cubat. They discussed the competing merits of Russian and European dance. After dinner, Diaghilev, who was twice Nijinsky's age, asked him to come back to the Europa Hotel where he lived.

"I disliked him for his too self-assured voice," said Nijinsky, "but went to seek my luck. I found my luck. At once, I allowed him to make love to me. I trembled like a leaf. I hated him, but pretended, because I knew that my mother and I would die of hunger otherwise."

This was not entirely true. By this time Nijinsky was the lead dancer at the Mariinsky Theatre and a guest dancer at the Bolshoi. He was also receiving expensive gifts from Lvov and the count. There was no way that his mother and he were going to starve. It seems that he was already used to being passed around, accepted that this was the way of the world and thought that having sex with such an influential figure in the world of ballet as Diaghilev would not harm his career.

And he was not wrong. Diaghilev's help and encouragement would make Nijinsky one of the greatest dancers ever to have lived. Together they would create legendary masterpieces of dance.

"How could I guess in that hotel bedroom that I should come to depend on Diaghilev as much as any one man ever depended on another?" he said.

In 1909, with dancers from the Mariinsky and the Bolshoi, Diaghilev formed the Ballet Russes and took Nijinsky to Paris. There the dancer caused a sensation, but he was struck down with typhoid fever after drinking tapwater. Diaghilev took a small furnished flat where he nursed Nijinsky back to health. He then suggested that they live together and Nijinsky agreed. The couple honeymooned in Carlsbad, where they enjoyed regular massages. Then Diaghilev showed Nijinsky the delights of Venice, where Nijinsky sunbathed and swam as Diaghilev looked on. He thought only the young and beautiful should strip off. At a party given by the flamboyant Marchesa Casati, who led panthers on chains, the flamboyant poet and, later, Fascist Gabriele D'Annunzio asked Nijinsky to dance. Isadora Duncan* asked him to have a baby with her. He declined both offers and went home with Sergei in a gondola.

Back in Paris in 1912, they outraged the critics with *L'Après-midi d'un Faune*. Everyone knows what a faun – not a young deer but a mythological creature, half man, half goat – gets up to on a hot afternoon. Nijinsky, wearing spotted tights, pursued nymphs around the stage who wore nothing under their flimsy tunics. According to the Press, it was an offence against public decency.

Next they put on Claude Debussy's* ballet *Jeux*, which also caused a scandal. It concerned a young man and two girls searching for a lost tennis ball.

"The search for the tennis ball is forgotten and the young man flirts, first with one girl, then with the other," Debussy said. "But as the first girl sulks and the young man hesitates, the two girls make love to each other to console themselves. Finally, the young man decides, rather than lose either of them, to have both."

This is a wholesome enough story, but in the hands of Nijinsky, it became positively risqué.

"Immorality passes through the legs of the girls and ends in a pirouette," Debussy wrote of the first performance. "Sensuality is overflowing its banks. These Russians are like Syrian cats."

The woman, who later became Nijinsky's wife, said: "Love becomes not the fundamental driving force, but merely a game, as it is in the 20th century. Here love is nothing more than an emotion, a pastime, which can be found among three as well as among the same sex."

When the ballet was performed in London, the critics missed all this naughtiness and their reviews concentrated on the fact that the ball used on stage was bigger than a regulation-sized tennis ball and that Nijinsky's tennis trousers were not cut according to the classic pattern. And still we can't win Wimbledon?

Nijinsky's tastes were changing. Though he continued to live with Diaghilev, the parts he was playing on stage began to stir in him heterosexual feelings. Of course, he was surrounded by pretty young dancers all the time, but most of them had lovers and he was painfully shy. However, he began visiting prostitutes.

"Diaghilev thought I went out for walks," he said, "but I was chasing tarts. I knew the tarts had no diseases, because the police kept them under observation."

But he was terribly ashamed of what he was doing.

"I knew what I was doing was horrible. I knew that if I was found out I would perish."

He would search out healthy ones. It became a compulsion. He would go out searching every day and, sometimes, have several a day. He found them simple and beautiful, and even had one while she was having her period.

"She showed me everything and I was horrified and said that it was a shame to do this kind of thing when a person was ill."

She said that if she did not do it she would starve.

He tried to control his passion by cutting out meat. Each time he ate meat, he found he was overwhelmed with lust, would pick up a girl and take her to a hotel which specialised in renting rooms for a short time for free love.

Diaghilev seems to have been blind to Nijinsky's growing heterosexual tendencies. He hired Miriam Ramberg, who immediately set her cap at him. Another young woman, however, had fallen for him. Her name was Romola de Pulszky-Lubocy-Cselfalva, the daughter of a Hungarian count. She had seen him perform in Budapest and Paris and, during rehearsals, would hide in a dark corner of the theatre to watch.

She had no training as a dancer, but she was determined to have Nijinsky, so she wangled an interview with Diaghilev. To hide her intentions, she raved about another dancer called Bolm. Diaghilev was suspicious, though, and asked her about Nijinsky.

"Oh, Nijinsky is a genius," she said. "As an artist he is incomparable, but somehow Bolm is more human to me."

He took her on.

Every day at 11, she had a private lesson with the dancing master Guiseppina Cecchetti. Nijinsky had his at 12. One day she sprained her ankle. When Nijinsky turned up, he took her foot in his hand, felt her ankle and said that she should be sent home. Meanwhile, Romola was cultivating a friendship with Miriam Ramberg, to learn more about him.

The Ballet Russes was going to London. Diaghilev went ahead. Although Nijinsky was supposed to travel separately from the rest of the company, Romola managed to travel on the same train and boat. They exchanged a few words in the corridor of the train and, on the boat, she braved the weather to be out on deck with him. It was hard going. She spoke very little Russian; he little French. And he was still attempting to disguise his inclinations from her. At Victoria, the train was met by Diaghilev in a jaunty straw hat. He gave Romola a dirty look when Nijinsky raised his cap to say goodbye.

When the company moved on to South America, Romola was dismayed to find that Nijinsky was not on board the *SS Avon* when it sailed from Southampton. She was overjoyed, however, when he joined the ship at Cherbourg. Miriam Ramberg had a cabin in second class, which she shared with another dancer. Romola had bought herself a first-class ticket and her state room was within sight of Nijinsky's. It was a long, hot voyage. Nijinsky was 24 and needed a sexual outlet. Diaghilev was not on board. He had no interest in South America and had decided to spend the summer in Venice, where he liked to pursue pretty, dark-eyed boys. It was inconceivable for Nijinsky to go below deck to second class for a little romance. And it wasn't that small. By the time they arrived in Rio de Janeiro, Nijinsky and Romola were engaged.

Ramberg was devastated. Like the rest of the company, she believed that Nijinsky was totally dedicated to Diaghilev. If he was going straight, he should have come to her. Now she had missed her chance. She stood on the prow of the ship looking down at the waves, howling: "I want to drown! I want to drown!"

In Rio, Nijinsky bought two wedding rings with their names and the date engraved on them, but when they travelled out of town for a romantic trip into the mountains, they needed a translator with them. They took Josefina Kovalevska, the former mistress of the Aga Khan*.

Several of the company tried to talk them out of the marriage, fearing what it would do to the Ballet Russes, but the couple would not listen. A trousseau was hastily assembled and a Catholic church booked. Nijinsky made confession to a padre who spoke neither Russian nor Polish, while Romola promised that she would try and stop her husband dancing anything "immoral" like *Schéhérazade*.

On September 10, 1913, they married in a civil ceremony at City Hall, then in a religious service in the Church of San Miguel. Afterwards, Miriam Ramberg warned Nijinsky to leave the Ballet Russes. She quit, changed her name to Marie Rambert, moved to London and never spoke to him again.

Nijinsky made a detailed confession to Romola about the relationship he had had with Diaghilev and sent her roses every morning. He sent a letter to Diaghilev, telling him of his marriage. He stressed that this would not alter their friendship, nor would it change his loyalty to the Ballet Russes. Diaghilev was so understanding, he said, that he would give them his blessing. Romola was not so sure.

A telegram had already arrived in Venice informing Diaghilev. He went hysterical and fired off a reply, forbidding the reading of the banns. Confirmation was received that the wedding had already taken place. It was irreversible. Diaghilev got wildly drunk, ranted and could not be left alone.

Their friends – even the newspapers – were surprised. Despite Diaghilev's Italian orgies, they all believed that the dancer and his muse were an item. Some were more sanguine, though.

"Was it a complete surprise to Sergei, or was he prepared for it," wrote one friend. "How deep was the shock? The romance was coming to an end and I doubt that he was really heartbroken."

There were more shocks in store. By the time they got on the ship back to Europe, Romola was pregnant. While a telegram from Diaghilev greeted the rest of the company at Cherbourg welcoming them back, Nijinsky received one giving him the sack. Back in Moscow, Diaghilev took a fancy to a young dancer at the Bolshoi called Leonide Massine. Diaghilev approached him, after which he not only took over from Nijinsky on stage but also in Diaghilev's bed. However, he, too, was summarily dismissed in 1920 when he fell in love with a young ballerina in the company. Diaghilev died in Venice nine years later.

Nijinsky started a dance company of his own in London, where he had befriended Lady Ottoline Morrell*, a frequent flier in my *Sex Lives of the Great Artists*. It failed. During part of the First World War, he was interned in Hungary as an enemy alien. In 1919, he had a nervous breakdown and retired. He was 29. He was interned again in Hungary in the Second World War and died in London in 1950.

Chapter Six

Howards End Away

The novelist E.M. Forster* was a leading light of the Bloomsbury Group, an effete intellectual and artistic circle that flourished in that area of central London in the first half of the 20th century. Many of its denizens were gay and included economist Maynard Keynes*, biographer Lytton Strachey* (author of *Eminent Victorians*) and artist Duncan Grant*, along with famous lesbians and novelists Virginia Woolf* and Vita Sackville-West*. All of these old duffers have moved out – they're dead – and a brave new breed of writer has moved in – of which I seem to be the only one. I live just off Queen Square – make of that what you will – just a spit from Bloomsbury Square itself.

I wrote most of my *Sex Lives…* books in the old Round Reading Room of the British Museum and I am writing this in the new British Library just over the Euston Road in St Pancras. During my daily commute, I pass numerous blue plaques bearing the names of illustrious Bloomsburyites. Essentially a Fitzrovian – having lived there twice – I apologise in advance for parading my local knowledge below. Now prepare for a New Bloomsbury Grope…

Edward Morgan Forster's father died when his son was a baby and he was brought up by his mother and two paternal aunts. There were odd mentions in the family of a deep, dark secret – that Forster's father had had a homosexual affair with a distant cousin.

Forster recalled becoming sexually aware at the age of five or six. In a section of his diary from 1935, he wrote of his early sexual experiences: "Prepuce being very long, I used to play with it."

His mother told him that this was "dirty" and he had to pray each night for God to "help me to get rid of the dirty trick". This was the extent of his sex education.

"For years I thought my 'dirty' was unique and a punishment," he said when an adult, though he scoured literature in the hope that others had "dirties" too. He was also conscious that he preferred men from an early age. A pale, snub-nosed garden boy called Ansell used to help him make houses out of straw stacks. They "often lay in each other's arms, tickling and screaming". In Forster's diaries there are also mentions of playing hide and seek with A's "billcock" which have never been fully explained.

Forster was then packed off to prep school. One afternoon in the spring of 1891, he was excused football and was told to go for a walk on the downs. He came across a man peeing. He then sat down with the man, who opened his fly and told him to take hold of his prick.

"Dear little fellow," said the man, "play with it … dear little fellow … pull it about."

"I obeyed with neither pleasure nor reluctance," Forster recorded in his diary. "I had no emotion at the time but was surprised at the red lolling tip (my own prepuce covering the glands even at erection) and was a little startled when some thick white drops trickled out."

Satisfied, the man lost interest, asked him casually where he lived and offered him a shilling, which he declined.

Forster wrote to his mother, telling her what had happened. She wrote to the school who tried to track the man down. Despite the general hysteria this generated, Forster did not seem the least put out. During the Easter holidays, his mother asked him whether he had cured himself of his "dirty trick". He said he had not and she became so distressed that he decided next time he would lie.

Forster had a close a friend at school called Howard. This should lead naturally to a joke about *Howards End* – Forster's most famous novel – which I am sure you can supply.

At Cambridge, Forster joined the Apostles, a debating group which later became the recruiting ground for the gay Cambridge spy ring. One topic that came up for debate was "Is self-abuse a bad thing?" Many of the Apostles voted "no". Forster was not among them, though he was a frequent and guilt-ridden masturbator.

After holidaying in Italy with his mother, he began writing. His protagonist was often a girl who was undergoing a sexual awakening while travelling with an elderly relative. After a visit to Greece, he began to slip into a more classical mode. Others read into this some sexual subterfuge, though Forster denied it vehemently. One of these stories, featuring a young man called Eustace, fell into the hands of a young man called Charles Sayle, who explained what he took to be the subtext to fellow-Bloomsburyite Maynard Keynes.

Sayle summarised the action thus: "B——- by a waiter in a hotel, Eustace commits bestiality with a goat in that valley … In the subsequent chapters, he tells the waiter how nice it has been and they try to b—— each other again."

Forster was not altogether flattered by this rendition.

"While alive to the power of my writing, to its colour, its beauty, its Hellenic grace, Charles Sayle could not believe his eyes," he wrote in his diary. "He was horrified, he longed to meet me. Of course, Maynard flew chirruping with the news. It seemed to him great fun, to me disgusting. I was horrified and did not want to meet Charles Sayle."

Apart from his "dirties" Forster knew little about sex. He did know that he was frightened of women, however. Either they were pretty and young and sexually threatening – brash and assertive like the girls at Girton – or married and had, consequently, crossed the sexual divide. He did not hate women and expressed none of the misogyny of his contemporaries and, later, some of his closest friends would be women. However, he came slowly and painfully to realise that he would never marry.

"I do not resemble other people," he wrote in 1907 when he was 28 and experiencing the first pangs of unrequited love for a man. Forster had no idea what to do about it. He was incredibly sexually naïve.

"Not till I was 30 did I know exactly how male and female joined," he admitted. Even then he learned from watching cows and other animals. But he was aware of where his tastes lay. In 1905, he recorded seeing the "two most beautiful things: bathers running naked under the sun-pierced foliage, and a most enormous beech, standing in the village like a god". The nude bathers were male and the scene is lovingly reproduced in *A Room With a View*.

He began visiting the British Museum to study the Greek artefacts, particularly the male nudes. It was these nudes that first drew him to Bloomsbury. Around this time he had a close friendship with Hugh Meredith, who was described by a colleague as "very much a ladies' man". But in their intimate dinners in the small restaurants in Marchmont Street (it's on my route between home and the British Library; I walk up and down it four times a day; there's a great Chinese restaurant and a pub where I have a Cuba Libra mid-afternoon – ooh, and there's a gay bookshop, you must go) and their walks around Coram's Field and Queen Square (see, I'm nearly famous) stirred something in Forster which, when he wrote about those times 60 years later, made him elevate their friendship into "an affair". And in Weybridge, where his mother had moved, he met the tall, handsome Indian student Syed Ross Masood and was much taken with his beautiful, brown, melting eyes and his forceful personality. But Forster was still wrestling with his own sexuality. He read copiously about the theory of "sexual inversion" and acted out the fantasies of his imagination in his gay novel *Maurice*, which was only published in 1971 after his death.

He began the book after visiting Edward Carpenter, author of *The Intermediate Sex*. Carpenter's partner, George Merrill, fondled Forster's bottom.

"I believe he touched most people's," said Forster. However, in his case it brought inspiration.

"The sensation was unusual and I still remember it, as I remember the position of a long-vanished tooth," he wrote. "It seemed to go straight through the small of my back to my ideas, without involving my thoughts … I then returned to Harrogate, where my mother was taking a cure, and immediately began to write *Maurice*."

He also began to spend weekends with cousins in Whitstable, where local residents were shocked by the unconventional and rowdy behaviour of Philip Whichelot, a flamboyant homosexual and, later, a chum of Quentin Crisp* – "P and Q," it is said, "flaunted around London together in their arty clothes." But this did not help Forster.

"However gross my desires," he wrote, "I find that I shall never satisfy them for the fear of annoying others."

But his dirty little tricks continued.

"I must try to be less lustful," he wrote in his diary, "not because

I don't like doing it, but because the habit induces unhappiness."

His friendship for Masood deepened, but it still had not been consummated.

"He is not that sort – no one seems to be," Forster remarked mournfully; Quentin's friend Philip already forgotten.

However Masood accompanied Forster on a holiday to Paris, causing Forster to ask: "Is the enigma him or his nationality?"

All the while Masood regaled Forster with tales of the merry times he had with women as a way to fend him off with giving him a definite "no". And, when he headed back to India in 1910, he wrote: "I have got to love you as if you were a woman or rather as if you were a part of my own body." Which part? "Pray pardon the singularity of the remark, but I hope it will help you to understand what I mean to convey by it – one of the dearest things I shall leave behind."

The following year they holidayed together at Tesserete, near Lugano. This time Forster's physical longing proved too much for him and he told his friend how he felt.

"Near the beginning, I spoke, seeing that after all he did not realise," Forster recorded in his journal. "He was surprised and sorry, and put it away at once."

Put it away? No passage to India then.

But Masood was playing both sides of the street. While it was clear to Forster that "he liked me better than any man in the world" he would run after any available girl. Forster said that he "did not mind", but later a note of peevishness crept in: "Masood is having an ugly waitress or visitor; for I think he had her, but thought me too much of a muff to be told."

Back in London, Forster became part of a gay underground that circulated homoerotic literature. He came across the autobiographic work of Kenneth Searight, an officer from the North-West Frontier, which detailed the gay delights of the Orient – especially the availability of young boys. So Forster booked a trip.

Strangely, when he arrived, he was immediately beguiled by the nautch girls, who sang and danced and reputedly provided other sexual services.

"The ladies had already arrived and salaamed us – one with a weak but very charming face and very charming manners: I was never tired of looking at her," he said. "The other was younger and fat with a ring through her nose indicating virginity. This made her arrogant, they said, and she didn't attract me. Both were short. One could easily 'lapse' into an oriental; I found myself discussing their points dispassionately."

Masood was sick and Forster nursed him. This gave them a chance to get intimate, but Masood's marriage plans were already being laid and Forster gradually resigned himself to his friend's heterosexuality. By this time Forster was 33 and he still hadn't had a shag.

All that was to change in Alexandria four years later. There, in March 1916, he met the Greek poet Constantine Cavafy, who encouraged him to put a toe in the water. In October of the same year, he told his confidante Florence Barger: "Yesterday for the first time in my life I parted with respectability ... I have felt that the step would be taken for many months. I have tried to take if before. It has left me curiously sad."

Sad? You're supposed to be gay. Maybe it was because there was a war on.

Details of who did what to whom have been lost, but Forster was spending a lot of time at the beach at Montazah where soldiers bathed and frolicked in the nude. One of them may have obliged him.

The following year, he chatted up the 18-year-old conductor on the tram that took him out to Montazah. His name was Mohammad el Adl and he resisted at first but, by September 1917, they were involved in mutual masturbation. Fellatio was not far behind, but they never got around to anything anal. They had broken up by the time Forster had got around to asking for it.

Nevertheless he found his first blowjob an emotional revelation. On October 3, 1917, he wrote: "I am so happy – not for the actual pleasure but because the last barrier has fallen; and no doubt it has much to do with my sudden placidness ... I wish I was writing the latter half of *Maurice* now. I now know so much more."

He rued all the people who, like him, have gone through their youth without knowing such joy.

"I have known in a way before, but never like this. My luck has been amazing."

Amazingly bad to have to wait until you are 38 before you first get sucked off.

The problem was that, like Masood, Mohammed was about to get married. Forster was not jealous. Indeed, he encouraged it. He liked woman and envied the comfort that marriage would bring.

They avoided being seen out together and sex, though it continued into July the following year, was infrequent. However, Forster built it up into a "great love affair" in his own mind and relished that he had had sex "nearly in a slum". The respectable middle-class Forster loved rough trade.

"I want to love a strong young man of the lower classes," he said, "and be loved by him and even hurt by him. That's my ticket."

Forster was pitifully self-conscious. He found that working-class people were not and he needed this release. He also needed to tell Florence Barger and other maternal women about it, to help assuage his guilt. He wrote to gay friends in London, boasting of having "an affair like Searight's". And he wrote to Masood, telling him how at home he felt in the mud of the Nile.

In January 1919, Forster left Alexandria and headed back to India. He was 40 and longed for sexual contentment.

"If I could get one solid night it would be something," he wrote. He longed to put an end to the "constant search for the perfect love object".

In India, he took a post as secretary to the Maharajah of Dewas, who publicly condemned homosexuality. Out of deference to the boss, Forster resolved to repress all sexual thoughts, but soon found that the heat "provoked me sexually ... and masturbation brought no relief". He tried to seduce an 18-year-old Hindu boy on an assignation on the road near the guest house – "the least I could do was to avoid any carryings on in the Palace" – but word got out and the plan had to be scotched. However, when Forster suggested tending his resignation, the Maharajah was sympathetic and supplied him with a young man called Kanaya.

"For a time all went well," said Forster. "I couldn't get from Kanaya the emotional response of the Egyptian, because he had the body and soul of a slave, but he was always merry and he improved my health."

But then Forster discovered that Kanaya had ambitions to become "catamite to the Crown" and boxed his ears for his silliness. After that, during sex, he found his passion was "now mixed with the desire to inflict pain". Forster said that he never felt that with anyone else before or after. It was not a desire to punish the boy because he knew he could not be reformed.

"I just felt he was a slave, without rights, and I a despot whom no one could call to account." Good game. Anyway, for the first time in his life he was getting regular sex.

But he had not forgotten Mohammed. Eventually, he headed back to Alexandria with one thing in mind and wrote ahead: "I promised myself that on my return I would get you to penetrate me behind, however much it hurt and although it must decrease your respect for me."

It was not to be. By the time he reached Port Said, Mohammed was dead.

This plunged Forster into mourning, but, returning to London, he was no longer content with being an unhappy homosexual.

"Half an hour in bed with a chauffeur who reminds me of Mohammed would cure it," he said. "I don't want love."

He got his way with Tom the chauffeur and moved into a small flat in Brunswick Square to be in the heart of Bloomsbury and free of his mother. He found himself in a midst of a little coterie of gays and lesbians and, by 1926, the list of his lovers had lengthened to 18, though most were fleeting encounters. He lovingly recorded each casual fondle and the mutual masturbation in the corner of the park (I guess he means Russell Square which is still a popular pick-up place with gays). The affair with Tom the chauffeur, though, was more long-lasting.

"Coarseness and tenderness have kissed one another," he said, "but imaginative passion, love, doesn't exist in the lower classes. Lust and goodwill – is anything more wanted?"

There was also a ship's stoker and a steward that he had met in Alexandria. In an effort to indulge the caring side of love, he helped these men financially and visited their families, but his lovers tended to be bisexuals with intellects far below his, making any permanent relationship impossible.

In 1926, he began an affair with a policeman called Harry Daley, who had been introduced to the joys of mutual masturbation as a child in Lowestoft. He was entirely guiltless and he passed this on to Forster. Together they would cruise Hammersmith Broadway, the centre of gay London at the time, but the fastidious Forster did not like the atmosphere of the "men's urinal".

On April 12, 1930, the Hammersmith set turned out in force for a party to celebrate the annual Oxford-Cambridge Boat Race. At it Forster met 28-year-old Bob Buckingham who had thin, sensual lips and a muscular body. Forster, being unathletic himself, admired athletes. He invited him back to his flat in Bloomsbury and things, well, bloomed. Buckingham was another policeman.

Nicked again. Now where did I put those handcuffs?

Their affair was physical to say the least. Forster told a friend: "It seemed a new sort of intercourse – more like sea lions diving around their tanks than anything describable in human terms." No, London Zoo's the other side of Regents Park.

Although Forster longed for a permanent relationship and hoped he had found it with Buckingham, he continued to entertain other lovers. He maintained a liaison with Surtees Newton, who he had met "by a certain corner" and proved "permanently more than willing". And he picked up another ex-policeman called Les, but as he already had his hands full, so to speak, he passed him onto a friend.

By March the following year, it was obvious that Buckingham was in love with Forster, who responded by reassuring his beau that he did not have a venereal disease. That June, Forster wrote to a friend, saying that the miracle had finally happened and he was going to settle down. There was a "plighting of troths". There was only one fly in the ointment – Buckingham's 23-year-old girlfriend, an accommodating nurse called May Hockey. The two were soon to marry. Forster was jealous, but he believed that Buckingham was so devoted to him that he would not give him up. And they continued having good, uncomplicated sex.

Buckingham told his new wife that he "had never known that Forster was homosexual" and May said she never thought of the friendship between the two men "as a sexual one". However, their letters make it plain that it was. After May gave birth to a son, she and Forster became friends. He became part of the family and it gave him, for the next 40 years, the domestic intimacy he had longed for all his life. When he died of a heart attack in 1970, he was holding May's hand.

Chapter Seven

Arabian Nights

T.E. Lawrence achieved fame as Lawrence of Arabia for his ability to handle Arabs and endure the hardships of the desert. He was uniquely talented in both departments. He never expressed so much as a passing interest in women and admired the Arabs' easy ways with homosexuality. For him, the hardships of the desert were not something to be endured, but enjoyed. He was a lifelong masochist.

His mother, the mistress of an Irish country gentleman, used to cane him on his bare bottom, even for minor infractions. As a means of discipline, this proved to be less than useless. From an early age he took his punishment like a man. The beatings he could take, but there were hidden fears.

"I always felt she was laying siege to me," he said of his mother, "and would conquer if I left a chink unguarded."

But what could that chink be? He later wrote that he was afraid of his mother getting "ever so little inside the circle of my integrity". This has a familiar ring to it. In his account of the war in Arabia, *The Seven Pillars of Wisdom*, he says of his anal rape by Turkish soldiers that he lost forever "the citadel of my integrity". Nuff said.

From an early age he never flinched from pain. He broke his ankle wrestling in the school playground and blithely returned to class though, when discovered, the break was so severe it kept him off school for a term. Later he broke two ribs, but wrote home saying: "They were not important ribs, only the little measly ones low down."

As a youth he showed no interest in girls and there was an incident of what was called "beastliness" at school. He was caught in a mutual masturbation session with another boy, for which he was nearly expelled. Instead he suffered another sound thrashing on the bare behind from his mother. He later claimed to have run away and joined the Royal Artillery. He said that he had no problem with the army's discipline, but that some of his fellow soldiers "frightened me with their roughness".

At Oxford, Vyvyan Richards fell in love with him, but Lawrence took no notice.

"He had neither flesh nor carnality of any kind," said Richards. "He never gave the slightest sign that he understood my motives or fathomed my desire ... I realise now that he was sexless – at least that he was unaware of sex."

From the incident at school this was plainly untrue.

What Richards offered was "my total subservience" for which he returned "the purest affection". But Lawrence did not want subservience. He wanted to be on the receiving end. And he might well have been.

Even before he went up to Oxford, he developed an attachment to Leonard Green, a friend of his older brother Robert at St John's. At 16, in defiance of college rules, he stayed in Green's rooms – where they discussed aesthetics and the work of Walter Pater. Green was a member of the Order of Chaeronea and a practising uranian. Lawrence read some of his verse and advised him not to bow to conventional morality or "develop a sense of sin or anything prurient". Later, Green published the uranian works *Dream Comrades* (1916) and *Youthful Lovers* (1919). Lawrence, too, read the classics and expressed an intellectual interest in Greek homosexuality, but he also read medieval literature and believed that sexual longings could be quelled by the scourge.

At Oxford it was remarked that Lawrence showed no interest in women and fell silent when other students talked about sex. Yet men were drawn to his company. While they were taking hot baths, though, he was taking midnight dips in the frozen Cherwell. He fasted for days on end, took walking and cycling holidays which were feats of endurance, and canoed around the city's sewers, firing his revolver occasionally to frighten the pedestrians walking above.

When he was 20, he proposed to Janet Laurie, a friend of the family. She laughed. They had never touched or kissed.

"He seemed hurt," she said, "but merely said, 'Oh, I see', and spoke no more about it."

It was the only time he made any sort of pass at a woman, or showed any interest in them.

"Do you really like naked women?" he asked the artist Eric Kennington. "They express so little."

Soon after his rejection by Janet, he started to learn Arabic and was sent out on a walking tour of Syria. Outside Aleppo, he was attacked. His own accounts of the incident are contradictory, but it is thought that he had been sexually molested during the incident.

After graduating, he returned to Syria to supervise a dig at Carchemish for the British Museum. He took on a slim, handsome 14-year-old servant boy with big brown eyes, who nursed him through a bout of dysentery. His name was Selim Ahmed, and may well be the mysterious "S.A." *The Seven Pillars of Wisdom* is dedicated to. The dedicatory poem begins: "To S.A.: I loved you." The original was deeply homoerotic and had to be toned down by Robert Graves, to whom Lawrence admitted his love for the Arab boy.

The locals called Selim "Dahoum" – "the dark-skinned one". This was ironic as he was light-skinned and probably had a dash of Armenian blood in him. Dahoum and Lawrence enjoyed wrestling together. When Dahoum came down with malaria, Lawrence returned the compliment and nursed him, sometimes holding him in his arms to comfort him.

Dahoum posed naked for Lawrence, who made a sculpture of him in sandstone, which was prominently displayed on the roof of the house they shared. This was shocking to the villagers because Muslim artists are forbidden to make any representation of the human form. It was widely believed that they were having a sexual relationship, though this too was prohibited by the *Koran*. They were undoubtedly close. Lawrence took him to England in the summer of 1913 and on an expedition to the Sinai in 1914.

Lawrence said that it was Dahoum who opened his mind to the peerless solitude of the desert. They also swapped clothing, so it was Dahoum who first got Lawrence into Arab costume. It was noted that Lawrence was practically beardless and had a girlish giggle. And when he appeared through a tent flap in his spotless white Arab robes, a British officer "stared at the very beautiful apparition" and said: "Boy or girl?"

Lawrence and Dahoum had another adventure together. When they headed off to a Hittite carving they heard had been unearthed, the pair were arrested at Halfati as draft dodgers and jailed. It is thought that Lawrence was beaten up and possibly whipped, but they managed to bribe their way out in the morning.

They were inseparable and, later, an Arab officer, Subi al-Umari, accused Lawrence of having sex with Dahoum at Karkamis. When Dahoum died of typhoid there in 1918, Lawrence turned away, pulled his kuffieh over his face and was heard to say: "I loved that boy."

When he was asked why he was so involved in the Arabic independence movement, he said simply: "I liked a particular Arab very much."

In *The Seven Pillars of Wisdom*, his warm acceptance of homosexual love and his disgust at its heterosexual counterpart is made very clear. He writes: "The public women of the rare settlements we encountered in our months of wandering would have been nothing to our numbers, even had their raddled meat been palatable to a man in healthy parts. In horror of such sordid commerce, our youths began indifferently to slake one another's needs in their own clean bodies – a cold convenience that, by comparison, seemed sexless and even pure." Elsewhere he finds "friends quivering together in the yielding sand with intimate hot limbs in supreme embrace".

They knew this was wrong, but life is hard in the desert.

"Several, thirsting to punish appetites they could not wholly prevent, took a savage pride in degrading the body, and offered themselves fiercely to any habit which promised physical pain or filth." Ah, bless.

When they took Aqaba, he put the local prostitutes under guard because "they are so beastly that I could not stand the thought to their being touched by the British: even though deprivation drove me into irregularities". He chastised Sheikh Auda Abu Tayi for taking "unhygienic pleasure" with his new wife. Another newly married warlord was asked how Arabs "could look with pleasure on children, embodied proofs of their consummated lust?"

So both wives and prostitutes were out of the game.

Lawrence said that it was impossible for an Arab man to love a woman, that they only used them as a "machine for muscular exercise" because the "man's psychic side could only be slaked" with another man. He took two servants for himself, who displayed "eastern boy-and-boy affection" – not because he needed them, of course, but because "they looked so clean". And naturally when they were naughty they were beaten, "a swinging half-dozen each".

Lawrence also ordered beatings of his men – especially those indulging in homosexual activity, rather than court martial them, even though flogging had been outlawed in the British Army 30 years before.

From Aqaba, Lawrence went on an undercover mission to Deraa.

"I went to Deraa in disguise to spy out the defences, was caught and identified by Hajim Bey, the governor," he said. "Hajim was an ardent pederast and took a fancy to me."

Lawrence was told that he was going to be Bey's pleasure that night and was taken to his bedroom. They had a wrestling match and Bey dragged Lawrence down on the bed.

"He then began to fawn on me, saying how clean and white I was, and how fine my hands and feet were, and how he was all longing for me and would get me off drills and duties, make me his orderly, and pay me, if I would love him."

Lawrence said he refused. Bey changed his tune and ordered him to strip. When he again refused, Hajim tore at his clothes. Lawrence pushed him off. Then he called his sentries who slowly pulled off his clothes until he stood there naked.

After taking a long, lingering look over Lawrence's naked body, Bey started to paw him.

"I bore it for a little, till he got beastly, and then I jerked up my knee and caught him hard. He staggered back to his bed, and sat there, squeezing himself together and groaning with pain..."

Bey called for more men to come and hold him. He spat at Lawrence and beat him around the face with his slipper. He sunk his teeth into the flesh of Lawrence's neck and drew blood. Then he kissed him. Afterwards, he took a bayonet and cut through a fold of flesh over his ribs. Blood ran down his side and dripped onto his thigh. Bey looked pleased and dabbled his fingers in the blood and painted it over his stomach.

Some say that Lawrence was forcibly sodomised at this point. Bey told his men to take Lawrence out and teach him a lesson. They took him out on the landing and beat him up, then one of them went to get "a Circassian riding whip" which Lawrence lovingly describes as "single thongs of supple black hide, rounded, and tapering from the thickness of a thumb at the grip (which was wrapped in silver, with a knob inlaid in black designs), down to a hard point much finger than a pencil".

The boy certainly had an eye for detail.

They whipped him savagely, then "would ease themselves, and play unspeakably with me … At last, when I was completely broken, they seemed satisfied." A corporal them kicked him and Lawrence smiled, "for a delicious warmth, probably sexual, was swelling through me". Then he lashed the whip into his groin. He tried to scream, but no sound came out. One of the men giggled, another said they had killed him. The two of them pulled his legs apart, "while a third astride my back rode me like a horse".

Some doubt has been cast on this version of events. The next day, Lawrence said he escaped and rode back to Aqaba, a four-day camel ride. It is hard to see how he could have done this if he had been so horribly maltreated. It has even been suggested that this was a sexual fantasy which he made up to disparage the Turks.

There is evidence that Bey preferred women and it is thought that, after being cruelly beaten, Lawrence gave himself to the garrison commander and then to his other tormentors. "They all had a go," he said on a number of occasions.

This experience was a revelation for Lawrence. After he returned to England, he told Robert Graves that he felt the urge to be whipped and liked being buggered. By 1922, he was attending flagellation parties in Chelsea, held by a German called Jack Bilbo, who was also known as Bluebeard. Fearing that he was going to spill the beans to a German magazine, Lawrence wrote to the home secretary, asking to have Bilbo deported. He was told that only the courts could deport someone and Bilbo left England of his own accord in 1932.

Meanwhile, Lawrence employed a strapping Aberdeen youth called John Bruce to beat him. The story was that Lawrence had a stern relative known as the "Old Man" or "Uncle R". He would write letters listing Lawrence's fictitious misdeeds, such as showing disrespect for the king or borrowing money from the "damned Jews". Each crime came with a tariff and unless the punishment was carried out, "Uncle R" threatened to expose him as a bastard – Lawrence was illegitimate.

"I have my mother to consider," Lawrence said.

Bruce beat him first with a birch cane, but that had no effect through Lawrence's trousers. So, off they came and he was beaten on the bare buttocks. Later, a metal whip was used. He would get an erection with the first stroke and the punishment only stopped when he ejaculated – sometimes as many as 75 strokes later.

"Uncle R" also ordered him to undergo privations, hard diets, physical hardships, emotional abuse, electric shocks and, compassionately, "Swedish massage". On one occasion, Bruce received a letter telling him to hire a cottage, three horses and a groom. Lawrence was then to spend a week swimming and riding. The week ended with a beating so merciless that the groom, who witnessed it, was physically sick.

He said that the Bedouin "hurt himself ... to please himself. There followed a delight in pain."

And he got more than his far share. On his way to the Versailles Peace Conference – where he appeared in Arab costume as advisor to Prince Feisal – the plane crashed, killing the two pilots. He cracked a shoulder blade and suffered other minor injuries, but despite his pain, he busied himself helping the other victims. On another occasion he ran for a bus with three broken ribs, saying they would "float back into place in time".

In the Majestic Hotel in Paris, he horsed around with fellow officer Richard Meinertzhagen, who grasped Lawrence and smacked his bottom. Afterwards Lawrence said "that he could easily understand a woman submitting to rape once a strong man had hugged her". Meinertzhagen said that Lawrence liked "big strong men" – Dahoum was big and very strong, so was Feisal.

After the war, Lawrence joined the airforce under an assumed name, aiming to lose himself in the ranks. When it was discovered who he was, he was discharged. There was also the matter of his attachment to a young airman called R.A.M. Guy, who was described by Lawrence's service friends as "beautiful, like a Greek god". Lawrence then returned to the army as a private in the Royal Tank Corps, so that he could be around other men's bodies in the "sensual cauldron" of the barracks. He liked fighting with the other men and talked of the "rank cruelty of the officers".

"There is as a glitter on their faces when we sob for breath," he wrote, "and evident through their clothes is that tautening of their muscles (and once the actual rise of sexual excitement) which betrays we are being hurt not for our good, but to gratify a passion."

He enjoyed the other men's sex talk, but "I … lamented myself most when I saw a soldier with a girl, or a man fondling a dog". Women to him were either prostitutes or "holy almost, despite the soilings they receive when men handle them".

Even when holy, they were not for him. His mother hoped that he might marry Kathleen Scott, the widow of the Antarctic explorer, who "developed a crush" on Lawrence when she sculpted him. He admitted that he liked her, but nothing had happened between them, she said, because she had heard that he was "the Royal Mistress" of Prince Feisal. He also developed a close relationship with another older woman, Charlotte Shaw, who had a sexless marriage to George Bernard Shaw. It was to her that he confessed that he had consented to sex in Deraa and he was "unclean", but there could certainly be nothing between the two of them. He had an obsessive dislike of all women under the age of 60.

"I take no pleasure in women," said Lawrence. "I have never thought twice or even once of the shape of a woman."

The idea of a man embracing a woman revolted him. He was even offended by couples dancing.

Sex "must seem an unbearable humiliation to the woman", he said. "I hate and detest this animal side. It must leave a dirty feeling."

On another occasion, he wrote: "Honour thy father and mother – when we can see crawling out of her that bloody and blinded thing (which was ourselves), the penalty of her fall to the sexual assault of the father?"

But then, maybe sex did not bother him that much.

"I'm deeply puzzled by this *Lady Chatterley*," he wrote. "Surely the sex business isn't worth all this damn fuss. I've met only a handful of people who really cared a biscuit for it." Well, I care, but I suppose it's my business.

However, there were sexual goings-on at the army camp in Bovington, Dorset, where he was stationed with the Tank Corps.

"Hut 12 shows me the truth behind Freud," he said. "Sex is an integer in all of us."

He also talked of "the orgasm of man's vice" in the services and admitted that "reports accuse us of sodomy, too".

When Robin Maugham was stationed at Bovington in December 1939, one of the tank instructors took him to an upstairs room in a pub which, he said, Lawrence used to rent. One evening he had gone there with him and he had "persuaded the lance-corporal to whip him and then to penetrate him".

Toward the end of his life, he was out riding his motorbike when he was asked to swing a car's starting handle. The driver had left the car in gear, so the handle flew back and broke his wrist. Without a murmur of complaint, he asked the driver to put it in neutral. He swung the starting handle again with his other hand, then asked someone to start his motorbike, got on and rode off with "his right arm dangling". In 1935, he was killed on that motorbike. After his death, it was revealed that a warrant had been issued for his arrest on charges of indecency with other servicemen. Shortly before he died, a plain-clothes police inspector had visited him and warned him what would happen if he did not leave the country immediately. This lead to speculation that his death, rather than being an accident, had been suicide.

Chapter Eight

Bounty on the Mountie

The actor Charles Laughton – famed for his portrayal of Captain Bligh in the 1935 movie *Mutiny on the Bounty* – was a respectable married man. In 1927, he had been cast to play the lead in the West End stage adaptation of Arnold Bennett's *Mr Prohack*. His secretary was to be played by Elsa Lanchester*, a young actress from Clapham. At rehearsals, they went to lunch in a cheap restaurant with the rest of the cast. Then the 28-year-old Laughton, who was already a star, asked her out to dinner. This time they went somewhere more expensive. Soon they were slipping away for Sundays in the country.

Toward the end of the run of the play, Elsa invited him to a party attended by a number of the Bloomsbury Group. She danced for them. He took her home in a cab, intending to drop her there and go on home, but on the doorstep – to both his and her surprise – he kissed her. She invited him in. Soon he became a regular visitor.

His landlady did not allow women in the rooms after hours, so he moved to the Garlands Hotel to be nearer to her room in Bloomsbury Square. At weekends they would stay in a pub called the Dog and Duck in Sussex, registering as man and wife. Soon, they were living together in a flat in Dean Street in a house where Karl Marx had once lived.

After that they moved to a top-floor flat in Percy Street and took a holiday together in Laughton's home-town of Scarborough, though, for the sake of appearances, they took separate rooms in the Pavilion Hotel. Then, in 1929, they decided to get married and tied the knot in a registry office on February 9 – a Sunday – to avoid the Press. Even so, a small number of journalists turned up.

They honeymooned in Switzerland and Italy and bought a cottage in the country. It seemed that they could not have been happier.

The following year, everything changed. One night a young man was stopped by the police, loitering outside the Laughtons' Percy Street house. At that moment, Laughton and his fellow actor Jeffery Dell arrived. The youth claimed that Laughton had picked him up in the park the day before. He had taken him home and promised him money – but had not given it to him. Laughton denied everything and the boy was arrested.

Inside, Laughton confessed to Elsa. For some time he had been having brief relationships with men and boys, which he had not dared to tell her about. Elsa appeared neither hurt nor cross. She simply said: "It's perfectly all right. It doesn't matter. I understand."

Laughton burst into tears.

In court, the judge warned Laughton about "misguided generosity" and a scandal was avoided. However, the strain told on Elsa. She suffered a hysterical loss of hearing for a week. Later, she asked Laughton what had really gone on. He described what he and the boy and done on the sofa. She swallowed hard and said: "Okay, but let's get rid of the sofa."

They never talked about his homosexuality again, but it ate into them. Sex between them stopped – Elsa had never wanted children anyway. Even so, they found they were still deeply in love.

Elsa accompanied him on his first tour of the United States. In Chicago, a thoughtless host treated them to a screening of a pornographic movie, which they found embarrassing and tasteless. Soon after, Laughton got a movie contract to play opposite the insatiable Tallulah Bankhead*.

Cecil B. DeMille* wanted Laughton for *The Sign of the Cross* (1932), an epic featuring gladiators, orgies and naked dancing girls. DeMille, a homophobe, wanted Laughton to play Nero* as an ancient version of Mussolini*. Daringly, Laughton played him as gay. He even wanted the emperor to be accompanied everywhere by a naked boy. DeMille drew the line at that and gave the boyish Elsa the part, though she only appears in a few shots.

Back in London, they moved from the suitably named Percy Street to Gordon Square, to be in the midst of the mostly gay Bloomsbury set. Then *The Private Life of Henry VIII* (1933), where he played opposite Merle Oberon*, made him an international movie star and won him an Oscar. He was soon so busy in London and Hollywood, that there was no time for even the most fleeting sexual encounter. Even if he had, he risked a painful experience. In 1934, he spent several weeks in hospital with a rectal abscess. Despite this lack of sexual activity, the Press made allusions about his sexuality. One reporter found him sprawled on the couch in his dressing room at Metro-Goldwyn-Mayer* "stroking the legs of the golden statuette given to him by the Motion Picture Academy".

Things improved during the shooting of *Mutiny on the Bounty* (1935), in which Laughton, as Captain Bligh, played opposite the handsome Clark Gable*, as Mr Christian. Laughton found him impossibly delicious, but Gable would not talk to him off the set as he felt that Laughton was acting him off the screen. As a result of the tension this caused, Laughton suffered from muscular spasms. Thoughtfully, the studio provided a muscular young masseur called Dennis. In his hands, Laughton's tensions evaporated. Other members of the cast noted that Laughton treated Dennis with the care and attention of an indulgent foster father.

In 1935, Laughton was alone in Hollywood when he was diagnosed with syphilis. It had been in his system for years, he was told. He was suicidal. Elsa was away in London and Laughton turned to Josef von Sternberg*, who stayed with him for three days. Then Laughton took a second test and got the all clear. The first doctor had mixed the samples up. In gratitude, he used his influence with the producer Alexander Korda* – who had just offered him the title role in *I, Claudius* – to get von Sternberg – whose career was on the wane in Hollywood – the job as director. The picture was a disaster. Merle Oberon*, Korda's mistress, found herself caught in between Laughton's masochistic homosexuality and the cold and sadistic Joseph von Sternberg, who strode around the set at Denham in riding breeches. The picture was finally halted when she received a cut on the face as the result of a car accident. It was never completed.

Back in Hollywood, Laughton had a new masseur, Bob, who, again, he treated like a son. He encouraged the young man to marry and have children, even if this meant that he would lose his services.

Laughton was always like this with his lovers. Distressed by his own homosexuality, he urged them to go straight. However, he did not seek out the company of well-educated gays, who might have helped him come to terms with his sexuality intellectually. Rather, he wanted the company of beautiful young men, perhaps seeking, for a moment, to escape from his own less-than-appetising flesh.

Despite his self-loathing, Laughton was happy appearing naked in company. He would strip off in his dressing room on a hot day and skinny-dip in other people's pools.

He got a certain pleasure from being kind to his lovers, though his happiness, he knew, lay with Elsa. She grew to accept his homosexuality, fulfilling her own sexual needs with a series of short-lived affairs. There was a mutual respect and tolerance between the two. Laughton would not discuss the situation though, fearing that if the words were spoken the structure would break. He longed for the time when his sexual urges would die, so that they could be content together.

"I do wish it would all pass," he said, "and we could go peacefully to beautiful places and beautiful countries."

In the meantime, they shared a love of country walks and memorised the botanical names of wild flowers they saw. They had the same taste in reading and food: plain English cuisine – stews, boiled beef, steak and kidney pie. They collected antiques and pottery and shared a sense of humour, lampooning the pompous people who surrounded them.

Laughton extended this tolerance to his profession. In the movie *They Knew What They Wanted* (1940), the wronged husband forgives his adulterous wife in the last reel. Joseph Breen from the Hays Office insisted that this did not comply with the Production Code, which required, he said that "the sinner must be punished". Laughton interjected: "Do I understand, Mr Breen, that the Code does not recognise the New Testament?" The "Mr Breen" here was said as if Laughton's Bligh was addressing "Mr Christian" on board the *Bounty*.

"Christ forgave an adulteress didn't he, Mr Breen," Laughton continued.

"Well, Mr Laughton," said a flustered Breen. "You may have a point there."

The end of the film was left unchanged.

Carole Lombard*, who was playing the part of the erring wife, was flat-chested and liked to work in rehearsals without her falsies. When Laughton turned up in costume, she turned to her maid, Bucket, and said: "Bucket, bring me my breasts, will ya?"

Lombard and Laughton did not get on. She mocked his portly figure, calling him "Moby Dick" and taunting him by insisting that she had it written into her contract that she "wouldn't have to kiss his fat lips".

Laughton turned to the young actor David Roberts for comfort, who encouraged Laughton to take pride in his appearance and made him feel attractive. Again Laughton encouraged him to marry, but his wife died in a car crash just four weeks after their wedding. So the affair with Laughton resumed. This was Laughton's first long-term gay relationship and it was to last for nearly 20 years.

Roberts often stayed at the Laughton's house on Pacific Palisades. Laughton took a Socratic interest in the young man, teaching him about literature and art while indulging himself sexually with him. Elsa had no problem with this. She was pleased that Charles had found some emotional stability in this relationship. She had no wish to end their marriage and, as before, found her sexual satisfaction elsewhere.

Laughton extended his pedagogic activities to other young actors and began teaching when movie parts began to dry up. He worked with the two prominent straights, Jean Renoir* and Bertold Brecht, though he annoyed Brecht at the opening of the 1947 production of *Galileo*. In the opening scene, Laughton appears in a shirt and loose trousers, prior to taking a bath. Unconsciously, Laughton began scratching his crotch through the trouser pockets and the audience began tittering. Brecht had the wardrobe mistress sew the pockets up.

David Roberts accompanied Laughton when he went to film *The Man in the Eiffel Tower* (1950) in Paris. They stayed at the Prince des Galles Hotel. Laughton befriended the ice skater Belita, who took him to a restaurant frequented by prostitutes. Laughton loved it.

In 1950, Laughton became a citizen of the United States and

acquired a new partner, a handsome young man called Paul Gregory. Gregory was an employee of the talent agency MCA and an ardent fan of Laughton's. He was watching the TV one night in a bar when Laughton appeared on the *Ed Sullivan Show*. He rushed over to the Broadway theatre, where it was being shot, and confronted Laughton and his agent Frances Head as they came out. Laughton pushed him aside and made off, but Frances knew him and arranged for them to meet over tea in the Algonquin Hotel the next day.

Gregory proposed a series of one-night stands across the US. Laughton would read – or rather recite – from the classics. He got $2,000, rising to $4,000, an engagement and numerous proposals of marriage from women of all ages. Gregory quit MCA to take personal charge.

Along the way Laughton picked up another handsome young friend, Steve Martin. Soon they were an item, but when Laughton took Tyrone Power* under his wing, they quickly drifted apart. However, they were back together when Laughton went to London to film David Lean's *Hobson's Choice* (1953) with Martin, who tagged along as Laughton's secretary. Laughton hated the trip. It alienated him from Gregory and he feared that his marriage was finally coming apart. However, when he returned to the United States, he managed to put everything back together again. Then, in 1954, he toured Canada, once more with Steve. It was a long time coming but, at last, "Bounty" got his Mountie.

The following year, he split from Paul Gregory and dropped Steve Martin, along with a young man called Victor, with whom he had had a brief and disastrous affair. Once again he sought comfort with David Roberts.

In 1959, Laughton and Elsa went to England, where Laughton was to play a season of Shakespeare at Stratford, taking over from John Gielgud*. When Elsa went back to California, Laughton met Bruce Ashe, a photographer's model and an aspiring actor. They met in an art gallery. Ashe was admiring a picture when Laughton came up and said: "Beautiful, isn't it?"

"Yes, I suppose it is," said Ashe with a sneer. "But what would you want to do with it?"

"Hang it up on the wall" was Laughton's reply. It broke the ice.

The two men left the gallery together and had lunch. Laughton was captivated by his beauty and revelled in his conversation. They had sex almost immediately. Soon Laughton was deeply in love in a way he had never been before and Ashe moved into his flat in Dolphin Square.

Laughton treated Ashe as the perfect English son – outside the bedroom at least – and taught him about art and literature. When Laughton's Shakespeare season finished, they spent all their time together. Laughton took Ashe to Rome where he was filming *Under Ten Flags* (1960) and introduced him to the glories of the ancient world. They then set off for the United States with Ashe as Laughton's pupil and paid companion. It was then that he started work with Christopher Isherwood* on a theatrical version of the *Dialogues* of Plato. The idea was to show the idealised love between the scholar and his pupil. Meanwhile Laughton was practising what he preached, swimming and sunbathing with his classical beauty Bruce.

When working with Isherwood, Laughton would occasionally break off and do some comic readings for light relief. One in particular, Isherwood recalled, was Laughton's reading of the Book of Job where Job is a Jew from Central Casting and God is a Nazi Gauleiter. It had them in hysterics.

That summer, Ashe returned to England for some modelling assignments. Now in his early 60s, Laughton's health began to fail and he became suicidal, but Bruce returned and they went to Japan together which seemed to revive him. At Christmas, Laughton, Bruce and Elsa went to Palm Springs. By this time Elsa had established herself as a stage actress and Laughton created and directed her one-woman show, which opened on Broadway to rave reviews. Afterwards he took Bruce on a tour of the United States.

In 1962, Laughton took Bruce and Elsa to the Cannes Film Festival. By this time, Laughton was very ill. Back in the United States, he could not longer remember where he had been with Elsa and where he had been with Bruce, he constantly got the two mixed up. He died quietly on the night of December 15, 1962.

Chapter Nine

I Am a Cabaret

Whe he was a child, Christopher Isherwood loved dressing up. It was a habit he was to get out of. At prep school, there was an outdoor swimming pool where the boys swam naked. He was already having trouble with girls. The headmaster's daughter, Rosamira Morgan-Brown – an attractive young woman who taught at the school – lost patience with him one day and slapped him across the face.

"I am sure it did me nothing but good," he said years later.

He enjoyed wrestling and stories about Sarah Bernhardt*.

His father Frank died in the First World War, going into battle with only a walking stick in his hand. It was a lot to live up to, that sort of stupidity.

At school he met Wystan Auden – that's the poet W.H. Auden to you – who was known as Dodo Minor. His older brother John's birdlike looks had earned him the nickname Dodo. A precocious child, Auden had discovered the key to the cupboard where his father, a doctor, kept his anatomical manuals and gave Isherwood his first lessons in sex, with graphic drawings on the blackboard.

Auden had been circumcised just before being sent to school, possibly to quell his precocious interest in sex. If so, it failed. It set him on a lifelong quest for rough trade, as working-class lads were less likely to have their foreskins lopped off. He missed his own foreskin terribly and, from adolescence on, he expressed dissatisfaction with the size of his own penis.

"Offered the choice between becoming the most powerful man in the world and having the biggest cock in the world," he said, "I would choose the latter."

He also claimed that it was men, not women, who suffered most from penis-envy, noting: "Cocks have personal characters every bit as much as their owners, and very often the two are quite different."

Auden's late circumcision, arranged by his mother it seems, left him with the idea that woman were potential castrators. He was afraid of the mythical "*vagina dentata*" – the vagina with teeth – that would bite his penis off. Auden believed that his mother had him circumcised because he was an early masturbator.

Following the death of Isherwood's father, Auden and Isherwood grew close, though Auden was two years younger. They would go on long walks together, had private jokes and developed a private language that only they could understand. Auden also had a crush on the school chaplain. The Reverend Geoffrey Newman headed the list of 15 men and boys he had been in love with, which he drew up in the 1940s, explaining that his "pseudo-devotee" phrase at prep school was in fact "unredeemed eroticism".

The two friends were parted when they changed schools. Isherwood later speculated that he might have been straight if he had gone to a day school or, even better, a co-educational school. As it was, he maintained that he fought off the homosexual assaults of other boys at his boarding school, Repton. He did, however, admit to having crushes on a number of other boys, including a long-legged blond hockey player. He had a full-blown fantasy while reading *Wuthering Heights* – he was Heathcliffe while the boy with the hockey stick was Catherine. He also befriended the admirably named Edward Upward and their friendship was dubbed the "Mutual Admiration Society".

Later, Auden initiated "romantic friendship" with John Pudney, who went on to became a poet. On long walks, he talked of "D.H. Lawrence*, Havelock Ellis, Wilfred Gibson, psychology, sexual hygiene, homosexuality and Socialism". Auden later regretted that he had not been more forthright in his sexual overtures.

Isherwood followed Upward up to Cambridge, where their friendship flourished. However, he had his first sexual experience with another student at Corpus Christi, locking the boy in a room and sitting him on his lap to ensure that there would be no escape. He then started a full-blown affair with Hector Wintle. He also began writing homoerotic short stories, including one about a mysterious form of alchemy that demanded repeated acts of buggery, but then dropped out.

Auden went to Oxford and promptly fell in love with an undergraduate called Bill McElwee. However, on a trip down to London, on a train they called the Flying Fornicator, he bumped into Isherwood in Kensington, where he was living with his widowed mother and trying to write a novel.

Up until this point, Isherwood's sexual experiences had been furtive. Auden regaled him with tales of his own shameless exploits. They soon realised that "transgressive" sex would serve their literary needs and, after a couple of months, began having sex together.

"For years we fucked like rabbits every chance we got," Isherwood told the poet Thom Gunn. There was nothing romantic about it. They did it for pure pleasure and, throughout the 1930s, went to bed together "whenever the opportunity presented itself". The shagging continued until 1939. Apparently, the Second World War dampened their ardour.

While Isherwood had a romantic yearning for younger boys, Auden was audacious. There would be gropings in the back of the cinema. He picked up a stranger on a train and, on one occasion, dropped coins in the boots of a sentry outside a royal palace and fellated him in the sentry box. He was even the victim of blackmail and had to pay £5 to a man who had caught him in bed with the future poet laureate, John Betjeman.

This began to cause consternation at home. During the Christmas vacation of 1926, his mother grew suspicious when he kept taking the grocer's boy to the movies. His father found some poems from his schooldays which describe, in loving detail, another boy's body when they went swimming. Auden's father explained that, while such feelings were common in adolescence, they were not a good idea in later life, particularly as homosexuality was illegal in England.

Isherwood was astonished that these matters could be discussed with such frankness and tales of Auden's exploits kept him awake at night. The two of them went off on a holiday to the Isle of Wight, where the locals mocked Auden's *outré* outfits. This embarrassed Isherwood, but Auden simply said: "Laughter is the first sign of sexual attraction."

He also took to smoking a pipe.

"Insufficient weaning, my dear," he said. "I must have something to suck."

And he mocked Isherwood's timidity when it came to sex. When a friend began calling him Bisherwood – a contraction of his middle initial and Isherwood – Auden contracted it further to "Bish", pronounced "*biche*", the French slang word for lesbian.

Even though Auden had been perfectly at ease with his sexuality since his schooldays, he took his father's words to heart and attempted celibacy during 1927. In his poetry, at least, he began to mention some heterosexual themes.

By the summer, he was writing again of a homosexual traveller who is "too curious" about love and "stiffens to a tower". That autumn, Auden wrote to his brother saying: "As a bugger, there are three courses open to me." One was "middle-aged sentimentalism" – in other words, he could become a schoolmaster, idealising "the glorious gift of youth" and occasionally laying a firm hand on a boy's strong shoulder. Otherwise he could become "a London bugger, sucking off policemen in public lavatories". Or else there was the "pursed mouth of asceticism". This, he thought, was the course he must adopt. Bad decision.

Auden's uncle Harry had been in trouble for some homosexual activities in Germany and it was decided that the best course for Auden was to undergo psychoanalysis. He did so under "one of those pleasant pornographic women" called Margaret Marshall.

Meanwhile, Isherwood went off to the Haute Savoie with Edward Upward, but at the sight of a sexy boy on a train, he abandoned Upward and went off on his own. In the spring of 1928, he travelled to Bremen.

"The whole town is full of boys," he wrote and was immediately enamoured of blond German youth.

In the summer of 1928, Isherwood grew close to Stephen Spender, while Auden mysteriously got engaged to a nurse called Sheilah Richardson in Birmingham – well, it's said that there are two things certain in this world, death and nurses. Almost immediately afterwards Auden left for Berlin, where he intended to spend a year learning German. Isherwood and others soon were getting explicit letters describing his adventures and the general wickedness of the city. There were, he said, 170 male brothels in Berlin.

Auden's liberation had come about through his meeting with John Layard, 16 years his senior and a disciple of the American psychologist Homer Lane, whose philosophy was that there was only one sin – being untrue to one's own nature. Auden immediately seduced Layard, giving the older man his first experience of homosexual love.

That Christmas, Auden returned to England to spread the word. He told Isherwood that the sore throats he suffered from were caused by the fact that he was lying about his nature. He told him that he had found a bar – "Cosy Corner" at 7 Zossenerstrasse – where he could turn his fantasies into reality. It was in the working-class area of Hallesches Tor and "juvenile delinquents" offered sex in return for presents or a little cash. Auden described a regular sex partner called Pieps, who he had picked up there, as a cross between a rugby player and Josephine Baker. Isherwood was particularly thrilled when Auden told him how Pieps could be provoked with a pillow fight into beating him up. He would emerge from their sex sessions covered with bruises. Isherwood had always loved the rough-and-tumble of wrestling and boxing at school and decided to set off for Berlin as soon as he could.

Auden broke off his engagement, explaining: "The attraction of buggery is partly its difficulty and torments. Heterosexual love seems so tame and easy after that. I feel this with Sheilah."

He resolved never to marry. He had had sex with another woman, an Austrian called Hedwig Petzold, a few years earlier and kept in contact with her until the end of her life. As to heterosexual love generally? "I am not disgusted with it, but sincerely puzzled at what the attraction is," he told novelist Naomi Mitchison. It was "like watching a game of cricket for the first time".

A sailor he met offered to help him out with a practical demonstration.

"We must get a woman up here and jazz her together," he told Auden. "Or I jazz her and you watch. You've done that? You'll get a kick out of it. I bet you find yourself jogging off when I jazz her."

It was Auden that now agonised over his sexuality. He disagreed with Proust's theory that homosexuality was a revolt against authority and that "the social ban on buggery makes it exciting" – pointing out that gay sex flourished when there was no such repression. He also thought that it flourished in the middle and upper classes because they slept alone. As poor housing forced working class boys to sleep with brothers and sisters, they did not associate such physical intimacy with sex. But middle- and upper-class boys, craving such physical intimacy, did.

Men were interested in penises – primarily their own, but they liked to see how it measured up to other men's, he said. He also identified his own homosexuality with motherhood. "I am my mother," he said. He was deeply confused. There was one thing, however, of which he was certain. When it came to heterosexual love: "Never, never, never again."

He did get married, though, in 1935, to Erika Mann, the strikingly beautiful AC/DC daughter of Thomas Mann, who was running an anti-Nazi cabaret called "The Peppermill". She wanted a British passport so that she could escape from Germany. She had first asked Isherwood, who was horrified that people might think he was trying to pass himself off as straight, and turned her down. So she turned to Auden.

"Delighted," he said. "What are buggers for?"

Isherwood had arrived in Berlin on March 19, 1929 and found heaven itself. As well as the brothels, there were 132 homosexual cafés registered with the police. Some were exclusively for lesbians. Others specialised in transvestism, or had a special attraction, like a genuine hermaphrodite, on the premises. There was a weekly paper for homosexuals call *Freundschaft* – yes, "Friend Shaft" – which featured the most fantastic advertisements. Then there was the *strich* or avenue, where prostitutes offered themselves for sale or rent. There were women in men's clothes, often holding a whip, and men in women's clothing – and a number of men or women who would go with either sex if the price was right.

Auden used Isherwood's arrival as the excuse for starting a diary, which is so obscene it has still not been published. First, of course, was a trip to Cosy Corner, a tatty bar where half-a-dozen boys sat at tables, drinking beer and eyeing up those who came in. Clients could inspect the merchandise in the lavatories or take a discreet feel under the table, slipping a hand into a trouser pocket that had conveniently been torn out.

"All these boys, as far as I know, were heterosexual," said Layard. "But they didn't mind playing around, and they liked a bit of money."

They boasted of their affairs with women and frequently consorted with female prostitutes. The fact that they were attractive to gay men both enhanced their masculinity and fed their vanity.

While Auden was taking a succession of lovers, he mocked Isherwood for his fidelity to one boy – Berthold Szczesny, known universally as "Bubi". He was not even a blond German but a dark-haired Czech.

Auden had split up with John Laynard and taunted him with the sexual prowess of his new boyfriend, Gerhardt Meyer.

"The cord from his balls to his spine was like a thousand volts," said Auden.

Laynard bedded Gerhardt in revenge, but he could not cope with the guilt.

"I had stolen Wystan's boy," he said. "I had gone against every rule, and then been impotent."

He went home, put a gun in his mouth and tried to kill himself. Somehow the bullet missed his brain and lodged in the skull. He took a taxi to Auden's place on the Furbingerstrasse, near a brothel, and begged him to finish him off. Instead, Auden took him to the hospital.

When the money ran out, Auden and Isherwood returned to England. Isherwood got a commission to translate Baudelaire's *Journaux Intimes* into English and he and Auden began writing a play together, which covered the themes of white slavery, cross-dressing and buggery. Then Isherwood got a job as a tutor in a remote Scottish village. To keep his hands off his pupils, he bedded the mothers. This was, he said, quite workable, but not as good as the real thing. And the real thing for Isherwood was sex with boys of 17 or 18.

In November, Isherwood was back in Berlin. He moved in with

Oscar Wilde: The unspeakable in pursuit of the fellatable.

Vaslav Nijinsky: Fancied a quick *pas de deux*.

Lawrence of Arabia: A sucker for a chic sheik.

Christopher Isherwood (left) and W.H. Auden: Get your glad rags on boys, it's Cabaret time.

J. Edgar Hoover: He always got his man.

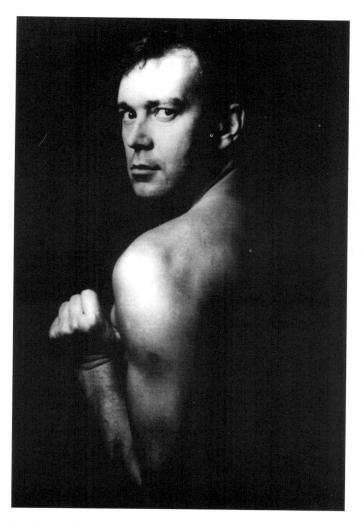

Joe Orton: Prick up your ears?

Yukio Mishima: It took guts, but one thrust and both he and his head came off with a single stroke.

Quentin Crisp: A stately homo of England.

Derek Jarman: Always making his movie.

Sir Noël Coward: A dedicated Thespian and Christmas came more than once a year.

the syphilitic Francis Turville-Petre in rooms rented from the Hirschfeld Institute of Sexual Science. The first such institute in the world, it was run by Dr Magnus Hirschfeld, a homosexual Baltic Jew and the author of such seminal works as *The Third Sex – Homosexuals in Berlin*, *Sexual Perversions*, *The Homosexuality of Men and Women*, *Transvestites* and *The Sexual History of the World War*. He campaigned for the legalisation of homosexuality and Isherwood was much impressed when André Gide* visited the institute to see a boy who had perfect female breasts. At night, Isherwood accompanied Turville-Petre cruising the boy-bars.

In the midst of a family row, Isherwood told his mother details of his life in Berlin. She began having crying fits and went into therapy under John Layard, who had now settled back in London. Isherwood took up with a promiscuous bisexual, Otto Nowak, who led him a merry dance. In the summer of 1931, Upward and Auden visited. Upward had become a school master and a Marxist, while Auden had taken up teaching and had been in hospital for a painful operation on an anal fissure – "the stigmata of Sodom", he called it.

Isherwood and Otto visited Spender in Hamburg, where another boy-bar scene was flourishing, and they invited Spender to come and sample the delights of Berlin. Isherwood moved in with Otto and his family briefly, but when Otto's mother went into a sanatorium for her TB, Isherwood moved to new lodgings at 38 Admiralstrasse, where he frequently entertained Spender.

Another resident was an American heiress, Jean Ross, who sang in a rundown nightclub and was the model for Sally Bowles. In looks and voice she was no match for Lisa Minnelli*, but Isherwood was fascinated by her outrageous clothes and her rampant promiscuity. Although they shared a bed on a couple of drunken occasions, she helped him smuggle boys in and out of his rooms. Money was tight, but he still had enough to indulge Otto and his other conquests with small gifts.

He also befriended the Berlin sales representative for *The Times*, Gerald Hamilton. A fat shyster who wore an ill-fitting wig and who had a taste for working-class boys, he was the model for Mr Norris in *Mr Norris Changes Trains*. He ate out on the notoriety the book gave him. He had also been a friend of the gay Irish patriot Roger Casement and, later in life, sat, in part, for a memorial statue of Winston Churchill*, as he was of similar build.

In the summer of 1931, Auden, Isherwood, Spender and Otto Nowak went on holiday to Ruegen Island in the Baltic. There was lots of nude sunbathing with Spender taking snaps, but there was a falling-out between Isherwood and Otto, who went dancing with girls and stayed out late. He resolved "not to live with Otto again for a long time". Spender suggested moving into Isherwood's lodgings, but Isherwood rejected this, saying: "I think it is better if we don't all live right on top of each other, don't you? I believe that was partly the trouble at Ruegen."

By this time Hitler and the Nazis were very much in evidence. Isherwood dreamed of going off to the Far East with Turville-Petre, but he wanted to move out into the German countryside and invited Isherwood to go with him. They headed for Mohrin, now Moryn in Poland. Turville-Petre employed Erwin Hansen – a friend of Hirschfeld's secretary/lover Karl Geise – as cook and housekeeper. A former army PT instructor, he was an active Communist and a practising homosexual. He brought Heinz Neddmayer with him as his assistant. His curly hair, big brown eyes and large lips caused Isherwood to dub him "nigger boy", but he soon took him as his lover.

Turville-Petre and Hanson soon got bored with the countryside and headed back to Berlin, leaving Isherwood and Neddmayer to their rustic idyll. In June, they went to Ruegen Island, where they caught up with Spender and a circle of like-minded friends.

On a visit to London, Isherwood met John Lehmann and his lesbian sister Beatrix, who joined him in Berlin. Auden introduced him to Gerald Heard, who was doing a series of radio talks for the BBC. He lived with Christopher Wood, who was young, rich and handsome. Wood and Isherwood immediately hit it off.

The South African novelist William Plomer took Isherwood to meet E.M. Forster, who showed him the manuscript of his unpublished homosexual novel *Maurice*. When Isherwood expressed his appreciation of the book, Forster leant over and kissed him. When *Maurice* was finally published in 1971, a year after Forster's death, Isherwood found that the royalties had been bequeathed to him and he used them to set up a fund for young British writers who wanted to travel in the United States.

With the Nazi Party now in power, the boy bars of Berlin were being closed down and Hirschfeld's Institute was trashed. Isherwood watched as his bust and books were burnt in front of the Opera – and cried "Shame!" very softly.

Isherwood again toyed with the idea of going to the Far East, but realised that he was in love with Neddmayer. Turville-Petre had rented the Greek island of St Nicholas and Isherwood, Neddmayer and Hansen set off to Vienna where they visited John Lehmann and the League for Sexual Reform. From there, they headed down the Danube on a streamer to Belgrade, then took a train to Athens.

Turville-Petre had assembled a small male harem on St Nicholas. He was having a house built but, for the time being, they had to live in tents. There were frequent orgies, but Isherwood was put off by the Greek boys' lack of personal hygiene. He was jealous of Neddmayer's entanglements with the local lads. The final straw came when one of the Greek boys was caught fucking the duck they were going to have for dinner.

Although Turville-Petre thought that St Nicholas was a buggers' paradise, Isherwood missed the company of women and escaped to Athens with Neddmayer. Things were not going well between the two of them, however. They sailed to Marseilles and Isherwood planned to dump Neddmayer when they got to Paris. Instead he took him on to London, giving him some awkward explaining to do to his mother. Neddmayer's tourist visa soon ran out, though, and he had to head back to Germany. Important business detained Isherwood in London, though he soon missed his lover.

When he heard that Neddmayer planned to return to England, he sent money and a letter outlining what he should say to the immigration officer to get an indefinite stay. Auden went down with Isherwood to meet the boat at Harwich. They waved to Neddmayer as the boat docked, but when the other passengers came out of the Customs House there was no sign of him. The immigration officials became suspicious when they found Isherwood's letter on him and he was deported. Auden said that the immigration officer was gay and had rejected the boy out of spite.

Isherwood went back to Berlin, collected Neddmayer and took

him to Amsterdam, with the aim of taking him on to Tahiti. Instead they had to make do with Tenerife, where they stayed in a pension run along the lines of a monastery by a gay couple, a German Nero-type and his partner, an Englishman who dyed his hair and "loathes women so much he has put a barbed-wire entanglement across an opening in the garden wall to keep them out".

Isherwood and Neddmayer travelled across Morocco, up through Spain to Copenhagen, then stayed in Brussels and Holland. Isherwood earned money writing for the *Listener*. Its literary editor was Joe Ackerley, a leading member of what Auden called the "Homintern" – a loose fraternity of intellectual gays, that included E.M. Forster*, Edwin Muir, Maynard Keynes* and Louis MacNeice.

They shared a house in Amsterdam with the drunken, snobbish Brian Howard and his German boyfriend Anton "Toni" Altmann. Isherwood got on well enough with the pleasure-seeking Howard, but could not stand the affected Toni. Forster visited with his policeman boyfriend Bob Buckingham, as did Spender, Hamilton and other like-minded friends. They celebrated Isherwood's birthday in an impromptu visit to Gevangenpoort Prison's museum of torture instruments.

With Spender and his latest boyfriend, working-class Welshman Tony Hyndman, Isherwood and Neddmayer set out for Portugal, where they thought they could live cheaply. They thought it best to leave, however, when the Spanish Civil War broke out. Isherwood had to go back to London. Neddmayer went to Paris, where he got in trouble with the police. He had lost his identity card in a brawl. An informant had identified him as a rent boy and he had been accused of seducing the deaf-and-dumb chambermaid at the hotel where he was staying. The police told him to leave France and he went to Luxembourg.

Gerald Hamilton, now in Brussels, said he could arrange a Mexican passport for Neddmayer. Isherwood caught up with Neddmayer in Luxembourg and told him the good news, but the police turned up at the hotel where they were staying and told Neddmayer that he was to be expelled. Isherwood called a lawyer in Brussels, who told him that Neddmayer should go back to Germany where he could get a visa to enter Belgium. Isherwood and Neddmayer had popped over the border before, just for the hell of it, and no one had checked their passports. This time though, the instant Neddmayer crossed the frontier he was grabbed by the Gestapo for being a draft-dodger. Then he was accused of "reciprocal onanism" with Isherwood. The court sentenced him to six years, followed by one year's work for the state and three years' military service.

In August, Isherwood holidayed with Auden in Dover. There was a large army barracks there and a number of the soldiers were happy to entertain gentlemen visiting from London.

In 1938, Auden and Isherwood went to New York where they were greeted by George Davis, who gave them bundles of dollar bills for the travel pieces they had contributed to *Harper's Bazaar*. Davis gave them a whirlwind tour of the city and offered to act as their pander. Isherwood asked for an 18-year-old blond with sexy long legs. Davis provided exactly what he asked for. Instantly Isherwood replaced his love of German blonds with the love of American blonds, and both he and Auden were captivated by the youth and vitality of the United States.

Auden grew jealous, though. It seemed that Isherwood was now having more sexual adventures than he was. In response, Isherwood began to withdraw his sexual favours.

Back in Britain, Isherwood went to see John Lehmann on the Isle of Wight. He had just come back from Germany, where he had managed to see Neddmayer – who seemed to be coping with his predicament rather well, but Isherwood's thoughts were now with his blond 18-year-old in Manhattan. He took up with Spender's old boyfriend, Tony Hyndman, and took him on holiday to Ostend, then he headed back to Dover with a bunch of similarly inclined friends to take advantage of the facilities there.

Whilst rubbing shoulders with Virginia Woolf* and W. Somerset Maugham in London's literary circles, he took up with 20-one-year-old Jack "Jackie" Hewit, a working-class lad from Gateshead. Since coming to London, he had become a regular on the gay scene on the first floor of Lyon's Corner House in Coventry Street. After a party at Brian Howard's, he had gone home with Soviet spy, Guy Burgess, who was then working at the Foreign Office. A tempestuous relationship followed. Ground down by

Burgess's drinking and constant infidelity, he sought comfort with Anthony Blunt, another member of the Cambridge spy ring.

They went for a short break to Brussels. Auden came, too. Jackie did the housework, while Isherwood worked. In bed at night, the sex was perfunctory. Jackie recalled that it was neither affectionate nor adventurous. This could have been because Brussels reminded Isherwood of Neddmayer – or it could have been because he had the clap, a painful condition in those days. Meanwhile, Auden took up with a Belgian boy. Isherwood made a quick trip to Berlin to find out what was happening with Neddmayer, then he and Auden set off back to New York. After seeing them off at Victoria, Benjamin Britten* and his boyfriend Peter Pears* took Jackie home to comfort him – "rather too warmly". For Isherwood, things blond and bold beckoned and Jackie knew he would not come back.

On hand to greet Auden and Isherwood on their arrival in New York was Auden's wife Erika Mann. The two poets moved into the George Washington Hotel and Isherwood took up where he had left off with his blond bombshell. Then they moved into an apartment at 237 East 81st Street.

On April 6, 1939, Auden and Isherwood were to give a poetry reading at the Keynote Club on West 52nd Street. The young Harold Norse mentioned this to his 18-year-old Jewish friend from Brooklyn, Chester Kallman, and said: "Let's sit in the front row and wink at them."

When Kallman first saw Auden, with unironed shirt, untied shoelaces and a notoriously slovenly appearance, he whispered: "Miss Mess."

He found his Yorkshire accent difficult to understand, but Auden recited his elegy to Yeats and was the star of the show.

"Overcome by the situation, we stifled giggles and continued to flirt outrageously with Isherwood, winking and grinning, and he grinned back," recalled Norse.

Afterwards, Isherwood gave Norse a visiting card, which Kallman purloined. Two days later, he turned up to see Isherwood. Auden opened the door and said: "It's the wrong blond." He had been hoping to see a young college-jock who had also come backstage after the reading. However, Kallman and Auden were soon deep in conversation.

Norse described Kallman at the time: "Both sexes merged with androgynous appeal: willowy grace combined with a deep, manly voice. Not at all effeminate, just young and blond, he was tall, unathletic, with slightly stooped shoulders, a spinal curvature and a heart murmur from rheumatic fever in childhood. His disliked all physical exercise except cruising, which developed his calf muscles. He picked his nose with long spatulate fingers, dirt-rimmed, and thoughtfully examined the product – a sure sign of a Brooklyn intellectual."

On a second visit, Kallman showed Auden his body and Auden fell head over heels in love.

Auden wrote to his brother: "At last, after all these years, Mr Right has come into my life. He is a Romanian–Latvian–American Jew called Chester Kallman, 18, extremely intelligent and I think, about to become a good poet … This time, my dear, I really believe it's marriage. The snag is I think I shall have to become an American citizen as I'm not going to risk separation through international crises. I write letters every day when I am away and so does he, have given up biting my nails and feel all warm and soft inside like a houseman. Not only can I talk to him as an equal, but he understands sex like no one I've ever met."

This was written in the first flush of love as later, they would prove to be sexually incompatible. However, they were together, on and off, for the rest of their lives. One friend said that Auden took Kallman on "as a sort of hair-shirt and put up with him as an article of undoubting faith". There was a lot of romance in their relationship, though. Chester "reigned over this province of formalised sensibility by appropriating the emotional world of 19th-century Italian grand opera. But he is not a screaming queen; his tone was moderate and much funnier." He wrote dirty light verse, but was "a real pain in the ass on many occasions and caused Miss-Master plenty of trouble".

Auden realised that they shared a similar need for emotional pain. As a neurotic and a Jew, Auden believed that Kallman was "tempted to desire suffering" – and he delivered this in full operatic style.

"After about an hour and a half of rowing, I got to a semihysterical state," Kallman wrote, "wherein I ran my hands through my hair and shouted 'I hate him' like a third act."

Their rows were legendary. Once, on the subway, with a crowd of passengers looking on in disbelief, they had a row which went like this:

Auden: "I am not your father, I'm your mother."

Kallman: "You're not my mother! I'm your mother!"

Auden: "No, you've got it all wrong. I'm your mother!"

Kallman: "You're not. You're my father.

Auden (now screaming): "But you've got a father! I'm your bloody mother and that's that, darling! You've been looking for a mother since the age of four!"

Kallman (yelling): "And you've been obsessed with your mother from the womb! You've been trying to get back ever since, so I am your mother! And you are my father!"

Auden: "No, you want to replace your father for marrying women who rejected you, for which you can't forgive him. But you want a mother who will accept you unconditionally, as I do…"

Kallman: "I'm your goddamn mother for the same reason! You're always sucking on me as if I were one giant tit."

Auden: "I must always have something to suck."

Kallman: "Not now, Wystan, not now."

Kallman was, of course, jealous of the close relationship Auden had with Isherwood, who used this as an opportunity to see less of Auden. He was beginning to feel overshadowed by him. Isherwood and his boyfriend took the Greyhound bus out to Los Angeles to visit Gerald Heard and Aldous Huxley* who had moved out there in 1937. Christopher Wood lent him $2,000 and Isherwood set up home in the Hollywood Hills. Domestic life with his American blond, Isherwood found, "reminds me very much of life with Heinz – except that he is even more serious, hates going out in the evenings, reads Suetonius*, Wells and Freud* and goes to art school."

And there was lashings of sex.

"Why do we have bodies? By the time they've been satisfied, there is only half an hour a day left over for talk. And talk is all that finally matters."

In fact, Isherwood was going off sex. Under the influence of Heard and Huxley he turned to Eastern religion and became a disciple of Swami Prabhavanda, who recommended sexual abstinence. Isherwood introduced Denny Fouts, a bisexual who Isherwood fictionalised as "the best kept boy in the world" in *Down There on a Visit*, to the Swami. Although the meeting was a disaster, Fouts moved in with Isherwood for a joint exercise in monastic living. Meanwhile, Isherwood's blond moved out. Isherwood hoped that he would go back to New York. Instead he rented rooms nearby.

Despite his devotion to Swami Prabhavanda, Isherwood found he could not give up sex and started having brief encounters on the beach. Then, in 1944, he was introduced to a beautiful young man by Denny Fouts and took him as his regular boyfriend. There was a brief reconciliation with his blond, but it was more of a friendship than a sexual affair. He eventually married and called his first son Christopher, as did Heinz.

Isherwood moved in with 24-year-old part-Irish, part Cherokee Bill Caskey, who washed dishes at Café J, a popular hangout near the beach. The rule of the house was that neither of them was to bring a sexual partner back while the other was in town. Caskey soon discovered that Isherwood could not keep to this – and gave up himself, too. They had a brief honeymoon in Mexico. They moved into Denny Fouts' flat and Isherwood cruised the beaches north of Santa Monica where orgies took place. He was particular fond of a stretch of beach called "The Pits" where he enjoyed numerous anonymous sexual encounters. He and Caskey also entertained at home. Greta Garbo* was a frequent visitor as was Cecil Beaton*, who was pursuing Garbo at the time.

Isherwood and Caskey were at a party at Charlie Chaplin's* house, when the well-known wit Nathalie Moffat called out: "Oh, Billy, do come and sit here. I just love pansies."

"Nathalie, my dear, your slang is out of date," he shot back. "The correct word is 'cock-suckers'."

The room fell silent and they were not invited back – though that may have been because someone told Chaplin that Isherwood had pissed on the sofa while drunk.

After a quick trip to England, Isherwood and Caskey set up home together in New York.

"Caskey is sweeter than ever, and I am very, very happy," Isherwood wrote.

He spent weekends on Fire Island with Auden and Spender, recapturing the spirit of their times on Ruegen Island. Then Isherwood and Caskey went off on a trip around South America.

In Argentina, they met up with Berthold Szczesny – "Bubi" – Isherwood's first boyfriend in Berlin. He had a couple of Isherwood's novels on his bookshelves, though he did not know enough English to read them.

While on the trip, Isherwood received a manuscript copy of Gore Vidal's* ground-breaking gay novel *The City and the Pillar*. Later, in Paris, they were sitting in a café in St Germain des Prés when Vidal came up and introduced himself. Isherwood and Vidal hit it off immediately and the three of them went sightseeing together, though Caskey found Vidal's game of naming historical figures and figuring out whether they were gay or not annoying. Isherwood and Vidal later dedicated books to each other. In Paris, they also ran into Auden and Kallman, who were on their way to Ischia.

Auden and Kallman seemed to have had an exchange of marriage vows and Auden began wearing a wedding ring, which Kallman soon discarded. With Kallman's father's consent, they went off to New Mexico to visit D.H. Lawrence's* widow.

"Wystan calls it our honeymoon," said Kallman. "Such a romantic girl."

Auden's state of rapture on the journey south was marred by Kallman's attempts "to establish closer contacts with sundry youths on the bus or at stops".

Auden managed to outrage the artists' colony in Taos with his lack of personal hygiene and his dismissal of all the poets and artists present as "second rate".

Margaret Lefranc and another woman were driving to California and offered Auden and Kallman a lift. Auden "made it clear that he hadn't much use for the company of women", but was stingy enough to accept the lift anyway.

On their return to New York, Kallman headed for Dizzy's Club on West 52nd Street.

"The dive was a sex addict's quick fix, packed to the rafters with college boys and working-class youths," said Norse. "Amid the laughter and screaming and ear-splitting jukebox music, it was like an orgy room for the fully clad."

Auden was seen there, sitting alone at the tables at the back where "he could observe boys kissing and groping under the bright lights". Too old to join in, he jotted down notes and sometimes wrote a verse or two.

He moved into a brownstone in Brooklyn with Paul Bowles, Benjamin Britten* and Peter Pears*, Louis MacNeice, Richard Wright and family, and Gypsy Rose Lee. Visitors included Salvador Dali*, Aaron Copland and Leonard Bernstein. Rows were frequent.

In 1940, he invited a handsome, young British merchant seaman to stay. Though he fell under Auden's thrall, he knew that Auden considered himself married "in the eyes of God" to Kallman.

"He was so blindly in love with Chester that he believed implicitly in his 'innocence' and fidelity to his marriage vows," said the seaman. This can hardly have been true, as the sailor and Kallman began to have an affair of their own, which Auden found out about soon after. In a fit of rage, he tried to strangle Kallman while he was asleep, but Kallman woke up and pushed him off. For years, Auden was quite unbalanced when it came to the subject of the British merchant navy.

Auden and Kallman continued their affair, though it was tense. After staying out in the Massachusetts countryside with Auden, Kallman said that when he got back to the city "I expect to spend three-quarters of my time flat on my stomach biting into pillows, listening to the music of the bedsprings".

After visiting Isherwood in California in 1941, Kallman rued that there weren't any "real men" in Los Angeles, then regaled them with this tale: "Just the other night I picked up a six-foot-two-and-a-half-inch merchant sailor in Brooklyn – wildly attractive, young, strong, perfectly built and large. I was all prepared for an absolutely relentless fucking but, as it turned out in the end, that is what I had to provide him with."

This was hard for Auden to take. He had come to believe, he said, that "sexual fidelity is more important in homosexual relationships than in any other; in other relationships there are a variety of ties, but here fidelity is the only bond".

Kallman continued to taunt him. He wrote from Los Angeles where he had gone to find work: "Sex has been spotty and silly consisting of quick ones and *morceaux de commerces* who decide that I'm their dear one."

On December 7, 1941, he wrote to say that he had just met a "divine soldier and his friend [who] just want to fuck all night long", but he had neither money nor a place to take them. Auden agreed to send money.

And Kallman's reaction to the attack on Pearl Harbor?

"It's all very depressing – and now war … and then to have these days of sheer sexual frustration. Is it asking so much to be fucked or even to indulge in the simplest childhood experiences with a more dangerous engine."

Even so, Auden cut out an old friend who told him he was foolish for getting involved with "a Brooklyn kike". Auden felt he needed to suffer to be an artist. Without it, "I should soon become like the later Tennyson." And Kallman provided suffering by a bucketful. Jealousy was grist to his mill.

"All homosexual acts are acts of envy," Auden said.

Of course, when it came to sexual fidelity, Auden did not practise what he preached. He arrived at *New Yorker* poetry critic Louise Bogan's apartment with "a whole cloud of mysterious little male presences all looking … like pressed flowers". He told her that he lived quietly in Brooklyn, "not seeing anyone for weeks." She added: "I think this is unlikely; but maybe he doesn't think the little pressed flowers are anybody."

Auden had a heterosexual affair. In 1945, he had hired a Brooklyn classmate of Kallman's, Rhoda Jaffe, as a typist. She came round to his apartment to work. While she was typing, Auden said, out of the blue: "I think we ought to have an affair."

It was consummated immediately. They were even seen out together, to everyone's surprise. Kallman rebuked Auden for going hetero, saying: "After all, I'm pure."

Despite his protestations, there were also rumours that Kallman slept with women but that he "never, never told".

Notwithstanding his occasional heterosexual slip-up, Auden was dubbed a "homosexual chauvinist" by Edmund Wilson, who said Auden was "homosexual to an almost fanatical degree – tells people that Eisenhower* is a queer and assured me the other day that Wagner's* Tristan and Isolde were really a couple of lesbians, because a man making love to a woman couldn't really get into that rapturous state – he would be 'thinking about something else'".

He said that he would rather go to bed with President Truman* than General MacArthur, enquired whether FBI chief J. Edgar Hoover* and Soviet foreign minister Molotov* were queens, and volunteered to throw shit on Labouchère's grave.

According to Auden, "all American writing gives the impression that Americans don't really care for girls at all. What the American male really wants is two things: he wants to be blown by a stranger while reading the newspaper and he wants to be fucked by his buddy when he's drunk."

After the war, Auden begun to get disillusioned with sex, though he still wanted it.

"I don't care about the excitement of the chase one bit any more," he said in 1947. "What I would really like would be a brothel where you simply go in, pay your money, and go home at a reasonable hour without any understanding on either side." And later: "Sexual experience never means a truly complete, but always a broken and divisive way of knowing one another."

His love for Kallman continued, though. After meeting Isherwood and Caskey in Paris, Auden started writing the pornographic poem "The Platonic Blow, by Miss Oral" which he wanted to dedicate to Kallman, who still tormented him by bringing home sailors and drag queens he had picked up in bars. Auden thought that Kallman's constant affairs were an expression of addiction rather than freedom. On the other hand, Kallman felt that Auden had robbed him of a life of his own, leaving promiscuous sex as his only form of self-assertion.

Auden and Kallman set up home in Ischia, where Auden became chaste.

"To my great delight I find myself completely untroubled by sex," he wrote. "Chester, too, is quite changed, and in consequence, our relationship is, for the first time, a really happy one."

His sex life was not quite over, though. In the summer of 1952, Auden asked a young American woman called Thekla Pelletti to marry him – even though he was not divorced from Erika Mann.

141

Thekla refused him. Auden had finally run out of puff. Though Kallman continued to bring back Greek boys after his holidays each July, they were still together when Auden died in 1973.

In 1951, Isherwood's Berlin stories were turned into a play called *I Am a Camera* – an expression of Isherwood's which meant that he merely recorded what he saw, like a camera, rather than getting involved in the action. It is disingenuous at best. Soon after its New York opening, Bill Caskey joined the Navy and shipped out to the Korean War. Isherwood went to London, then on to Germany where he met up with Otto and Heinz.

After a quick holiday in Bermuda with a young American, he headed for San Francisco, where Caskey was on shore leave. This was the last gasp of their affair. Back in Los Angeles in 1953, Isherwood met two attractive brothers Ted and Don Bachardy at a St Valentine's Day party. Forty-eight-year-old Isherwood took paternal interest in the boys at first, then fell in love with 18-year-old Don.

At the time, Isherwood was living in the summer house of Dr Evelyn Hooker, who was doing a comprehensive study of homosexuality in California. Don moved in, but Hooker's husband, a professor of English at UCLA was afraid of a scandal and Isherwood was asked to leave. Poison-pen letters circulated and there were threats that Isherwood would be reported to the police. Bachardy thought this was rum. To cover their tracks, Isherwood and Bachardy moved in with a married couple.

Isherwood was working on the script of *Diane* (1956), a movie based on the life of Henry II's mistress Diane de Poitiers starring Lana Turner*, at the time, which prevented him from having a hand in the film version of *I Am a Camera* (1955).

After several trips around the world, Isherwood and Bachardy settled into a serene domestic existence which lasted for 20 years. During his stay in California, the actor Charles Laughton* was a near neighbour. He and Isherwood sat down to write a play together based on Plato's life of Socrates.

In 1964, David Hockney moved out to California and quickly became friends with Isherwood and Bachardy.

"David, we have so much in common," Isherwood exclaimed on meeting Hockney. "We love California, we love American boys and we're both from the North of England."

Hockney wondered wryly what, as a working-class lad from Bradford, he had in common with the upper-middle class milieu of Isherwood.

Isherwood must have been thinking of his relationship with Don when he wrote in *A Meeting by the River*: "I don't believe such closeness is possible between a man and a woman – deep down they are natural enemies – and how many men ever find it together?"

In 1972, *I Am a Camera* had transmogrified into the film *Cabaret* (1972) with Lisa Minnelli*. Along the way, Isherwood was appalled to discover that he had made Sally Bowles pregnant – yuck! This prompted him to come out on American television. He was upset to have missed Auden's memorial service in Westminster Abbey and was convinced that Kallman had deliberately chosen not to inform him about it. After the death of Auden, Kallman went into a rapid decline and died within months.

In 1976, Isherwood celebrated his sexuality in the book *Christopher and his Kind* which is dedicated to Don Bachardy. He died in California in 1986.

Chapter Ten

Jean Genet, Let Yourself Go

It's true. Honest. The title of David Bowie's hit "Jean Genie" in 1972 – the year he came out – is a pun on the name of gay French author and playwright Jean Genet, though the song is about Iggy Pop, who you will have to make your own mind up about.

Abandoned by his mother as a child, Genet liked to spend time in the company of women and girls. He baked cookies, invented recipes, designed frocks and organised otherwise all-girl tea parties. Well, that's a bit absurd, but there was another side to him. At the age of ten, he was caught stealing and us sent to a notorious reform school, Mettray. With its harsh regime, communal showers and invasive body searches, it turned him from an effeminate gay into an altogether butcher type. Throughout it all, he was conscious that he was sexually attracted exclusively to men.

In the courtyard at Mettray, there was a huge dummy ship where boys were taught to tie knots and furl sails. This inspired the adolescent Genet's imagination. He dreamed of being a cabin boy on a pirate ship, where he would be roughly violated by the captain and other crew members and would be forced to climb the mast naked. In French, the word *frégate* – frigate – also means a boy who is the passive partner in a sexual act. So Genet loved frigging in both senses of the word. No designing frocks and all-girl tea parties here then.

He describes his time at Mettray in his acclaimed novel *The Miracle of the Rose*. To avoid being passed around the other boys, he took an older boy called Villeroy as his protector.

"I loved Villeroy and he loved me," Genet wrote. "I was his wife… We were children searching for our pleasure, he with his awkwardness and I with excessive cunning."

Although Genet found no tenderness with Villeroy, he enjoyed his animal grace.

"When we made love, when he had enough of my eyes," he wrote, "I would work my way down to his cock. In passing, my mouth would loiter around his neck and chest in order to glide slowly down to his stomach."

He would suck the medallion that hung around his neck and slowly withdraw it. Then "I'd suck his dick", said Genet, never one to mince his words. "After I'd swallowed his semen and kissed the tangled hairs on his body, my mouth would rise back up to his."

When Villeroy left to join the navy, Genet gave himself to another tough guy called Divers, who told him bluntly: "I'd like to get into your pants."

"I understood," he said, "that he wanted to bugger me because I was the most sought-after kid in the whole colony."

Although he loved all the sexual attention – he called himself "a high-born lady" – Genet and Divers married at midnight in the chapel, while the other couples of his block looked on. It was, he said, "the most beautiful day of my life". Plainly Divers did not feel the same. A week before Divers moved on, he sold Genet to VanRoy. Deprived of a mirror, it was only later that Genet realised that he and Divers looked alike.

In Mettray, everything became sexualised for Genet. He particularly enjoyed the punishment cells, where boys were kept naked in cages and doused with cold water. Hard work in the surrounding field gradually "masculinised" Genet and, as he grew to manhood, he became the protector rather than the protectee and became the frigger instead of the *frégate*.

He ran away several times, then, when he was 19 he joined the army and was posted to Damascus, where he fell in love with a 16-year-old "little hairdresser".

"Everyone in the street knew I was in love with him," he said. "And the men had a good laugh over it."

No matter how sordid the setting, Genet was always a romantic. He claimed he never went for anonymous sex.

"I could only make love with boys I loved," he said. "Otherwise I would make love with certain guys just for money." Which is it Jean, love or money?

He was also having sex with a Foreign Legionnaire in the garden beside a mosque in Meknès each evening and hankering after fellow soldier Armand. He was the son of La Goulue, a lesbian dancer at the Moulin Rouge who had posed for Toulouse-Lautrec*.

Quitting the army, Genet moved to Barcelona where he worked as a prostitute. He would hang out in a cabaret called the Criolla, where both women and transvestites danced for the pleasure of an audience of men, and the bordello of Madame Petite, whose medieval torture chamber, Chinese pagoda, Japanese rooms, Moorish rooms and Louis XVI boudoirs catered for all tastes and became the model for the brothel in his masterpiece *The Balcony*. He went to see the Black Virgin at the abbey in Montserrat, which reminded him of a young hoodlum opening his fly and pulling out his black penis. He also cruised the toilets of the Ramblas, competing for clients with two young *maricones* – queens – with a monkey.

He tried to compete by dressing as a woman, but he was seated at a table with French officers when a real woman of about 50 asked him when he first realised he was homosexual. In the resulting confusion, he managed to pick one of the officer's pockets. He also got arrested for prostitution in Barcelona. The police searched him and found a tube of Vaseline, which they took to be a tool of the trade.

Poverty forced him to re-enlist, but after he had taken the signing-on bonus, he stole the suitcase of two black officers and deserted. He decided to live by theft "but prostitution was better suited to my nonchalance. I was 20 years old," he said. By this time, literary ambitions had set in and he began devouring homosexual pornography.

He joined up again and supplemented his soldier's pay by working as a prostitute in Marseilles. There, he fell in love with an undercover cop who, two years later, stepped in and saved him from a beating at the hands of fellow officers. When Genet was released, he confessed his love. The policeman was flattered, introduced Genet to his wife and even let him suck his cock from time to time.

Genet deserted again and went travelling. He recalled being in a gypsy camp in Serbia and seeing two beautiful 16-year-old women.

"They slowly lifted to their waists their long panelled dresses, one green, the other black with red flowers, and made me look at their unshaven sexual organs," he recalled. He was appalled.

In Brno, Czechoslovakia, he met a beautiful young man who was the lover of a fat industrialist – though he insisted he was "the man" in the relationship. They robbed the industrialist and joined a counterfeiting ring in Katowice, Poland, where they got arrested. Genet was sentenced to two months in jail; his friend got three. Curiously, in a letter written after he got out, he reveals some heterosexual feelings toward the young wife of the fat industrialist. Although the woman was Jewish, he also developed an erotic fascination for Hitler*.

Genet crossed Germany into Belgium, where he worked as a prostitute. It was there that he suddenly realised that, unlike prison and the army, where men had sex with other men through a lack of women, some men were gay by their very nature .

One night, he tied up a client, robbed him, hit him in the face and threatened him with a knife, writing delightedly that it was "the first time I saw the face made by someone I'd robbed". Robbing his customers became a regular part of his act and he teamed up with two heterosexual friends to indulge in some lucrative queer-bashing.

He moved on to Paris, where he was jailed for breaking into cars. Meanwhile, he was still writing to the industrialist's wife. Arrested a second time, the authorities realised that he was a deserter and, after five months in jail, he was handed over to the military authorities.

When he finally got out, he worked as a prostitute servicing sailors in Toulon. Then he joined the gay underworld in Montmartre. Living by theft, he was in and out of jail, and when Hitler* invaded France, Genet was delighted. After all, the Germans had never put him in jail, while the Poles and French had.

During the war he began writing. Along with a series of poems he wrote the novels *Miracle of the Rose* and *Our Lady of the Flowers*, and the play *Heliogabalus**. His work is militantly homosexual and he made no secret of his orientation.

"Yes, I am a homosexual as everyone knows," he told an interviewer in the 1950s. "But I'm one with rigour and logic. What is a homosexual? A man for whom, first of all, the entire female sex, half of humanity, does not exist."

He was not an apologist for homosexuality. Nor does he not write in defence of homosexuality. Rather he presents it as pure evil – an evil which he eagerly embraces.

His growing literary reputation put him in touch with such seminal figures as Jean Cocteau*.

"Jean Genet brought me his novel," Cocteau wrote in his journal. "Three hundred incredible pages, in which he pieces together the mythology of 'queers'. At first glance such a subject is repellent (I reproached him for it this morning). Subsequently, I wanted to ask his forgiveness for my stupidity."

Even though he had signed a multi-book deal with a publisher, Genet could not give up stealing. He returned to jail, where he met Lucien-Guy Noppé. He completed *Miracle of the Rose*, which is dedicated to "Guy N…" and later bought him a thousand-franc suit. Genet was now 34 and crossed the line from femme to butch. He now took the active role in sex and was attracted to younger, smaller men with pretty faces, fine features, milky skins, slicked back hair, tattoos, bad teeth and bad grammar, petty criminals with tough-guy ways and expressions that alternated between snarling and pouting.

Guy Noppé was ten years younger than Genet and had entered Mettray three years after Genet had left. He was a car thief and Genet recognised him as a younger version of himself.

"Guy was the soul of the cell," he wrote. "He was this adolescent, white and curly-haired, buttery … Every time he spoke to me I felt the meaning of this strange expression: 'in his loins a load of spunk.'"

He wrote to Cocteau begging him to send food parcels to Guy, who he was afraid was dying of hunger. When Genet was released, he was back in jail within a month. This time, however, he was kept in solitary confinement and only caught fleeting glimpses of Guy. Meanwhile, he worked on the play *The Nude Warriors* and *Funeral Rites* – in French it is *Pompes funèbres* which is a common phrase for "undertakers". However, *pompes* is slang for "blowjob", so the title could be translated as *Funeral Fellatio*.

When he was 35, Genet said that prison had lost its erotic

charm for him. Earlier, he had been attracted to it because homosexuality flourished there. In his work he eroticises prison itself, but once Guy had been freed, it no longer had any charm for him.

"Now that prison is stripped of its sacred ornaments, I see it naked," he wrote, "and its nakedness is cruel."

Genet was paroled in 1944, but lived in fear of returning to jail until he was given a presidential pardon in 1949. He made friends with a woman called Olga Barbezats. He would be seen in her bedroom, wearing only a towel and one of her beaded head-dresses. The cook would serve them breakfast in bed, where they would chat endlessly. He said that she was the only woman he could marry, but when he asked her, she pointed out that she was already married.

On holiday with Olga and her husband in the Dolomites, Genet would wander into their bedroom in his underpants. When they went swimming, she tried to hide behind her husband while changing, but Genet dodged from side to side to catch a glimpse of her naked. On another occasion, he persuaded her to pull down her top and show him her breasts.

"Not bad," he said.

For his lady friends, he would often act out in mime his methods of picking up boys – to hysterical effect. They found him very seductive.

Genet fell in love with the young poet Olivier Larronde, who was 16 at the time. He paid for his room in the Hôtel Eden in Montmartre and gave him spending money. Every morning for three or four months, he would visit the Hôtel Eden and try and seduce him, but Oliver was not attracted to him. At this time, Genet split his actives into two sides – *la côté amour* and *la côté vice*. While Oliver was definitely *la côté amour*, he found *la côté vice* in rough trade. And he could not bear the two sides to mix. Once, he picked up a young thug and took him back to his hotel. After sex Genet asked: "How much?" The bloke said that he did not want any money, he had done it for his own pleasure. Disgusted, Genet threw him out.

Genet got to know Jean-Paul Sartre and Simone de Beauvoir, who described him as "the homosexual burglar-poet". He called her a "tough bitch", while she continually criticised his "silly fairy entourage". Many saw Genet as Sartre's "pet queer". He once asked Sartre: "As you are not a homosexual, how can you love my books?"

Typically, Sartre replied: "It's precisely because I am not a homosexual that I love them."

Later he wrote *Saint Genet*. In it he said that Genet had never completely come to terms with the change of roles in homosexual couplings, recalling that Genet had said to him: "The so-called active pederast remains unappeased in the midst of his pleasures and keeps a nostalgia for passivity." Then again, Sartre got most things wrong.

A later lover remarked that Genet liked being with men with whom he could quickly reverse roles from active to passive.

Sartre also recalled that Genet had told him that he detested flowers. "It's not roses that he loves, it's their name," he said.

But Genet was never really at home in intellectual circles. At a reading of Rimbaud's "The Drunken Boat" at the Théâtre Hébertot, Genet leapt up and shouted: "In the name of Rimbaud, go fuck!"

And he did not get on with his publisher. He told Claude Gallimard: "Your employees treat me like a buggerer."

Indeed, Gallimard published some of Genet's early work without their imprint on it – just a line saying that it had been published in "Bikini, at the expense of amateurs".

In January 1945, Genet met 20-year-old Jean-Pierre Lacloche. He was immediately attracted to the dark, muscular paratrooper, but Lacloche promptly seduced Olivier Larronde. Genet was jealous. Neither man wanted Genet who had gone prematurely bald and there was a fight where Genet got beaten up by Lacloche.

"Genet was as bad a fighter as he was a thief," said Lacloche. "He consoled himself with black American soldiers, just as during the war he'd slept with blond Germans."

But Genet said he "could never sleep with a Jew" – though he always said that he could never steal from a Jew either.

"The Israelite is the very symbol of a martyr," explained Sartre. "Since Genet wants his lovers to be executioners, he could never bring himself to be sodomised by a victim."

Larronde and Lacloche moved in together, but the relationship was never smooth. Lacloche took numerous mistresses, which caused Lacloche torments of jealousy. Meanwhile, Genet was hanging out with Diaghilev's* former private secretary, Boris Kochno, and his lover Christian Bérard.

Genet gave Kochno a signed first edition of *Our Lady of the Flowers* with a gushing dedication. Later he said that he regretted this and pretended to be very upset by it. Lacloche took him seriously, went over to the apartment Kochno shared with Bérard and tore the first pages with the dedication out. He delivered them to Genet with a flourish.

"It was an act of love towards Genet on my part, since I was also friends with Bérard," Lacloche said. Genet promptly made it up with Kochno and wrote him a new, even more fulsome, dedication. He also wrote one for Lacloche thanking him for his assistance.

In the spring of 1945, Genet met 18-year-old Lucien Sénémaud, a pretty boy with full lips and slicked-back hair – a fellow thief who resembled Genet as a youth. Genet wrote him a poem called "The Fisherman of Suquet" – the port of Cannes where Sénémaud had fished as a child. In the poem, Sénémaud is portrayed as a virile young god. In one passage, tiny pilgrims explore his body and "scrabble up the wooded slopes of your thighs, where even during the day it's night".

Later, a thief – Genet – gives the fisherman a blowjob and begs him to "inflate your presence, which is inside me". And I thought it was rude to speak with your mouth full. The climax is followed by it shrinking and going limp, while the thief tries to breathe life back into the weary organ.

He gives him another blowjob in "A Song of Love", but in *The Thief's Journal* he recalls biting Sénémaud until he bleeds. After that, I think I would politely decline if fellatio was offered again.

What excited Genet was that Sénémaud was not gay. He saw him with "terrible girls" and wondered: "What other sluts is he going to go out with?"

In fact, Sénémaud had an affair with a beautiful actress he had met through Jean Cocteau*. The affair ended when Sénémaud was arrested for theft. He fell in love with a woman and later married.

In Cannes in 1947, Genet met 22-year-old André B. He was half-

French, half-Russian and Genet called him Java because he worked on a yacht called *Le Java*, belonging to the Count de Loriole, and had its name emblazoned across his chest. It was Genet's chance to get back in touch with the darker side of love. Java had been a French SS man, the bodyguard of a German general in the Waffen SS, and had his blood group tattooed on his forearm SS-style. With another friend of Genet's called René, and Genet's encouragement, Java went into business shaking down homosexuals. A good-looking boy, he would lure men back to a room where René would be waiting.

Genet admired Java's massive build and was fascinated by his amorality and his omnivorous bisexuality. They moved in together, but fought. Java tried to read one of Genet's books once, but fell asleep. Genet grew angry and accused him of living just for women and food.

Although he was living with Java, Genet was still seeing Lucien Sénémaud and the three of them became firm friends. Sénémaud also had a girlfriend at the time, called Ginette Chaix, who did not seem to mind that her boyfriend was also sleeping with Genet. When she fell pregnant, they married with Genet and Java as their witnesses at the civil ceremony.

Both Sénémaud and Genet continued their life of crime, stealing compulsively. Genet particularly enjoyed the exploits of Java and René, considering the whole subject of robbing homosexuals a huge joke and coaching others to do the same.

Genet and Java lived together from 1947 to 1954, but they only had sex when they were drunk. Then it was very intense. Otherwise Genet would hire male prostitutes.

Meanwhile, Java would disappear for days on end with girlfriends, returning to a jealous row. Genet hated it even more if Java made love to a woman on their bed. He once found pubic hair on the pillow and threw a tantrum. Even so, when Java went out with women, Genet wanted to know every detail of what they got up to. Sometimes he was tantalisingly close at hand. When they went to stay with some rich friends in the country, Java slipped off to sleep with the maid.

Genet was stalked by Violette Leduc, a lesbian who made a habit of falling in love with gay men – which would be quite unsatisfactory on all sides, I would have thought. She eventually got an introduction and, after a lunch date, wangled her way up to his room – which, with its overflowing ashtrays, unmade bed and scattered manuscripts became some sort of shrine in her imagination. However, she was disappointed that air was not heavy with the smell of semen.

"No traces of cocks here," she concluded, but was delighted to discover that both she and Genet used the same Elizabeth Arden face cleanser. Then Sénémaud turned up, who she swooned over – another rugged homosexual, she thought. On another occasion, she had a row with Genet, crawled across the floor, smothered him with kisses and begged his forgiveness. I would have thought that this would have put him right off. Nevertheless, a strange love triangle then developed between Genet, Leduc and Genet's new publisher, Jacques Guérin.

After Sartre and Cocteau petitioned and won a pardon for Genet from President De Gaulle – who Genet later described as a "soft cock" despite his rigid bearing – Genet set off for Italy, which was "an immense whorehouse where fags from all over the world rented, by the hour, by the night or for the duration of the trip, a man or boy". Genet met and fell in love with "a 21-year-old hoodlum" called Decimo. The writer, Alberto Moravia said he was "a skinny queen with bandy legs and no appeal", but Genet considered him beautiful, even if Valentino*-style features were obscured under a thick layer of talc. He was far from the tough-guy type Genet usually bedded. Genet described him to a journalist as "a young Italian with the figure of a girl and Mongol eyes".

Again Genet played the active role sexually with Decimo and depicted him naked on all fours with his rump raised invitingly. It is said that this was the one time Genet was really in love. He even tried to kill himself over Decimo and was so hurt when they split up that he left him off his list of great loves.

There was, as usual, a criminal element to the relationship. Genet asked Moravia, then Italy's most famous writer, for his help to get Decimo's brother out of jail where he was languishing for what Genet called "a minor crime". It turned out to be armed robbery.

Decimo generally refused to leave Rome, where he worked as a prostitute, though he did consent to a paid trip with Genet to Venice. It was then that Genet realised that he was being taken for a ride. Decimo dropped him as soon as he found someone with more money. Genet attempted suicide, but Java rode to the rescue, threatening to smash his face in if he tried it again.

Genet, however, remained depressed. Homosexuality was a curse, he decided and he entered into a long correspondence with Jean-Paul Sartre about the nature of the condition, in which Sartre points out that, in Genet's novels, the heterosexual reader is forced to become a homosexual for the duration of the read. The only gay man Genet had any time for at this point was Michelangelo, who "sought his rigour only in pederasty". Genet now had writer's block and he blamed his professional sterility on his homosexuality.

To make things worse, in 1954, he was charged with producing pornography and offending against public decency for two works he had published in 1948. One of them was illustrated with Cocteau drawings showing sailors with huge erections buggering each other. Genet was given a suspended sentence and fined.

Ironically, his creativity was sparked again when he began an affair with Pierre Joly, a 20-year-old drama student with black hair, blue eyes and pale skin who drank a lot and hung out in the gay night-spots of Saint-Germain. Genet supported him for a while, while he got down to writing *The Balcony*. This was actually inspired by the artist Alberto Giacometti*. A heterosexual, Giacometti was a regular user of prostitutes and brothels. While Genet sat for him, Giacometti regaled him with tales of the whorehouse. Meanwhile, Joly complained to a young lover that he was fed up with Genet's sexual demands and left him. A series of absurdist plays followed.

In 1955, Genet met the acrobat Abdallah Bentega, who was 18 – he was 46. Abdallah was half-Algerian, half-German and semi-literate. Genet paid for lessons on the high wire for him. They moved in together, but Abdallah was soon called up into the French army. As this would have probably meant him being sent to fight in Algeria, which was in the throes of its war of independence from France at the time, Genet encouraged him to desert and the two of sought refuge in Belgium, Holland, Italy,

Germany, Austria and, finally, Greece. Genet loved Greece, saying that it gave him the same "erotic charge" as the Arabic countries. However, it is said that he was slightly shocked by Greek morals. He picked up a young Greek policeman and took him back to his hotel. When the policeman had put his clothes back on, the naked Genet held out a handful of money and the policeman took it.

"You, a guardian of the law, are paid to maintain public order," Genet protested, "and here you are accepting money from a naked queer."

The policeman shrugged, smiled and pocketed the money. This was not the reaction Genet had hoped for. He wanted guilt. It was he who was supposed to be the bad one.

Abdallah, it was said, was a mixture of the masculine and feminine with "a soft voice and a gracious way of carrying himself, he always expressed himself with a great deal of delicacy and modesty". He was not a very satisfactory lover, though. Genet complained that he giggled every time he kissed him. They only slept together occasionally and, during their European tour, he had a homely Greek girl called Erika in tow. Genet was not best pleased.

But there were compensations. He wrote to a gay friend: "The Greeks? I lay four or five of them a day on the grass and on their tummies. Beautiful arses, beautiful cocks, hairy bodies, beautiful eyes, beautiful tongues – tongues that come and go around my dick."

Along the way, he continued working on books and plays to pay for the costumes and equipment for Abdallah's high-wire act and became addicted to Nembutal and other prescription drugs. Wearing a costume designed by Genet himself, Abdallah began to perform, but in 1959, in Ghent, he fell and injured his knee. It was the end of his career.

With Genet now more famous than ever, the relationship became strained and Genet found himself drawn to 22-year-old Jacky Maglia. He had known Genet since he was eight or nine. Genet had encouraged him to desert from the army too, and he was forced to live outside France. As he had stolen cars, Genet thought that he should become a racing driver and bought him a

Lotus. Strings were pulled to get him into the Italian racing club and he won races in Chimay, Belgium and at Monza.

Abdallah was reduced to running errands for Jacky. Erika left him. He took an overdose of Genet's Nembutal and slashed his wrists in Genet's apartment. Genet was staying in a hotel on the Left Bank at the time. The body was not discovered for two weeks, when the smell of Abdallah's rotting corpse finally alerted the neighbours. Jacky then fell in love with the daughter of a Norwich policeman. Genet encouraged them to marry and built the newly-weds a house.

After Abdallah's death, Genet stopped writing, though his translation rights world-wide were fetching ever higher prices. In 1968, he travelled to Japan, where Jacky was now living with his second wife, Isako. On the way, Genet had a sadistic fantasy about a young Japanese girl and felt that he might be able to write again. He was particularly impressed by the Noh theatre, where men dress as women, and one actor presented him with his fan.

After a trip to Tangiers, Genet went to Chicago where he met William Burroughs, Terry Southern and Allen Ginsberg. He went to bed with Ginsberg, but after finding that he did not have an erection got out of bed and left. Genet returned to Tangiers, where he enjoyed Arab boys stroking his penis and watching them suck each other off.

Back in France, Genet took a fancy to the 11-year-old son of the actress Chantal Darget and asked whether he could take the boy around the world. His mother's answer was a very firm no.

After Genet wrote the play *The Blacks*, he was contacted by the Black Panthers, who invited him back to the United States. Genet was much taken with the Panthers' National Chief of Staff, the very heterosexual David Hilliard. One night, after taking too many Nembutals, Genet danced in a pink negligée for Hilliard and three other Panthers. It is not known what they thought of this display but his translator said it was "sickening".

In 1974, Genet was in Tangiers when he saw a young man sleeping on the street. He woke him gently and asked if he was French. No, he said, he was Moroccan and his name was Mohammed El Katrani. They travelled together to Rabat, where Genet got him a passport. They moved to Paris where they lived together, first in a hotel and then in an apartment in the suburb of Saint-Denis.

Mohammed enrolled in drama school but had little or no aptitude. Few of Genet's friends liked him, so he dropped them. Later, he built a house for Mohammed and his new wife, and one for Jacky and Isako when Jacky decided to return to France. He also indulged a young circus performer called Alexandre Bouglione and planned to build a house for Bouglione and himself. By this time, he had cancer of the throat.

In 1982, he took up with a 16-year-old boy who resembled Lucien Sénémaud – though Genet boasted that he looked like Mick Jagger. Genet was then 71 and rode around on the pillion of the youngster's motorbike. The relationship ended when the boy persuaded Genet to pay for him to go to Greece. Genet then discovered that he had taken his girlfriend at Genet's expense and was furious. Afterwards, Genet travelled through Lebanon and Jordan, where he enjoyed the company of the young *fedayeen*.

Returning to Morocco in 1983, he began writing *Prison of Love* – that's *Sex*, Jean. He knew the end was near and flew back to Paris where Jacky and Isako nursed him until he died on April 15, 1986. He was buried in Morocco a few days later.

Genet had paid for the upkeep of Abdallah's grave for 22 years, but had neglected to make any provision after his own death. The very same day Genet was buried, Abdallah's remains were dug up and flung into a communal pit. Such is love.

Toward the end of his life, Genet told a colleague: "I don't have readers, but thousands of voyeurs who spy on me from a window that gives onto the stage of my personal life… And I'm sickened by this interest that is awakened by the scandalous person I used to be."

Well, you didn't have to write about it, mate.

Chapter Eleven

Gee Man

As director of the Federal Bureau of Investigations from its creation in 1924 until his death in 1972, J. Edgar Hoover* was the man who had the dirt on everyone. When asked why he did not sack Hoover, President Lyndon Baines Johnson* famously said: "It is better to have him inside the tent pissing out, than outside the tent pissing in." The real reason was that Hoover knew that Johnson had a long-term lover and an illegitimate son in Texas, plus a series of peccadilloes elsewhere. Johnson had once famously boasted: "I had more women by accident than Kennedy* had on purpose."

Johnson may have referred to Hoover as "that queer bastard", but they were close. Johnson had befriended Hoover when he came to Washington as a young congressman in the 1930s. Hoover would come over for Sunday brunch and, though childless himself, baby-sat Johnson's children. He also lent Johnson his secret files for a little light bedtime reading. This allowed Johnson to control the House of Representatives, then the Senate – and, finally, gave him the presidency itself.

When John F. Kennedy* won the Democratic presidential nomination in 1960, Johnson was not on the ticket, but he had read Hoover's file on Kennedy. Early in the Second World War, Kennedy had been in Naval Intelligence in Washington. Hoover's G- – that is, Government – men had bugged the hotel room where he enjoyed assignations with a former Danish beauty queen who had Nazi connections. This almost got Kennedy cashiered as a security risk, but Kennedy's rich and powerful father Joe* pulled strings and got him posted to the Pacific where he became a war hero.

At the 1960 Democratic Convention in Los Angeles, Johnson

went to Kennedy, told him what he knew and said that, if Kennedy did not put him on the ticket as vice-president, he would ruin Kennedy's "family man" image and lose him the Jewish vote. Kennedy was forced to concede.

"I'm 43 years old," Kennedy said. "I'm not going to die in office. So the vice-presidency doesn't mean a thing."

Johnson saw it differently.

"I looked it up," he said. "One out of every four presidents has died in office. I'm a gamblin' man, and this is the only chance I have got."

It turned out he was right.

When Kennedy got into the White House, he wanted to get the tapes back. He did not succeed. This explains why, despite the acrimony between Hoover and Bobby Kennedy*, the attorney general, Hoover was not removed from office. Hoover even had a picture of JFK on a pleasure cruiser surrounded by naked girls, so his position was unassailable.

President Richard Nixon* tried to sack him, but emerged from the meeting ashen. Hoover had photographs of Nixon in Hong Kong in the mid 1960s with a young Chinese woman called Marianna Liu*, who was a suspected Communist agent. At the request of the CIA, the Hong Kong Special Branch had used an infrared camera to film Nixon and Liu making love through his hotel bedroom window. She later became a permanent resident in the United States, living in Nixon's home-town of Whittier, California.

So Hoover knew about everyone else's sex life, but what do we know about his?

Well, the man never married. He largely eschewed friends and, when he took a vacation, he went with his similarly unmarried deputy Clyde Tolson. It all looked very clean and above board. There were rumours, of course, but it was generally assumed that they were two deeply repressed homosexuals. However, the biographer Anthony Summers believes that, in private, Hoover secretly practised homosexuality and transvestism – and produced a lot of evidence to back his claims.

The Mafia boss Meyer Lansky, it seems, had the dirt on Hoover – possibly even photographs – and boasted that he had "fixed" the

FBI boss. Hoover also wrote flirtatious letters to top agent Melvin Purvis – the man who shot down John Dillinger* – which drooled over the "slender, blond-haired, brown-eyed" Clark Gable*. Although Purvis bungled Dillinger's arrest, Hoover praised him to the skies for his "almost unimaginable daring". When Purvis married, however, his name was dropped from the FBI story and no one dared mention him within Hoover's hearing. From then on, Hoover maintained that it was Clyde Tolson who shot John Dillinger, not Melvin Purvis.

The official line on Hoover's sex life was given by Helen Gandy, who served as his secretary for 53 years. She said that, when Hoover was 24 and working in the War Emergency Division of the Justice Department rounding up suspected Bolsheviks, he was seeing a girl called Alice, the attractive daughter of a prominent lawyer. After the war, Hoover hoped to get a job in his firm.

On Armistice Day, November 11, 1918, a friend of Hoover's was getting engaged. He and Alice were invited to the celebration at Harvey's Restaurant, a well-known Washington watering hole, and Hoover decided that it should be a double celebration. He sent a note to Alice, asking her to meet him beforehand at the Lafayette Hotel, where he intended to propose. She never turned up and soon married another man, who had fought in the war. For the rest of his life Hoover nursed a broken heart. Or so the story goes.

In 1928, Hoover personally hired the handsome 28-year-old Clyde Tolson after his application form turned up with a photograph attached. His references said that he was "not at all dissipated" and that he showed "no particular interest in women". He was destined for higher things. Tolson made it from rookie to assistant director of the FBI in just three years. While everyone else called Hoover "Mr Hoover", Tolson called him "Speed", "Eddie" or "The Boss". The usually formal Hoover called Tolson "Junior". They lunched together every day at the Mayflower Hotel and dined together five nights a week at Harvey's. They had much in common. Both were unusually close to their mothers and Tolson, like Hoover, had been rejected by women, twice. His childhood sweetheart had married another man when he moved to Washington and at law school, his girlfriend fell pregnant to another man and married him, leaving Tolson devastated.

Even in the early 1930s there were rumours that they were an item. Journalist Ray Tucker noted Hoover's "mincing step"; others remarked on Tolson's "soft, pampered face – struggling for masculinity" which "had for decades been the flower to the bristled cactus" that was Hoover.

It was noted that Hoover wore perfume – which he vehemently and disingenuously denied. He kept dainty china next to his crime-fighting trophies and he loved flowers. Foreign journalists said that he was "different" from the police chiefs in other countries. The American Mother's Committee once made the terrible mistake of naming Hoover one of the "Fathers of the Year". This gave the newspapers the chance to point out, pointedly, that "Mr Hoover is a bachelor". Even *Time* magazine said that he was "seldom seen without a male companion, most frequently solemn-faced Clyde Tolson".

Cutting-edge camper Truman Capote* offered to write an article called "Johnnie and Clyde" outing Hoover and Tolson. It did not get published. FBI agents were ordered to intimidate the Press when homosexual rumours flourished.

Fashion model Martha Stuart, who hitched a ride to the Cotton Club in the FBI chief's limousine on New Year's Eve 1936, noticed that Hoover and Tolson were holding hands in the back seat. Hoover was a racist and, at the Cotton Club, complained loudly that a black man was dancing with a white woman.

"Well, I'd like to dance with you," said a drunk and lachrymose Tolson.

Stuart was young and naïve and asked Art Arthur, a colleague of the columnist Walter Winchell*, about them. He told her that Hoover and Tolson "were queers or fairies – the sort of terms they used in those days," she said.

Hoover and Tolson were regular guests at the Sunday brunches given by Winchell, who was the only man Hoover allowed to call him by his first name "John". One Sunday, Hoover turned up alone, saying that Tolson was sick. After he left, people said that Tolson was not sick at all. Hoover had caught him in bed with another man and there had been a fight.

Within the Bureau, there were jokes about "Mother Tolson" and "J. Edna Hoover". And when one agent named his son "J. Edgar" in 1939, another said: "If it had been a girl, she'd have been called

Clyde." Some people in the administration were bolder and even teased Hoover himself. Attorney General Francis Biddle, walking past Hoover's office with his assistant James Rowe, asked loudly: "Do you think Hoover is a homosexual?"

"Shush," said an embarrassed Rowe.

"I only meant a latent homosexual," said Biddle loudly again.

In an attempt to scotch these rumours, Hoover and Tolson made lewd remarks about women and included smutty, heterosexual jokes in their speeches. Hoover gave a plastic pen with a picture of a woman on it whose clothes fell off when you turned it upside down to Biddle's successor Howard McGrath, while Tolson gave Hoover an inflatable Jayne Mansfield* doll on his 70th birthday. It did no good. At a dinner for the United States' highest law officers, the featured entertainer, one of the Duncan sisters, tried to sit on Hoover's lap. He fled. A taxi driver who picked them up after Hoover had met Tolson at Washington National Airport said that "he never saw so much kissing and ass-grabbing in all his life".

Early in their relationship, Tolson shared an apartment with a young man called Guy Hottel and, in 1938, Hoover took him on as an agent, making him head of the Washington field office. Together Hoover, Tolson and Hottel went away on "inspection tours" which were little more than glorified junkets. They liked to stay at the Flamingo Hotel in Miami where, according to Hottel, they "had a court with sides on it, and you could go up there and sunbathe all you wanted in the nude". And though Hoover and Tolson were sometimes seen in the company of the opposite sex, Hottel was very clear about one thing, "they didn't date them." Once Hottel asked Tolson to make up a foursome with two women he had met. When Tolson agreed, Hoover threw a jealous tantrum and Hottel had to break into the hotel suite's bathroom to calm him down. This was a regular chore, as Tolson was still attracted to women.

Tolson had a crush on 1930s model Anita Colby, but it did not go anywhere. In 1939, he began seeing a waitress called Edna Daulyton. One night they were having dinner at the Mayflower when Hoover came in and joined them.

"I was shocked," she said. "He behaved in such an ugly way to me. And there was a closeness between him and Clyde that I didn't understand – something that didn't seem quite natural. It was only afterwards that I heard the stories."

Clyde and Edna never got past the hand-holding and kiss-on-the-cheek stage. Concerned that he was not even trying to get to first base with her, she asked him straight out: "Is there something funny between you and Hoover?"

"What do you mean?" said Tolson. "Are you saying I'm some sort of abnormal faggot?"

Well, yes, Clyde. It would have been a normal inference, as Hoover continued to join them for dinner, even when they found a discreet hideaway down by the Potomac. Soon after, they stopped seeing each other.

Later that year, Tolson fell in love with a woman in New York and there was talk of marriage. Hoover got Hottel to talk Tolson out of it. Plainly, if Tolson had got married there would have been no more meals *à deux* and Tolson's career would have suffered. Interestingly, Hoover was seeing women himself at that time. His mother had just died after a prolonged battle with cancer.

He seemed to favour older women and was seen in the company of Lela Rogers, mother of Ginger*, who was seven years older than him. Politically far to the right, she had been the first woman in the Marines and edited the Corps newspaper *Leatherneck*. He showered her with gifts. They made regular visits to Florida and there were rumours of marriage right up to 1955, when one of their vacations was interrupted by a summons by the president and Lela went off to LA in tears.

Hoover was also in "hot pursuit" of screenwriter Frances Marion, who was also seven years older than him. She had been married before and could not marry him because of her kids. Then there was movie actress Dorothy Lamour, who Hoover had met when she was a 20-year-old hat-check girl in the Stork Club. He was 19 years her senior. She had just divorced her first husband when his mother died. According to friends they were serious, but they split because their careers were not compatible. He was later a regular, if intimidating, guest at Dorothy's home when she married again in 1942. After that he gave up.

Two years after his mother died, Hoover moved into a house he had had built for himself on Thirteenth Place, NW. He was visited there by Churchill's* wartime personal representative in

Washington, William Stephenson, who commented on the proliferation of male nudes, often in suggestive poses, all over the place. And when he met Hoover with Tolson, he said that he immediately recognised them as a gay couple. Later, Hoover toned down the décor, adding pictures of nude women - including Marilyn Monroe's* famous calendar shot - to the walls of the bar in the basement.

In 1946, Hoover consulted a doctor about his sexuality. Unable to unburden himself because of the intolerable risk to his public position, he grew paranoid and withdrew from the consultation. Other psychiatrists have concluded that Hoover was a bisexual, but of a "strongly predominant homosexual orientation" or a bisexual "with a failed heterosexuality". I think that means you're gay.

Hottel eventually got married. Tolson was his best man. After quitting the Bureau, Hottel turned to drink. In his cups, he was talking about "sex parties at Hoover's house, you know, with boys". A local police inspector looked into this and concluded that Hottel was not making it up.

"He had attended some of the parties, let's put it that way. According to him, some of the top boys who were holding the top jobs at the FBI were participating," said the officer.

Once, it seems, Hoover was nearly caught out. Ex-FBI man Jimmy Corcoran claimed that, in the 1920s, Hoover had been arrested on sex charges in New Orleans. The case involved a young man and Corcoran was sent to Louisiana to straighten things out. After he quit the Bureau, Corcoran became a political lobbyist and was caught in a sting operation. Corcoran was then able to force a reluctant Hoover to return the favour and straighten things out for him. Soon after, Corcoran died in a mysterious plane crash near a Caribbean island owned by one of Hoover's associates.

Movie producer Joe Pasternak said that Hoover would come down to the racetrack at Del Mar each year with a different boy.

"He was caught in the bathroom by a newspaperman," Pasternak said. "They made sure he didn't speak ... Nobody dared say anything because he was so powerful."

Tolson and Hoover were often seen together sharing a box at Del Mar racetrack. According to Henry Hay, the founder of the Mattachine Society, the United States' first gay rights organisation, they were seen in "boxes owned by gay men, in a circle in which they don't have people who weren't gay. They wouldn't be in that crowd otherwise. They were nodded together as lovers."

Asked to comment on anti-gay campaigner Anita Bryant in 1978, Ethel Merman, who had been a friend of Hoover's since 1936, said: "Some of my best friends are homosexual. Everybody knew about J. Edgar Hoover, but he was the best chief the FBI ever had." Hoover had been dead for six years by them.

While hiding his own sexual identity, Hoover was only too happy to persecute other gays. In 1943, he set up the Undersecretary of State, Sumner Welles*. Disliking Welles' liberal tendencies, Hoover claimed that he had "absolute proof that Welles is a homosexual". The story spread that he had propositioned the staff on a Pullman train. President Franklin D. Roosevelt*, a personal friend of Welles, tried to stand by him, but the whispering campaign eventually forced Welles from office.

As well as being gay, it was also rumoured that the racist Hoover had black blood in him. He had no birth certificate and asserted that both parents were "white", but most people were not so sure.

"There were two things that were taken for granted in my youth," said Washington insider Gore Vidal*, "that he was a faggot and that he was black."

He was certainly no more sympathetic to the civil rights movement than he was to gay liberation. He made no effort to improve the lot of African-American people in the South, saying that he "was not going to send the FBI in every time some nigger woman says she's been raped".

Hoover accused Adlai Stevenson* and Martin Luther King* of being gay – though he had copious tapes of King making love to women who were not his wife. And, at the time of Watergate, he said that Nixon's aides Haldeman*, Ehrlichman* and Dwight Chapman* were lovers and attended gay parties in the Watergate building.

He made bold statements about hunting down "sexual deviants in government service" and told the House Appropriations Committee that "no member of the Mattachine Society or anyone who is a sex deviate will be appointed to the FBI". Meanwhile, the word was sent out for FBI agents to penetrate homosexual rings across the country. This continued for 23 years, long after it had been concluded that the gay liberation movement was in no way subversive. So I guess he must have enjoyed it. Meanwhile, ordinary people who made a crack about Hoover being gay were likely to receive a visit from the FBI.

The Bureau, of course, had to be whiter than white. One agent was publicly chastised for possessing a copy of *Playboy* magazine. The FBI was, as a matter of public policy, against pornographers and "peddlers of filth". Hoover took this very seriously and took time out of his busy schedule to review the pornography his agents had seized in private screenings in the Blue Room, the small cinema in FBI headquarters. His desk was often scattered with the most lurid pornography, often involving naked women in degrading positions and involving "all sorts of abnormal sexual activities". Hoover was particularly miffed when FBI agents neglected to bring him the latest surveillance pictures showing African-American radical Angela Davis having sex with her boyfriend.

As well as persecuting homosexuals and trying to "smear" straight men by alleging that they were gay, Hoover also had it in for straight men who liked to fool around. In 1949, Hoover sent a report to President Harry S. Truman* informing him of a youthful affair of his administrative assistant Dave Niles and that his press secretary Charlie Ross and a friend had "chased a couple of gals around the deck" on a boat trip. Truman was not impressed. This was only weeks after he had received a detailed briefing on Hoover's sex life. Truman did not give a damn about it, saying that it was none of his business. He told Hoover: "I don't care what a man does in his free time: all that interests me is what he does while he's on the job." Perhaps you would like to rephrase, that Mr President.

But on the job was exactly where Hoover was falling down. A young Justice Department employee had just been caught handing summaries of FBI reports to the Soviets – and, with the Cold War nearing its height, Hoover himself was vulnerable to Soviet blackmail.

Hoover's personal passion was the suppression of subversion and, during the McCarthyite witch hunts, it was Hoover who recommended Roy Cohn to Senator Joe, who was also allegedly gay. A lifelong homosexual, Cohn, like Hoover, took a delight in attacking gay rights groups and fellow gays – until he died of AIDS in 1986. However, the FBI had originally been set up to fight organised crime and Hoover's closet gayness let him down there too, I'm afraid.

Hoover and Tolson New Year's Eve spat in the Cotton Club in 1936 could hardly have escaped the attention of the owner, Owney Madden, and his partner Frank Costello, who was a close associate of Lucky Luciano* and Meyer Lansky. Winchell, a compulsive gossip, also knew these mobsters. Among the crime syndicate bosses, Hoover's homosexuality was "common knowledge". One of Lansky's associates said: "I used to meet him at the racetrack every once in a while with lover boy Clyde, in the '40s and '50s. I was in the next box once. And when you see two guys holding hands, well come on … They were surreptitious, but there was no question about it."

In 1948, Jimmy "the Weasel" Fratianno was at the track and pointed out Hoover to Mafioso Frank Bompensiero.

"Ah, that J. Edgar's a punk," said Bompensiero loud enough for everyone to hear. "He's a fuckin' degenerate queer." At that time, "punk" was US prison slang for a catamite.

Meeting in the men's room later, Hoover said to Bompensiero: "Frank, that's not a nice way to talk about me, especially when I have people with me." But he did nothing about it.

It seems that the mobsters got to know about Hoover's 1920s bust in New Orleans through local crime boss Carlos Marcello, who had infiltrated the city police force and local authorities. Marcello was a close friend of Meyer Lansky. According to Mafia courier Irving "Ash" Resnick, Lansky was the man who put it all together and "nailed" Hoover. It was even said that Lansky even had pictures of Hoover and Tolson together in some gay situation.

"That was the reason, they said, that for a long time they had nothing to fear from the FBI," claimed Resnick

When Resnick visited Florida, he would stay in a bungalow next door to the one occupied by Hoover and Tolson.

"I'd sit with him on the beach every day," said Resnick. "We were friendly."

Lansky would often eat in the same restaurant as Hoover and Tolson in Florida, but Hoover avoided his gaze.

"The homosexual thing was Hoover's Achilles' heel," said one of

Lansky's men. "Meyer found out and it was like he pulled the strings with Hoover."

The FBI never interfered with any of Lansky's operations. It is said that Hoover pulled the strings that got the permits for Bugsy Siegel to open the Flamingo in Nevada, which was backed by Lansky.And when Lansky ordered Bugsy Siegel to be whacked because of the casino's losses, the FBI did nothing. Hoover also helped Lansky's gambling operations in Cuba and the Bahamas. When Lansky eventually faced prosecution, it was the IRS who brought the charges, not the FBI.The case eventually unravelled and Lansky, head of a crime syndicate for over 60 years, lived as a free man until his death in 1983.

A number of CIA men also said that they had pictures of Hoover and Tolson "engaged in homosexual activity".

"What I saw was a picture of him giving Clyde Tolson a blowjob," said one. "There was more than one shot, but the startling one was a close shot of Hoover's head. He was totally recognisable."

These pictures were in the possession of CIA counter-intelligence chief James Angleton, who insisted that they were perfectly genuine. It seems likely that these were the same pictures that Lansky had. Naval Intelligence and the OSS – the forerunner of the CIA – had close ties with the mob during the Second World War to prevent sabotage in the dockyards and help in the invasion of Sicily. Lansky's men were even asked to keep an eye on an upmarket gay brothel in Brooklyn for the US government, who feared its distinguished clientele might be a target for enemy espionage and blackmail. Hoover and OSS head William "Wild Bill" Donovan got involved in a turf war when the OSS, then the CIA, took over the FBI's overseas espionage duties. As usual, Hoover's response was to search for dirt on Donovan, who responded in kind – and hit pay dirt in 1946.

That by no means was the end of it, however. In 1957, an outbreak of gang warfare forced the government to do something about organised crime. As Frank Costello was one of its victims, Hoover was emboldened. However, an associate of Costello's, Lewis Solon Rosenstiel – a leading distiller before and after Prohibition and one of the richest men alive – was able to straighten Hoover out.

Rosenstiel's wife Susan said that, after they were married, she soon became aware of her husband's strange tastes. He did not seem interested in having sex with her, but rather, dressing her up as a little girl. Then, one morning, she walked into his bedroom and found in him bed with Roy Cohn. Rosenstiel made a joke about wanting to be alone with his attorney.

She said: "I have never seen you in bed with Governor Dewey" – another of Rosenstiel's lawyers – and walked out.

After that Cohn flaunted his homosexuality around her, telling her that the Archbishop of New York, Cardinal Spellman*, was gay and fondling a congressional aide in her presence. Later, her husband and Cohn took her to a party at the Plaza Hotel on Central Park. She was then ushered into one of the hotel's biggest suites where she could not believe what she saw – the head of the FBI in full drag.

"He was wearing a fluffy black dress, very fluffy, with flounces, and lace stockings and high heels, and a curly black wig," she told Anthony Summers. "He had make-up on and false eyelashes. It was a very short skirt and he was sitting there in the living room of the suite with his legs crossed."

Cohn introduced him as Mary, but Susan Rosenstiel was too shocked to laugh. Of course, Hoover did not make a very convincing drag queen. He needed a shave.

Then two blond boys of about 18 or 19 came in and everyone moved into the bedroom. Hoover stripped down to his garter belt and the two boys gave him a Swedish massage. One of them – wisely – wore a pair of rubber gloves.

Cohn and Hoover watched while Rosenstiel got it on with the two boys. Then Cohn fucked them. Mrs Rosenstiel was feeling sorry for them at this stage as Cohn "couldn't get enough". She did not see Hoover have anal sex with them though, saying that he confined himself to playing with their genitals. Despite the invitation being extended, she did not join in. She did get the impression, however, that they got an extra thrill out of a woman being present. When the Rosenstiels left, Cohn, Hoover and the two boys were still hard at it.

"That was really something, wasn't it, with Mary Hoover?" Cohn said later, and he told her that it was he who had supplied Hoover's extraordinary outfit. Her husband warned her that if what she had seen got out, there would be terrible consequences. She feared for her life.

The following year, her husband bribed her with a pair of expensive earrings to attend another "party" at the Plaza. This time Hoover wore a red dress with a feather boa, like a 1920s flapper. Just as had been the case before, two boys came in. This time they were wearing leather. Hoover got one of them to read a passage from the Bible, while the other one, clad in a stout pair of Marigolds, played with him. Suddenly Hoover seized the Bible, threw it to the floor and ordered the other boy to join in.

That night, the Rosenstiels had a row and she was not invited again, though later she saw Hoover with Cardinal Spellman on their Connecticut estate.

Now, amusing though this story is, I am not sure that I believe it. The story comes from one source – a mobster's moll. Not only would Hoover have been putting himself in a position where Rosenstiel and Cohn could blackmail him, but it is also very difficult to keep such activities quiet in a hotel. I know people do strange things for love and take extraordinary risks for sex, but Hoover loved the FBI more than anything in the world. He clung on as its director long after retirement age. Being caught over a youthful indiscretion in New Orleans is one thing, so are compromising pictures falling into the wrong hands, but deliberately putting yourself under the thrall of blackmailers is quite another. I include this anecdote because the mental picture of the burly, pot-bellied, pug-faced, 58-year-old Hoover in a cocktail frock is simply too funny to miss.

Some had even claimed to have seen real pictures of Hoover in drag – lying on a bed and at a party. They were said to have been stolen from Hoover's home and did the rounds of the gay scene. There was no intention of using them for blackmail. They were just passed around as a curiosity. Again, those who said they had seen them confirmed that "Hoover made an ugly-looking woman", but also insisted that the man wearing an evening gown and blond wig was "easily recognisable as J. Edgar Hoover". How they must have laughed.

By this time, Hoover and Tolson were no longer getting it on. They had been together for 30 years. Tolson's health was deteriorating and he had lost his youthful beauty. Hoover was still robust, though, and still a powerbroker. In the 1960 presidential election he backed JFK*, because in the 1920s when Joe Kennedy* had been a movie producer he had lent Hoover some Hollywood starlets to be seen in public with to help quash the scuttlebutt that he was gay. In truth, Hoover was a Johnson* supporter. Johnson's house, he said, "was a place where you could get the best chilli con carne and the best mint julep in Washington". And there were pictures of the two men hugging each other on Johnson's ranch in Texas.

The moment Kennedy was elected in to the White House – against all expectations – he re-appointed Hoover. Kennedy told columnist Igor Cassini that Hoover was gay and he loathed him, but he was being blackmailed and there was nothing he could do. Of course, Hoover was being blackmailed, too, and when Kennedy was assassinated, the FBI quickly established that it had nothing to do with the mob.

There are reports that, in 1969, Hoover and Tolson used to stay in a bungalow in La Jolla, California, next-door to Billy Byars, the producer of X-rated movies featuring adolescent boys. Byars used to procure for them. On three or four occasions, he sent a couple of 15-year-old boys to them. They would meet at a bar, then drive up into the hills where the boys would get into their limo and "do their business". In a paedophile prosecution in the area a year later, Hoover's name came up repeatedly.

By 1970, *Washington Post* columnist Jack Anderson was on the case and had tracked down the shrink Hoover had consulted about his sexuality 24 years before. He also wrote about Hoover's almost voyeuristic interest in "who was sleeping with whom in Washington" and promised to hand over compromising documentary evidence to a congressional committee. Hoover's entire career was soon being trashed. Now Hoover found himself being hounded, just as he had hounded others.

When Nixon was informed of Hoover's death on May 2, 1972, he said with some relief: "Jesus Christ, the old cocksucker."

Within minutes, Hoover's house was being combed for incriminating material. Much of what was found was destroyed. Among those things that survived are numerous photographs, nearly all of Tolson, in a bathrobe, lounging by the pool, bare-chested on the beach, sleeping. At Hoover's funeral, as he had no wife, Tolson accepted the flag from the coffin. He died old and lonely three years later.

Chapter Twelve

Mr Show (Off) Business

In 1959, the nominally partial Queen's Bench Division court in London found the *Daily Mirror* guilty of libel for implying that Liberace was gay. He was awarded £8,000 in damages and, as always, was laughing all the way to the bank.

Of course, you could hardly find a finer example of red-blooded All-American manhood that Wladziu Valentino Liberace (or "Lee" to close friends and confidantes). Born in Milwaukee in 1919 of immigrant parents, his father was Italian and his mother Polish. And, of course, he was the son that every American mother wished she had – or should that be the daughter that every American mother wished she had? He was the survivor of a pair of twins.

"He took all the strength from his little brother," his mother said. "That was a sign."

Even so, he was a sickly child and, in the freezing Wisconsin winter, came close to death from pneumonia four times. Each time, he was nursed back to health by his doting mother, but she was normally occupied in the family grocery store, so he was left in the care of his older sister, Angelia, who introduced him to the world of dolls, princesses, fairies and dressing up. He began learning to play the piano at the age of four.

Pretty soon Wladziu became Walter because his playmates could not pronounce his Polish first name. However, most local boys shunned him for being sissy.

The Depression hit the family hard, but Walter flourished at school. He was respected for his ability to play the piano and tap dance, as well as for his ready wit.

Every term the school held "Character Day", when pupils were supposed to turn up dressed as a famous figure. Liberace excelled, even appearing one time as Greta Garbo*, complete with blond wig, slinky gown and a full face of make-up. Even on a regular school day he was a snappy dresser, wearing a suit and spats while other boys turned up in baggy sweaters and slacks.

In typing class he outperformed the girls and was up for any sort of theatrical activity. He arranged cookery classes for the other boys and made corsages for the Prom. It was noted that he showed little interest in dating, though he had a crush on a ballet dancer, whose recitals he played for. However, she married and left Milwaukee.

He beat a dozen girls to win a local music contest, so his music teacher put him forward for the state championships in the hope that it would stop him being so all-fired cocky. He won.

Liberace was disturbed by his sexual orientation. A Catholic, he would go to church and pray that something in him would change so that he could "look at girls with the same lust they inspired in other boys". His prayers were very nearly answered.

He formed a band with a few friends and began playing in beer gardens, though he was too young to drink himself. His older brother, George, began instructing him on the finer points of sex. He had never got beyond a few furtive kisses. Then, one night, he found himself playing in a darkened hall for three female strippers, who brushed past him provocatively as they left the stage naked. He also got to watch a pornographic movie before the place was busted.

Things got better.

One night, a busty Blues singer called Miss Bea Haven persuaded brother George to leave the 16-year-old Walter behind in the club to play for her as she entertained two men she knew to be big tippers. Afterwards she drove him home, but on the way she pulled to the side of the road, parked, and began to fondle him. "My" she said, "you're a big boy."

Before he knew what was happening, she had opened his fly and was sucking on his erect penis. Then she straddled him and they both enjoyed a few brief moments of intense passion.

"It was very fast, like would you believe about five strokes?" he said. Yes, Lee, I believe.

Walter was still on top of the world when he got home. It was only when he got indoors that he noticed the lipstick stains on his white pants. He spent the rest of the night scrubbing them with soap so that Mom would not find out what he had been up to. The way things turned out, she would probably had been quite pleased.

Liberace was quick to boast of his first sexual experiences. Not surprisingly, no one believed him.

Miss Bea invited him up to her apartment several times and was amazed that the youthful Liberace could come over and over again, but then she found a singing job in Cleveland and moved on.

Though it was blissful at the time, in retrospect Liberace's initiation into the wonderful world of sex seemed ever-so-slightly sordid. His partner had been an overweight nympho, who was old enough to be his mother and their lovemaking had none of the romance he had expected from the movies.

This first sexual experience put him right off sex with women. He didn't like girls at all, but he wanted to avoid being called a "fag", so he dated, even though the thought of being physically close to a girl made him feel sick.

Another alley soon opened up, however. When he was playing the Wunderbar in Wausau, Wisconsin, in the fall of 1939, he noticed that the men coming in together were not the usual after-work blue-collar crowd. He was naïve and it took him some time to recognise that they were gay. Suddenly, he discovered that he was not alone.

There was one guy in particular he could not miss.

"He was the size of a door, the most intimidating man I'd ever seen," said Liberace.

Every time Liberace looked out into the audience he'd be there smiling at him. Then he began to show up in other places where Liberace worked. He would buy the young musician drinks and tell him how much he liked his music.

"One night he asked to drive me home. That's the night I lost my virginity," said Lee. I thought you'd lost your virginity with Miss Bea Haven … Oh, I see what you mean. The guy was a football hero from the Green Bay Packers.

Liberace's Packer was first person he could unburden himself to. The two men became very close. The Packer introduced him to other gay men, often from other cities. Liberace began collecting telephone numbers, which became the basis of a gay network that would stand him in good stead for the years of touring to come.

Liberace's parents were having problems with their sex lives too, as Liberace found out when the celebrated conductor, Leopold Stokowski, came to Milwaukee. Liberace had bought two tickets – one for himself and one for his father – but his father refused to go with him.

"So I went to the concert," said Liberace, "and there, sitting two rows in front of me, was my father with another woman. That's how I found out he'd had a mistress for years ... It was a terrible shock to me. To think that my father was living with two women! I couldn't conceive of that. It made a tremendous mark on me at the time, because I really took it very emotionally."

The woman was a Pole called Zona Smrz. Mom took umbrage, kicked her husband out, divorced him and married the lodger – Alexander Casadonte, who came from her first husband's village in Italy. There was some talk that the affair had begun before the separation. Meanwhile, Dad married Zona in 1941. Casadonte died in 1945. Mom never married again and moved in with her son.

Liberace was exempted from the draft during the Second World War because of a back problem, hmmm. Instead, he went to play the Persian Room at the Plaza in New York. The Big Apple was totally liberating. He found that attractive young men would strike up a conversation with him and take him to parties and the theatre. For the first time he could openly express his homosexual desires and his affections for other men. Soon, he moved out to Los Angeles. He worked in the bars of Hollywood and Long Beach, which were full of eager young men, both in and out of uniform, with well-stuffed pockets and looking for an evening of pleasure.

Touring the West Coast, Liberace found himself besieged by adoring young men backstage. He began to wear outlandishly camp costumes. When he was criticised, he responded by dressing ever more extravagantly.

"You have seen in movies and plays how a badly dressed, ordinary-looking woman can be transformed into a most attractive woman by beautiful clothes and the latest style of hair-do," he said in his own defence.

In fact, though he denied it, Liberace sprayed grey on his temples, to appeal to the more mature women in the audience.

And, of course, he loved his Mom and told the world about it. Naturally, he took a lot of stick for it, but he entered the *Guinness Book of Records* for earning $138,000 for a concert at Madison Square Gardens – the highest salary ever paid to a solo pianist.

Of course, Liberace had to claim to be straight, despite his camp appeal. One whiff of a gay scandal would finish his career. So, in 1954, he wrote a piece called "The Girl I'll Marry" for a fan magazine.

"I have been engaged three times and, in each instance, I felt I was very lucky to have had the experience," he wrote. "Later on, as each romance in turn did not seem to work out, I felt I was fortunate that it did not culminate in marriage. There were different reasons in each case for the break-up. All three of the girls had sex appeal, too, and yet this rather intangible quality figured in our romantic problems."

Yes, Lee, we understand.

The first woman was a ballet dancer, he said, who had "all the qualities of sex appeal for which a man could ask". They had wanted to marry immediately, but it was the Depression and he felt he had to establish himself first. She found a job out of town and married someone else.

The next was a sexy singer. A girl who just wanted to have fun, she thought nothing of cancelling an engagement to go to a party and expected him to do the same. She even had him attend a beach party the night of his concert at the Hollywood Bowl. Such an irresponsible attitude toward work – and his fans – was not for Lee and he broke the engagement off.

Then there was a woman of independent means and spirit – too independent. They soon found that they could do without one another.

The problem was that these engagements had been very secret indeed. None of his friends or family knew anything about the women concerned. In fact, around that time, Liberace was having an affair with a young actor called Rock Hudson*. It did not matter to Liberace that Rock was not the type of young blond he generally preferred. He even had an Indian boy once.

Liberace ended the article with some tips for the girl he would marry.

"The exciting woman is the one who makes a genuine effort to take her natural beauty and enhance it by the proper use of cosmetics, make-up, girdles, or bras," he said. Well, at least Lee knew all about making the best of your appearance – if you did not mind looking like something that had just fallen off a Christmas tree, that is.

For publicity purposes, Liberace often appeared out with TV star Betty White. When they arrived at a movie premiere in a windstorm, she expected him to help restrain her huge bouffant dress – but he was too busy holding onto his bouffant hair.

There was a predictable storm of innuendo in the Press, but try as they might, reporters could not track down some willowy young man in his entourage. Liberace, meanwhile, hid behind his role as a mother's boy and continued to rue his three failed "engagements".

"Resentment of my women fans ruined each of them," he explained through his famously cheesy grin. "None of my fiancées could understand or accept the adulation of my fans, an understanding that is so important in a complex career like mine."

Even so, Liberace declared very publicly that he was still looking for love – brave little soldier.

"I keep my eyes open every day," he proclaimed. "Any minute I might walk into a hotel lobby and find her sitting there."

He was looking in the wrong direction, though. Love was just across the street. When he moved into a house in Camellia Avenue, North Hollywood, the 18-year-old Joanne Rio lived directly opposite in number 4209. Her mother was a Chicago Blues singer who sang under the name Mildred LaSalle and her father was Eddie Rio, a dancer with the Rio Brothers, who had performed in Broadway musicals and in vaudeville. He had retired from the stage to head the Los Angeles branch of the American Guild of Variety Artists.

As a teenager, Joanne had watched him play the piano through a window and met him on the street a couple of times when he was out walking his poodle, Suzette. Nothing happened and, eventually, they both moved on. Four years later, Liberace was in the audience of a show at the Moulin Rouge, where Joanne was a chorus girl. By now she was a beauty, who would later double for Elizabeth Taylor*. Dressed in a scanty negligee, she was performing a bump-and-grind routine which involved the ringing of hand bells. Recognising her old neighbour at ringside, she sent him a note saying: "You can ring my bell anytime."

Liberace invited her over for a drink and drove her home.

"He walked me to the door and shyly asked to see me again," she said. "Then he bowed and squeezed my hand. It was like a caress."

They began dating, but their relationship remained chaste. Liberace was often away performing, as it were. Her nightly appearances at the Moulin Rouge meant that she presented little by way of an obstacle to his social life, even when he was in LA. One night, she dashed from the dressing room to attend a reception for him after a concert at the Hollywood Bowl. Amid a crowd of celebrities, he stuck by her side. And, at the midnight supper, she was seated in the place of honour – next to Mom.

At the end of the evening, he walked her to her car. His poodle tagged along.

"Give me a kiss, Suzette," she said to the dog. "If you don't, your master won't."

She was in for the shock of her life.

"Lee took me in his arms and kissed me soundly," she recalled. "Wow! I blushed. But in the back of my mind I knew that was exactly what I wanted."

I think I want to be sick.

They began appearing at parties and premieres together. There were rumours of an engagement and a forthcoming marriage. These were promptly denied. Liberace was not ready for marriage, he said. He wanted to play in Europe and make movies. With that kind of schedule there was no time for nuptials.

The gossip columnists were frantic. A terrific self-publicist, Liberace milked it for all it was worth. He told one journalist the mom-and-apply-pie story that he had first seen Joanne in church.

"She seemed like a very nice girl," he said. "Of course, when you're dating, you don't want a goody-goody girl." You can say that again, Lee. "You want someone who is fun and has sex appeal. I realised that when I saw her at the Moulin Rouge. By the way, we still go to church."

As for Joanne, she said that Lee was "the perfect all-round man any woman would be thrilled to be with. He's so considerate on our dates. He's just the end. He never forgets the little things that women love. He brings me orchids. He lights my cigarettes and he opens doors." Aren't we forgetting something else women love? "He makes you feel that when you are with him, well, you really are with him."

He was also off on a five-week tour and his tours were a riot of casual gay sex.

Soon, they announced that they would marry after a year – "if she really loves me and is willing to wait". He had professional commitments and he did not want to split up over career differences like Marilyn Monroe* and Joe DiMaggio*. They were both Catholics and wanted their marriage to last.

Publicly Mom was all for her precious son's marriage to a good Catholic girl, but privately, she had her doubts. She did not like the look of some of the young men he brought home with him. They hung around Liberace's piano-shaped swimming pool in their bikinis, drank his liquor, played loud music and generally made themselves at home whether he was there or not. Mom called them "the hillbillies". Sometimes she called the police to get rid of them.

"I don't like the hillbillies," Mom said. "I wish you could get rid of them."

"Oh, Mom, they're harmless," he said. "They amuse me and relax me. It's the only time I can be myself."

It's not true. He also enjoyed the gentle art of sewing.

Then there were the fans to consider. Around 6,000 letters a week poured in, begging him not to marry. How could he abandon his mother? How could he abandon his fans? And there were, of course, numerous competing proposals of marriage – after all, Joanne was only marrying to boost her own career, they said.

"Am I jealous? I love it," Joanne said in a series of ghosted articles in the *Los Angeles Mirror*. "I am happy that so very many women see the same fine qualities in Liberace that I do and love him for them."

Liberace pointed out that his namesake, Rudolph Valentino,* had been married twice, yet his fans still adored him. In fact, Lee, Valentino married two lesbians and neither marriage was consummated. Maybe that's what Lee was hoping for.

179

However the real fly in the ointment was Joanne's father. He had been around in showbiz long enough to rub up against a lot of gay men. He suggested to Joanne that she might find the marriage less than satisfactory because Liberace was, well, not very manly.

"Oh, Daddy," she said. "He's just a mama's boy. Everybody knows that. He'll change."

Then an old friend in the business phoned Rio Snr and told him about "an incident involving Liberace that had the makings of a scandal, but had been hushed up". His duty as a father was clear. He told Joanne. At first she was disbelieving, then inconsolable.

Next time Liberace came round, Rio put his arm around his shoulder and told him that the marriage could not go ahead. He wanted grandchildren and his daughter had the right to have a family of her own. As Catholics, divorce was out of the question. The engagement was off and millions of middle-aged women across the United States breathed again.

When Liberace published his autobiography in 1973 he said that publicity had killed off the affair – but it was Joanne's publicity seeking not, of course, his own that was to blame.

"What finally hosed me down and cooled me off was the discovery that Joanne had been paid a tidy sum by a newspaper syndicate to let them publish details of the romance," he said. "These pieces contained many intimate details, confidences and personal confessions that two people share when they're in love (or think they are). When these are set down in cold print they tend to make both parties look somewhat ridiculous."

Joanne, who was married to fashion designer David Barr by then, sued, alleging that he had portrayed her as "an untrustworthy person" and "an opportunist who would exploit any personal relationship".

In his defence, Liberace made a deposition, which stated: "As far as I am concerned, Joanne Rio does not exist because this is something that happened 20 years ago. We all agreed it was like a ghost coming out of the past to haunt me. I see nothing in the book that was damaging or derogatory to Miss Rio. As I remember it, she was a very pretty girl, a very nice girl. I liked her very much. I wanted to marry her, and that's exactly what I said in my book.

The reason I didn't marry her was because of these goddamn articles and her father screaming at me and calling me all kinds of names. I suddenly realised I had found out in the nick of time that all was not going to be sunshine and roses."

He also said that he had heard from a columnist on the *Los Angeles Mirror* that she had received a "tidy sum" for the articles, which had upset him because they were "silly like a puppy love, school-girl kind of thing, not a grown-up adult thing".

However, Joanne was also upset because in his autobiography he had implied that she "had been intimate with him and accordingly was unchaste".

In her deposition for the case, she said that, after excerpts of the autobiography had appeared in the *National Enquirer*, friends had asked her:"Was he homosexual? Did you go to bed with him."

She replied:"I dated him, but I never went to bed with him."

When she had read the *Enquirer* she had become quite hysterical.

"Why was he degrading me to justify why he never got married?" she kept asking."Why was he lying about me?"

If the case had gone to court, he risked cross-examination about his sexual orientation. So, eventually, the suit was settled for a "substantial amount".

After the affair was over, Liberace launched himself into a movie career, moving into Judy Garland's* dressing room at Warner Bros. His one movie, *Sincerely Yours* (1955), was panned by the critics and died at the box office. Apart from a few cameo roles, his movie career was over.

The gossip columns linked his name with that of Frances Goodrich, the pretty young heiress to a Californian orange fortune. Liberace said that the romance foundered when the family insisted that he give up the piano and take up the fruit business. Then came skater Sonja Henie, who he met at a party a Ciro's. She came to the wedding of Liberace's sister, Angelia, and presented the happy couple with two ice sculptures – one of Liberace at the piano, one of her on skates. Naturally they melted before the newly-weds had time write a thank-you letter. Soon after, she married a Norwegian multi-millionaire. As another one slipped through the net, Liberace was encouraged to take up horseback riding to improve his image, but he had always been more of a bare-back rider.

Liberace headed for Europe. On the *Queen Mary* he met Nöel Coward*, who said, with perfect punctuation: "I've seen your act… You do what you do – very well."

At Waterloo, Liberace was greeted by crowds and Britain's formidable Press pack.

"Do you have a normal sex life?" asked one reporter.

"Yes," replied Liberace. "Do you?"

He played to packed houses, but the Press savaged him for his "smirk-and-smarm act" and his "deplorable taste". One paper suggested that he be "stoned with marshmallows". However, William Connor, in his Cassandra column in the *Daily Mirror*, went further:

> He is the summit of sex – the pinnacle of masculine, feminine and neuter. Everything that he, she and it can ever want.
>
> I spoke to sad but kindly men on this newspaper who have met every celebrity coming from the United states for the past 30 years. They say that this deadly, winking, sniggering, snuggling, chromium-plated, scent-impregnated, luminous, quivering, giggling, fruit-flavoured, mincing, ice-covered heap of mother love has had the biggest reception and impact on London since Charlie Chaplin* arrived at the same station, Waterloo, on September 12, 1921.
>
> This appalling man – and I use the word appalling in no other than its true sense of terrifying – has hit this country in a way that is as violent as Churchill* receiving the cheers on VE Day.

William Connor did not stop there. He said that Liberace "reeks with emetic language that can only make grown men long for a quiet corner, an aspidistra, a handkerchief, and the old heave-ho.

"Without doubt, he is the biggest sentimental vomit of all time. Slobbering over his mother, winking at his brother, and counting the cash every second, this superb piece of calculating candyfloss has an answer for every situation."

He called his act a "slag heap of lilac-covered hokum" and no one anywhere had "made so much money out of high-speed piano playing with the ghost of Chopin gibbering at every note". He concluded by saying:

> There must be something wrong with us that our teenagers longing for sex and our middle-aged matrons fed up with sex alike should fall for such a sugary mountain of jingling claptrap wrapped up in such a preposterous clown.

Liberace was taken aback. At a press conference he complained of the "degenerate attacks" he had suffered which implied that he was an "unmanly man". Reading them had made his mother ill and if her health did not improve he would have to take action. Besides, how could he be an "unmanly man" – look at all the female fans he had. However, the American newspapers were beginning to put this down to the cult of "Momism".

When he played in Manchester he was greeted with placards that read: "We Want He-Men, Not Momma's Boys" and "Send the Fairy Back to the States". And Teddy Boys in Sheffield shouted: "We don't want Yankee fairies!" and "Queer, go home!"

Jokes about Liberace's sexuality appeared in London cabarets and a song that first appeared in a stage revue, then on television, contained the lines:

> My fan mail is really tremendous,
> It's growing so fast my head whirls;
> I get more and more,
> They propose by the score –
> And at least one or two are from girls.

Liberace became so paranoid that, when he was approached backstage by a man from his home town Milwaukee who said "We're so proud you are one of us", he pushed the man away and screamed: "I am not a homosexual."

He decided that he had no alternative but to sue and on October 22, 1956, the High Court issued writs against William Connor and the *Daily Mirror* for libel. Liberace told reporters: "It was just too much for any man to stomach. If I didn't have the contract dates in the immediate future and my appearances did not depend on my hands, I would knock Cassandra's teeth down his throat. And I ain't kidding."

The case took three years to come to court. Meanwhile, back in the States, *Hush-Hush* magazine asked: "Is Liberace a man? If not, what?" This was a question that had been bothering the United States for years, it said, and it reprinted the entire Cassandra piece from the *Daily Mirror*. Not to be outdone, the famous scandal sheet *Hollywood Confidential* ran a picture of Liberace with the screamer: "Exclusive! Why Liberace's Theme Song Should Be 'Mad about the Boy'!"

According to the story, a handsome young press agent who had been hired to organise a Fourth of July bash for Liberace had caught up with the showman in Akron, Ohio. Alone in his suite in the Sheraton-Mayflower Hotel, the eager young agent told Liberace: "Whatever you want, I'm your boy."

Liberace took him at his word. After they had loosened up with a drink, he found Liberace sitting on his lap. Then there was an impromptu wrestling match.

"Once, during the scuffle, the press agent let out a yelp of pain," said the article, "and no wonder... For Luscious Libby, it was strictly no-holds-barred. Finally, with a combination of wrist-lock and flying mare, the publicity man wrenched loose from his host's embrace and fled from the suite, leaving Liberace sprawled on the floor."

Later, the same press agent had to fly to California to obtain Liberace's signature. Lee took him to dinner at Trader Vic's and ran his fingers over him in the back of his car, attempting an arpeggio on the piano-key upholstery.

Then, in a suite in Dallas, there was a return match.

"The floor show reached its climax when Dimples, by sheet weight, pinned his victim to the mat and mewed in his face: 'Gee, you're cute when you're mad.'" The bout ended – not with two falls, two submissions or a knock-out – but when the agent's friend, who had been filled in beforehand, burst in like "the US Cavalry riding to the rescue in the nick of time". The moral of the story, the *Hollywood Confidential* said, was: "Hit the road when a client tries to turn public relations into private relations."

Liberace sued, demanding $25 million in damages. Maureen O'Hara was also suing *Hollywood Confidential* at the time, over an allegation that she had sex with a Mexico boy in the back seats of Grauman's Chinese Theatre. They got together with other Hollywood stars and the studios and pursued the *Hollywood Confidential* for criminal libel. After a 14-day trial, the paper was forced to agree to stop delving into the private lives of the stars. Liberace continued with his private suit. After he proved that he was not in the places mentioned at the times the incidents were said to have occurred, the *Hollywood Confidential* coughed up $40,000. There was still the Cassandra case to face, however.

Liberace dressed soberly for his appearance at the Queen's Bench Division. In British courts, all the fancy dressing up is done by the judge and the barristers. Liberace's counsel's cross-examination was simple and to the point:

Question: Are you a homosexual?

Answer: No, sir.

Question: Have you ever indulged in homosexual practices?

Answer: No, sir, never in my life. I am against the practice because it offends convention and it offends society.

Question: Was there anything sexy about your performances at all?

Answer: I am not aware of it if it exists. I am almost positive that I could hardly refer to myself as a sexy performer. I have tried in all my performances to inject a note of sincerity and wholesomeness. I am fully aware of the fact that my appeal on television and in personal appearances is aimed directly at the family audience.

Question: Do you ever tell dirty stories?

Answer: I have never been known to tell any so-called dirty stories. I have told of experiences that happened to me that might have been termed double-meaning in referring to some of my sponsors. Among them was a very famous paper company who among their products make toilet tissue. I mentioned them among my sponsors and the audience found it very funny. But the audience in no way found it offensive.

The defence counsel was not nearly so slick and allowed Liberace to establish that he had received 27,000 Valentine cards that year and around 12 proposals of marriage a year.

Question: Including one from a lady who offered to put down
   $200,000?
Answer: Yes.

The defence counsel said that Liberace had arranged to be
showered with bouquets when he arrived at Southampton.
Liberace denied it. Instead he said that women were screaming,
sobbing, fainting, throwing themselves at him and trying to kiss
him through the window of the train. But, like Oscar*, he was
caught out lying about his age – but not under oath. His publicity
material said that he was born in 1920, not 1919. When this was
pointed out, he said: "We find it desirable to make the birth date a
round figure. I borrowed the idea from Jack Benny*."

He was questioned about his interview on CBS Television's
Person to Person. When veteran interviewer Edward R. Murrow
had asked him about Princess Margaret*, he said: "I would like to
meet her very much, because I think we have a lot in common.
We have the same tastes" – in diamonds and tiaras, perhaps –
"in theatre and music, and besides, she is pretty and she is
single."

He said that he was "not referring to the Princess as a marriage
prospect". A titter ran through the courtroom, but he said he was
looking for a girl "just like Mom".

Did he have sex appeal? "No, I consider sex appeal as something
possessed by Marilyn Monroe* and Brigitte Bardot*. I certainly do
not put myself in their class." There was more laughter.

He denied using perfume or scented lotions – just "after-
shaving lotions and underarm deodorants". It was plain that the
defence could not get the better of him. Unlike Oscar, he never
got flustered and he seized the opportunity to declare from
the witness stand that the Cassandra article had "cost me
many years of my professional career by implying that I am a
homosexual".

That night he was appearing in concert in Finsbury Park.
Glitzed up and brimming with confidence, he told the audience: "I
had such a marvellous time out here that I'm ashamed to take the
money." Then he added with a wink: "But I think I will."

On the stand the following day, William Connor was asked: "Did you at any time have any intention of imputing homosexuality to Liberace?"

"None at all," was his reply.

He also denied knowing that "fruit" was American slang for a homosexual, but the case was lost. The *Daily Mirror* was ordered to pay £8,000 in damages and £14,000 in costs.

Liberace put the money towards a house in Palm Springs where he could hang out with his hillbillies far from the eyes of the gossip columnists. His love life now assumed a regular pattern. He formed a temporary liaison with one of his young men, lavished gifts on him and basked in his youthful gratitude, then dumped him when it was time to go back to work. The desert community turned a blind eye to such peccadilloes among the stars who came there to relax, but his brother George was worried.

Though George never criticised Lee for his homosexuality – being an inveterate womaniser himself – he said: "Goddamnit Lee, how can you keep saying in public and in courtrooms that you're not a homosexual and then you hang out in the Springs with a bunch of faggots? You're gonna get nailed some day."

Liberace was outraged. There was a very public feud. Mom stepped in, ruing that "Lee lives in Palm Springs most of the time, surrounded by a gang of what I call hillbillies and freeloaders …

"We are simple people from Wisconsin," she said. "You can only live in one house at a time. Lee has four houses in Palm Springs – and you can only rent houses there for a few months of the year. You call that an investment? Give me the old bankbook. That's what counts."

Publicly it was made to look as if the two brothers had fallen out over real-estate investment. Eventually, behind closed doors, they patched it up.

In the more liberal atmosphere of the 1960s, Liberace felt he could let go a little. Appearing in ever more camp outfits, he said: "Actually, I never wear clothes like this offstage – oh, no, I'd be picked up for sure."

After his shows at Las Vegas, there would be all-male drinking parties in his suite. And he "tricked around" gay bars, relishing quick casual encounters.

"In the 1960s, you could often see Liberace cruising the Akron store on Sunset Boulevard with his little doggie in hand, dressed all in white – Lee I mean – trying to pick up Mexicans in the store's parking lot," said a TV producer who knew him. "He wasn't discreet. He was daring and rather outrageous about it. He'd stand in the lot and try and pick up young men in their cars. Most didn't recognise him."

He even dared to show his face in England again. Arriving with 35 pieces of luggage, he was immediately asked by waiting reporters about the Cassandra affair.

"Why don't we let sleeping dogs lie," he said.

Back in Hollywood, Liberace became close friends with Mae West – already a gay icon – and they discussed the art of showmanship.

"You know how I got that sexy walk of mine?" she said. "I put a half-dollar between my buttocks and tried to hold it there."

"Maybe I should try that," said Lee. "But I don't think I'd get the same result."

Confronted by pressmen on the way to see a puppet show where they were both caricatured, they were asked what they planned to do after the show. Mae said: "Mr Liberace invited me to come up and see his house. I'm gonna look at his golden organ."

In the 1970s, when everyone else was coming out of the closet, Liberace jumped back in and locked the door. And he chose San Francisco, of all places, to do it. At a press conference in 1973 he said: "As I told a British court in 1959 when I won a $20,000 judgement against a London newspaper, my sexual feelings are the same as most people's. I'm against the practice of homosexuality because it offends convention and society. The only reason I never got married is probably because I come from a family of divorce. My parents, first of all. It put me off marriage. It was a deterrent."

He went on to say that he was tired of people writing stories about him that were "dishonest and cancerous with innuendo".

"The only reason they started is because I was the first in my field to dare to be a nonconformist, to wear the fancy clothes I do … Now if I were to emerge on the scene, I would probably go unnoticed. A lot of people nowadays can wear sequins on their eyelids and nobody puts a sexual label on them."

If that was not disingenuous enough, he went on with some real porky pies.

"I could have given up many, many times, professionally and personally. Why, I've been pronounced dead three times. I've had the last rites of the Church. I've been the victim of an international kidnapping attempt. Mind you, I wouldn't trade my life for that of anyone else. I'm a person who was put on earth simply to bring happiness and love to people. And I get it back in abundance. It's what makes me go on living and doing my thing."

This last bit of flimflam was ignored. The headline in San Francisco was: "I Am Not A Homosexual, Says Liberace."

Later, Liberace was interviewed for *The First Time* by Karl Fleming and Anne Taylor Fleming. He was supposed just to talk about the loss of his virginity. Instead, he talked about masturbation, his father's mistress, his family's sexual conservatism and his brother. Then he launched, with some vitriol, into the San Francisco press conference: "This son of a bitch says, 'Do you feel the same way about homosexuality that you did when you fought your trial in London?' I said, 'Whatever I said in the high courts in London, I meant, and if I said it then, I say it now.' So he took this one line out of 12 days of testimony and quoted it completely out of context, without any explanation at all. For me to say something like that today would be stupid. It made me appear that I'm down on gay people. Shit, I resented it."

Even if Liberace did not come out in 1973, his autobiography did. Fifty of its 312 pages are devoted to his defence of the Cassandra case, vindicating him of the taint of homosexuality. The book mentions Frances Goodrich, Sonja Henie, Joanne Rio and the girl next-door in Milwaukee. It also covers his time in the roadhouses of Wisconsin.

"Needless to say," wrote his ghost writer, a well-known writer of radio variety shows, "before the joint I was playing was hit by the police, I had ceased to be a virgin and found out exactly the meaning of the word 'prostitute'."

Well, that could be read in a number of ways, but I guess it is meant to convey that he is a good, red-blooded, all-American, heterosexual chap.

His autobiography also rued the fact that, as a long-term bachelor, he was a poor prospect as a husband. However: "Should the right woman come along, one who clearly loves me enough to take a chance on me and if I feel that deeply for her, I'm sure we both will know that 'this is it'."

George was now back on the bandwagon. On a TV award show, he said: "Everyone asks about Lee's love life. Well, of all the girls that he loved and lost, every one calls Lee their 'little cave man'. One kiss and he caves in …" Why, he'll do anything if they stop.

Accepting the award, Liberace said: "I guess you know now why George never talked on our television show."

Lee's taste was more toward young, blond, blue-eyed men with taut torsos and well defined muscles. These were ten a penny in gay circles in Las Vegas and West Hollywood. He was particularly fond of male strippers and stayed in contact with former lover Chris Cox who ran the Odyssey, a gay club in Los Angeles. From the age of 50, he cut down on casual promiscuity and took on a series of live-in lovers who provided comfort on tour and companionship on his long vacations in his holiday homes in Palm Springs and Malibu. When they left him, he would be devastated. Once, his chauffeur recalled that he cried all the way from Palm Springs to Los Angeles, a distance of 100 miles. Otherwise, he would get bored with an airhead and pay him off with jewellery and cash.

As he got older, lovers were ever more difficult to replace. He began to put on weight, despite Spartan diets, and he was going bald, though the fact was hidden by ever more boyish wigs. Plastic surgery ironed out the wrinkles and make-up was applied by the bucketful.

In 1977, he met 18-year-old Scott Thorson backstage after a show. He was blond, blue-eyed, tanned and athletic. Six-foot-three-inches tall, he weighed just 13-and-a-half stone, or 190 pounds.

"You look like Adonis," said Lee. "My own blond Adonis."

Lee then took his current boyfriend and the producer of his show Ray Arnett, Scott Thorson and Bob Street, Thorson's intimate companion and a friend of Arnett, out for a drink. During the conversation, Arnett said: "Lee, I'm sure Bob and Scott would love to see your house. Could I bring them by tomorrow?"

Liberace effortlessly consented.

The following afternoon Liberace appeared from his bedroom to give them a guided tour of his house. They must have been particularly impressed by the bathrooms. Fearful of the sight of a naked toilet, Liberace had them disguised. The one in his master bedroom in Palm Springs had been transformed into a throne, literally.

He also introduced them to his five "children" – that is, his dogs. They had eye trouble, he said. Scott immediately volunteered that he worked with animals and knew of a new ointment that would clear up the problem. Liberace was delighted to hear this and gave Scott his private number.

Next day Scott called from LA. He had the medication.

"Why don't you bring it up here?" said Liberace.

A fortnight later, Scott drove up to Las Vegas in his Ford Capri and caught Liberace's Friday-night show. Afterwards, he took Scott home with him and they had sex. Saturday, they lazed around the house. On Sunday, Lee gave Scott $300 and told him to go to Los Angeles and get his stuff. Scott was moving in. They were living in each other's pockets.

Scott had never heard of Liberace, who was doing no TV at that time, before he fetched up in Las Vegas. He too was from Wisconsin, but had been brought to California by his mentally unstable mother, whose regular breakdowns meant that much of his childhood was spent going in and out of orphanages. He lived with a gay man when he was at high school, then moved in with his half-brother Wayne Johansen, who was a bartender in San Francisco. From then on his life revolved "around a few gay friends in northern California". As a sideline, he trained animals for use in the movies, but he was unemployed when he met Bob Street and had sex with him. Then they took off together to Las Vegas.

Liberace showered Scott with jewellery, fur coats and cars. The boy's awe at his new-found wealth gave Liberace a vicarious thrill. It did not go unnoticed. A journalist at the opening of the Liberace Museum asked him why Scott was wearing almost as much gold and diamonds as the 58-year-old showman himself.

"I did not wear a lot of jewellery before I met Lee," he said. "But if you're with Lee, you've got to keep up the image. And it's fun. It's become a company thing, a trademark for all his employees."

A trained observer might have drawn a different inference.

Scott began to appear in public with Liberace at parties and in restaurants. Even during interviews he was never far away and, in a series of fancy chauffeur outfits, he drove Lee around.

His constant presence annoyed other acquaintances, particularly when he interrupted conversations with old friends. Debbie Reynolds* snapped at him and told Lee that he should not have people around him who did not know how to behave.

"I know," said Lee. "But you know how lonely it gets on the road."

According to Thorson, Liberace had "an insatiable sex drive" which was undiminished even though he was in his 60s. Thorson said he spent more time thinking about sex than about his act. When the impotence that comes with age began to affect him, he had "a silicone implant that made him semi-erect all the time". Although sometimes this was the best he could manage, he was still fanatical about sex, using popular gay drug, amyl nitrate, or "poppers" as they were known, to increase his pleasure.

"He wanted sexual encounters a couple of times a day," Thorson said.

He also used pornographic movies to turn himself on.

"Each time Lee viewed one of his tapes he wanted to have sex."

Before Thorson came into his life, Lee had a consuming interest in hard-core porn and would show porn movies at his all-male parties. He was fascinated by the variety of sex acts he saw, but "nothing made him hotter than a three-way".

"No matter how hard he tried, curiosity about the mysteries of sex and his own sexuality obsessed him."

Unfortunately, Thorson said that gay porn turned him off.

Liberace took Thorson on a sightseeing tour of Hamburg. Thorson said that Lee "sat, riveted by the action, as a series of acts – homosexual and heterosexual – unfolded in front of us". Closer to home, he loved to visit porn shops. Thorson remembered Liberace taking him to one in Fort Lauderdale "where you could watch sex flicks to your heart's content – heterosexual, homosexual, sex acts featuring animals or children – they had it all" in What-the-Butler-Saw machines. Thorson said that Lee "gleamed as he took it all in" and soon he "was going from viewer to viewer, grinning all over the place".

"The bookstore also had private cubicles in the back with what are known in the gay world as 'glory holes'," said Thorson. "For a small fee a man could rent one of these cubicles, put his penis through the 'glory hole', and wait for a response."

Thorson thought that Liberace was crazy. What would he do if a reporter saw him in there? "How would you explain that to all the little old ladies?" he asked.

Liberace was a "danger queen", Thorson thought, who got off on risking getting caught.

Thorson also claimed that in their five years together he never gave Liberace anal sex, even though he begged him. However, there were a lot of other things they got up to. Lee, said Thorson, "preferred to have a variety act – on stage and behind closed doors."

For four years, Liberace thought he had found a lasting love, even so, he could not keep his hands off other men.

"When he had a few drinks he would come on to teenage boys as though I wasn't there," Thorson said. He was "a Dracula who never wearied of the taste and touch of youth".

He constantly caught Lee with his hand in another man's fly. They experimented with having an open relationship so that Liberace could "indulge in the sexual experimentation he craved". This foundered on the rock of jealousy, which Scott tried to alleviate with drink and drugs. His behaviour became erratic. Finally, Liberace decided that he should say bye-bye to Scott, like he had had to do to so many others, but Scott refused to leave the penthouse on Beverly Boulevard he shared with Liberace. Early one morning, in April 1982, he woke to find four burly men surrounding his bed. They sprayed Mace in this face, beat him and threw him out. The locks had already been changed so he could not get back in. Six months later, Scott whacked Liberace with $380-million "palimony" suit.

Thorson appeared in the Los Angeles County Courthouse in a ruffled shirt and a brocade dinner jacket, saying that he and Liberace had developed an intimate sexual relationship soon after they met. At the time, he said, he was a flourishing composer, dancer, animal trainer and trainee vet. He gave all that up to become Liberace's exclusive chauffeur, bodyguard, secretary, confident, lover and cohabitee. In return, Liberace gave him room and board, and $7,000 a month plus between $20,000 and $30,000 to care for the pets.

Liberace was to keep him in the style to which he had become accustomed for the rest of his life, adopt him as his son, give him half his real estate and personal property, and a prominent burial next to the Liberace family plot in Forest Lawn Memorial Park in Glendale. He also filed a civil suit against Liberace and the four men who chucked him out of the Beverly penthouse.

Liberace's lawyer dismissed Thorson's suit as a publicity stunt. There was "absolutely no truth in it". Thorson was merely a "disgruntled former employee who was fired … because of excessive use of drink and drugs and carrying of firearms". Thorson's suit was, Liberace said, "character assassination".

He later claimed that Thorson had threatened him by saying: "If you think the Billie Jean King [lesbian tennis player] scandal was something, wait till I get through with you."

He claimed to have been unaware of Thorson's drug abuse, but found drugs hidden in cans of shaving cream, deodorant and hair spray. Guns were sent through airports in the baggage. If the authorities had discovered the drugs and guns, it would have reflected badly on the entire company. Thorson had become a Jekyll-and-Hyde figure. He also had hallucinations, where he was convinced that people were out to kill him.

Thorson struck back with a front-page article in the *National Enquirer*, saying that he was a fresh-faced 17-year-old virgin with no homosexual tendencies when Liberace picked him out and that the affair had finished when he had caught Liberace with an 18-year-old boy. They also called each other "Libby" and "Boober". You couldn't make it up. The following week, he told the readers of *Enquirer* that Liberace was almost totally bald, had had two major face-lifts and dressed like a slob at home.

Not to be outdone, the *Globe* ran an article said to be based on an interview with Wayne Johansen, which said that Thorson had had gay sex from the age of 11, had been a gay prostitute since the age of 16 and had even gone to bed with his stepfather before he died. Thorson filed an $18-million libel suit against the *Globe* and Liberace, who he claimed had put them up to it.

In deposition, Thorson had to admit that he was 18 when he

met Liberace and that he had never been employed as a composer or dancer. He had used cocaine in 1980 or 1981, but never in the presence of Liberace, who himself used amyl nitrate. He then described their first sexual encounter.

"When he took me in his arms, it revolted me at first," he said. "I was unaccustomed to full make-up."

Asked whether he was wearing make-up during the deposition, Thorson said: "Maybe. Probably am. Why? Why not?"

Question: Was it your expectation that you would become a legally adopted son of Liberace?

Answer: Yes.

Question: And continue in a sexual relationship with him after the adoption?

Answer: No.

Question: Is that when you thought the sex would stop?

Answer: Our relationship later on went from a sexual relationship to – he always thought of me more as a son.

Aha. Incest. Liberace had also said that he had always wanted children and that Thorson reminded him of his alcoholic younger brother Ruby. Thorson also said that Liberace had arranged for a plastic surgeon to give him a cleft chin.

Despite his paternal and fraternal feelings, Thorson said that in March 1982, he still "made love to Liberace regularly", but that he became upset because he thought Liberace "was in Palm Springs having sex with his two male house guests from France".

"The thought of this outraged me because I loved Liberace and I considered this type of conduct a violation of our trust," he said.

Liberace did not testify at first because, he claimed, the papers had not been served on him. The process-server insisted that she had served them at the Westbury Music Fair on a man wearing a brown business suit who she was sure was Liberace. The judge found for Liberace on the grounds that: "That man would not be caught dead in a brown business suit."

When he was finally deposed, Liberace said that he had heard about Thorson's use of cocaine in 1981 and that he had urged him to stop and seek medical help. He grew irrational and threatened to kill him. He was particularly disturbed that Liberace was entertaining two house guests from France.

"He shouted all kinds of obscenities at me," Liberace testified. "I refuse to name those obscenities. Let's just say that they were obscenities of the dirtiest kind you can imagine."

Help came in the form of a California Supreme Court ruling in Marvin v. Marvin, the first palimony case. Michelle Triola Marvin had sued actor Lee Marvin over monies she had lost during their long cohabitation, even though they weren't married. The courts tried to give her some, but Lee Marvin fought it all way to the California Supreme Court which ruled that "the courts should enforce express agreements between non-marital partners except to the extent that the contract is explicitly founded on consideration of meritorious sexual services" as this constituted prostitution.

The Superior Court judge in Thorson v. Liberace dismissed the case on March 1, 1984, on the grounds that any agreement that Thorson claimed to have constituted was a contract for prostitution and therefore, illegal and unenforceable. Overjoyed, Liberace told *Newsweek* that Thorson's suit was essentially "blackmail". Thorson then took out a $36.2 million libel suit against Liberace and *Newsweek*.

Eventually, in 1986, Liberace paid Thorson off with $95,000, on top of the $75,000, plus two dogs, a gold Rolls Royce and the other trinkets, he had already given him. By then, he had found a new boyfriend – 19-year-old Cary James, a fresh-faced Floridian who had been in the troupe of dancers and singers who supported Liberace's Las Vegas show.

Despite the fact that his stage outfits were now so extravagant that they bordered on drag and his act was laced with gay innuendo, he refused to come out because his own audience would never "accept people who were totally gay or came out on Johnny Carson".

"I've seen careers hurt by this kind of thing," he said. "Look at Billie Jean King."

When asked where he stood on the issue, he said: "With a name like Liberace, which stands for freedom, I'm for anything that has the letters L.I.B. in it, and that includes Gay Lib."

He was also asked whether he had ever watched a

pornographic movie. He admitted watching *Inside Jennifer Welles* – where an amorous adventuress has 72 gentlemen in one night, including the entire staff of a Chinese restaurant. It could be seen as a rather odd, distinctly heterosexual, choice – unless Liberace actually imagined himself in the role of Jennifer. However, that does not fit with what other witnesses tell us. The hustler John Rechy, who was part of his retinue, said that sexually "he was an incredibly, incredibly aggressive man". Another lover concurred: "Oh, Lee was a top. He liked to fuck."

Whether Liberace could really manage 72 men in one night is open to debate, but he certainly liked a lot of sex.

"Some people say that fucking saps your creative energy. I don't believe it," he said. "A healthy sex life keeps you young and vital. And it should be frequent. I don't mean three times a day, but frequent. Some of these sports managers tell their players no sex before the night of the game. That's a lot of bullshit. It's healthy to get your rocks off in a passionate way. Well, a lot of people have hang-ups sexually. I feel sorry for them."

But when pressed further, he clammed up.

"I don't think entertainers should publicly air their sexual or political tastes," he maintained. "What they do in the privacy of their own home or bed is nobody's business."

So let's respect that then. He died of AIDS in 1987.

Chapter Thirteen

What the Butler Saw

J oe Orton was the *enfant terrible* of the English stage in the 1960s. He wrote a series of black comedies which included *Entertaining Mr Sloane*, *Loot* and *What the Butler Saw*. These outraged audiences with their unconventional sexual undercurrents. Orton is better remembered now, however, for the fact that his prodigious young talent was snuffed out in a blood-soaked murder-suicide by his friend and long-term lover Kenneth Halliwell.

The couple first came to public attention in May 1962, when they were convicted of stealing and defacing library books. According to the *North London Press*: "In a book on the life of Dame Sybil Thorndike, there was a photograph of her sitting on a chair in a room, but the picture of a man's torso had been pasted in front of her face to show her looking at the man." In fact, she was looking directly at the man's genitals.

A female nude was pasted on a book of etiquette by Lady Lewisham. Other books were given mildly obscene blurbs. One, of a Dorothy L. Sayers whodunit, read: "When little Betty Macdree says she has been interfered with, her mother at first laughs, but when sorting though the laundry, Mrs Macdree discovers that a new pair of knickers are missing and she thinks again. On being questioned, Betty bursts into tears. Mrs Macdree takes her to the police station and, to everyone's surprise, the little girl identifies PC Brenda Coolidge as her attacker. A search is made of the women's police barrack. What is found there is a seven-inch phallus and a pair of knickers of the kind used by Betty. All looks black for kindly PC Coolidge ... What can she do? This is one of the most enthralling stories ever written by Miss Sayers. It is the only one in which the murder weapon is concealed, not for reasons of fear but for reasons of decency. READ THIS BEHIND CLOSED DOORS. And have a good shit while you are reading!"

In the contents page, *The Collected Plays of Emlyn Williams*, *Night Must Fall* became *Knickers Must Fall*. *He Was Born Gay* curiously became *He Was Born Grey*. *Up the Front, Up the Back* and *Fucked by Monty* were added. They had also stolen a large number of lavishly illustrated books which they cut up to decorate the walls of their bedsit with louche collage.

No motive for the crime was given in the court, though a senior probation officer speculated that "both defendants were frustrated authors". This was true. They had recently finished collaborating on the unpublished novel *The Boy Hairdresser*, but the world was not ready for a book about gay love in the salon.

Summing up, the prosecution said: "In some 30 years of experience, I have never seen anything of this nature before."

They got six months.

Born in Leicester in 1933, Orton was interested in the theatre. At the age of 14, he joined the Leicester Dramatic Society. He found girls confounding. They rejected him and stood him up, or simply did not give him the sexual attention he craved. By the age of 16, he was writing in his diary: "I'm really mad tonight. Penny said she would come to dancing school tonight and was to meet me outside the library. I turned up, but did she? No, she didn't, and I waited like a fool in the howling wind and pouring rain."

A few weeks later: "This really is the last straw. D.L. and I went to the theatre and we saw Penny with Dickie B, George B and some other boy, 14 I think. Well, if she prefers their company to mine, she's welcome to it. I have finished with her completely."

He had no luck elsewhere, though. Four weeks after he wrote: "My opinion of women is going down. At present it is zero. Dot [Dorothy Crashley] never turned up at all [for a date]. Am completely fed up with girls. Brought two sticks of greasepaint."

The only success Orton tasted during his adolescence was on stage. He got great reviews for his amateur productions, but still the women were not impressed.

"I feel so fed up, fed up with girls," he wrote in his diary on his

17th birthday on New Year's Day 1950. "I'll be damn glad if I do have to go in the Army. At least, it'll be a change."

Instead, he eradicated his working-class Leicester accent and won a scholarship to the Royal Academy of Dramatic Arts. Almost as soon as he found digs in Gower Street, he took up with Kenneth Halliwell, another RADA student. Seven years older than Orton and already bald, Halliwell had been actively gay from the time he was at school. At first, Halliwell was like a surrogate brother to Orton – both were lonely outsiders – but Orton was still pining for a girl called Joyce Holmes who he had left behind in Leicester.

Three weeks after arriving at RADA he wrote to Joyce, saying: "What do you thing of 'free love'? I think it is cute. Some of the types in this place, seven-eighths of them, look at you as if it's an insult to be a virgin (I'm still pure, but only just)."

Orton had a strange preoccupation with Joyce's "virginal qualities". He mistakenly thought that she had been to a convent school and this turned him on. That summer vacation, during a production of *Measure for Measure* in Leicester, he kissed Joyce in the lighting booth. She was not impressed and dismissed him as "just a boy". He was – he was Kenneth's boy. At his first term at RADA, he wrote: "I completely lost my confidence and my virginity." Within a month he had moved into Halliwell's flat in West Hampstead and into Halliwell's double bed.

At first Halliwell was the stronger personality. He would stroke Joe in front of friends and call him "my pussycat".

"Halliwell was like a Svengali," said another flatmate. "They'd argue because they weren't having sex. Kenneth wanted to, and Joe refused. Kenneth could be a little sadistic with him."

Orton put up with this because Halliwell was the first person to pay him any serious sexual attention – how unlike all those unresponsive girls – but Halliwell had a problem. Unsure of Orton, Halliwell became possessive and intervened when other men showed an interest.

While Orton's acting talent blossomed at RADA, Halliwell's withered. He turned to writing, but showed little aptitude there either. Joe took an interest, however, and started making suggestions that Halliwell incorporated. Having discovered this talent, he began writing pieces to perform in class at RADA. He also set to work on *Head to Toe*, where the protagonist, Gombold, explores a giant's body inside and out and fights a war between the clefts of his massive buttocks "for the independence of body parts". Meanwhile, Halliwell's novel, *Priapus in the Shrubbery*, was rejected by Faber & Faber.

Together they wrote the science-fiction caper *The Mechanical Womb*, the homoerotic *The Last Days of Sodom* and *Between Us Girls*, a tale of prostitution in modern-day Mexico. All these were rejected, but Charles Monteith, an editor at Faber, met up with them, but got the impression that Halliwell was the literary figure while Joe was "simply his young, pretty and rather vivacious boyfriend".

This was not the impression that the prison psychiatrist, who interviewed them in Wormwood Scrubs, got.

"I think your friend is a homosexual," he warned Orton.

"You don't say," said Orton feigning shock.

For Halliwell, prison was the last in a series of defeats and within six months he tried to slash his wrists. For Orton it was a springboard.

When they were released in September 1962, they went back to the large bedsit Halliwell had bought in Noel Road, Islington, to give them somewhere to write. Orton re-wrote *The Boy Hairdresser* as a play called *The Ruffian on the Stair*. The following year it was accepted by the BBC who broadcast it in 1964. That year saw his first West End hit with *Entertaining Mr Sloane*, which was followed the next year by *Loot*.

His success brought him to the attention of the Beatles; their manager Brian Epstein, who was gay, was soon in touch. The idea was for Orton to write their next movie for them – they had had hits with *A Hard Day's Night* (1964) and *Help!* (1965). Orton wrote *Up Against It*. Everyone loved the script, but the characters were all sexually ambiguous. It was thought that the gay undertone would hurt the Beatles' image and they dropped out of the project.

Despite his growing fame, Orton was not afraid to go out cottaging and recorded his encounters in loving detail in his diaries. On March 4, 1967, for example, after leaving the theatre, he dropped into a public lavatory in Holloway Road. He nipped in next to a labourer and grabbed his penis. The man responded and started playing with his, so he unbuttoned the top of his jeans so that the man could feel his balls. Another man entered and they froze, fearing that it might be the police, but the man flashed his cock and the action continued.

A second man put his hand down the back of Orton's trousers. Another man came in, got down on his knees and sucked Orton's dick, while, nearby, another penitent was administering a blowjob on another man. Two other cocksuckers came in and took over, and one satisfied customer left. Orton's jeans had now been pulled down. One man was trying to push his penis between his legs from behind, while a bearded man was sucking him from the front. The real thrill for Orton, however, was that they were only feet away from passers-by going about their everyday business.

Orton was now fondling the labourer with both hands. He could feel the man getting terribly excited and he kissed him on the mouth. Orton came, squirting into the bearded man's mouth, then pulled up his jeans. The bearded man said, wiping his whiskers: "I suck people off. Who wants their cock sucked?" The labourer obliged, while Orton took the bus home.

Things at home were not good. Orton's meteoric success depressed Halliwell and it was plain that their passion was dying. One night in early May, they took some Valium and had an amazing sex session, but that only caused more problems. Usually, things were not working in that department and Orton was puzzled.

"I can fuck other people perfectly well," he told Halliwell. "But up to now, I can't fuck you."

To cheer him up, Orton took him on holiday to North Africa. In Tangiers they stayed in the flat where Tennessee Williams had written *Suddenly Last Summer*. It did not do the trick. The availability of sex was a threat rather than a treat to Halliwell. He was no longer young and pretty, and anonymous sex with street boys lacked the intimacy he craved. Joe, on the other hand, was like a kid in a sweet shop, sucking on every last gum drop.

Joe enjoyed fucking and being fucked. One afternoon, as an Arab boy was coming in his anus, he thought that this was a wonderfully undignified position for an internationally known playwright to be in. And, while he had his own cock up a Moroccan boy's arse, he mused on how this powerful, erotic experience put some of the more damning reviews in the London papers into a new perspective. Another thought plagued him, though. If he had boys of the age as those he was fucking in North Africa back in England, he would spend the rest of his life in terror of his parents or the police. Even so, Orton bragged loudly about his experiences in the bars. The graphic detail of these tales often scared other tourists away. Orton was delighted by this reaction.

"They have no right to be occupying chairs reserved for decent sex perverts," he said.

"You shouldn't feel guilty. Get yourself fucked if you want to," Joe told a friend who was having trouble coming to terms with his homosexuality. "Get yourself anything you like. Reject all the values of society. And enjoy sex. When you're dead, you'll regret not having fun with your genital organs."

Joe was thoughtful enough to arrange for young boys to service Halliwell too, but Kenneth just accused him of being a procuress and said that he was perfectly capable of getting his own sex. Something else was worrying him, too – Orton's growing heterosexual feelings. Joe had been out walking with a beautiful Nordic girl called Vipsil. They went to the Casbah to buy souvenirs and chatted.

"I enjoyed the looks of envy as I walked along with her," he said. "I possessed the most beautiful and desirable girl in town. I was curiously excited by the fact."

The action scarcely slackened when they got back to London. On June 6, 1967, he went back to the gents on Holloway Road. A couple of men came in. One gave another man a blowjob, while the other dropped his trousers and offered Orton his arse. Normally this sort of saturnalia was what Orton enjoyed but, this time, he considered it too dangerous. When three men came in, he made off with the man who had been administering the blowjob. They went back to his place in Highbury, where he sucked and nibbled Orton through his underpants.

The man admired his body.

"You've got a grand cock," he said.

It was then that Orton realised that he had missed all the sex talk in Morocco. He put his tongue down the man's throat and pulled him onto the bed. Pulling the man's legs in the air, he lubricated his cock with a bit of spit and shoved it up the man's arse. He cried out: "No, no."

But Joe reckoned that was just a sex kink.

"I'm going to fuck you," he said. "Keep quiet." And rammed it home harder.

He was right. After a while the man asked him to move so that he could see his cock going in and out. Then he stroked Joe's balls until he came. Then he conceded: "I needed a good fucking."

Afterwards, he suggested a threesome with another man. Joe washed his prick and went home.

The following month, Orton picked up a middle-aged man in a gents. They were walking back to the man's flat when he asked Joe if he wanted it stuck up his arse. Joe said he wasn't keen. The man then said he didn't suppose that Joe was going to suck him off either. Joe agreed, he wasn't.

"You just want to shoot your gun, like me," the man said, turning back toward the lavatory.

On the way, he said to Joe that, if that was all he wanted to do, he should pick up rich queers in the toilet, ones who had cars and houses. They liked to be fucked up their arse in their rooms.

Back in the lavatory, a Greek man suggested he take Joe to the park and shag him. Joe thought this was a bad idea, but did it away. There were other men shagging in the park, but he was afraid that there might be a maniac on the loose. The Greek suggested that they did it up against a tree. Joe told him to be quick, because it was light and they could be seen.

"No, no one will notice," said the Greek.

Joe dropped his trousers and the Greek fucked him. After he came, he tossed Joe off. Then he offered him £2. Joe refused, saying he had plenty of money. Next time, they should shag in a room, the Greek said, and maybe Joe could fuck him, too. Joe said it would be a pleasure and they parted.

On July 28, 1967, Orton took Halliwell for a day out in Brighton. They took a walk along the pier and saw a number of near-naked boys. This made Orton sad. Then he became mad when he saw a beautiful 15-year-old in red swimming trunks lying face down and he cursed England. If he was in an Arab country and saw a boy like that he could take him home and fuck him. Halliwell told him off for this display and sunk into a deep depression.

Two days later Orton was out cottaging again. He met a respectable middle-class man who flashed his cock. Joe got his out too and let him feel it. The man was afraid to take him back to his place in case the neighbours saw, but he pointed out a dwarf in the corner who gave people blow jobs and summoned him over. They all went home refreshed.

On August 1, Orton went home to see his family for a couple of days. Alone Halliwell grew more depressed. He was now addicted to anti-depressants. On August 6, Orton and Halliwell were seen backstage at the Criterion, where *Entertaining Mr Sloane* was still playing. Halliwell was seen to be moody and depressed. It did not lighten his mood that *What the Butler Saw* was about to go into production. Nothing about it amused. Orton's final play reaches its farcical climax with Winston Churchill's* penis being discovered in cigar box.

> "How much more inspiring if, in those dark days, we'd seen what we see now. Instead we had to be content with a cigar – the symbol falling far short, as we all realise, of the object itself," says Rance who discovers it.
>
> Geraldine looks in the box,
> "But it is a cigar!" exclaims Geraldine.
> "Ah, the illusions of youth," says Rance.

Orton originally wanted Churchill's penis – or at least a facsimile – to be displayed. But the Lord Chamberlain, who still censored the theatre back then, would not allow it. The producer Oscar Lewenstein was against it, too.

"What am I saying about Churchill, though?" asked Orton.

"You're saying he had a big prick," said Lewenstein.

"That isn't libel, surely," said Orton. "I wouldn't sue anybody for saying I had a big prick. No man would. In fact, I might pay them to do it."

In the first production of the play, which occurred in 1969, after Orton's death and the demise of the Lord Chancellor's office, Ralph Richardson edited out the penis and flourished a cigar. This found its way into the published version of the play. The penis was only reinstated by Lindsay Anderson in his 1975 production.

Plainly, Halliwell did not get the joke. On August 8, he called his psychiatrist, who was just off on holiday. Isn't it always the way? Orton and Halliwell were invited to a late-night screening of Yoko Ono's film *Bottoms* – which you would have thought would have interested them both. Halliwell was ill, however, and they did not go. Between two and four in the morning, Halliwell beat Orton's head in a frenzied attack with a hammer. He then took a massive overdose and died within 30 seconds. Orton died later of his wounds. He was still warm when they found him.

Their bodies were discovered by the driver who was going to take Orton to Twickenham Studios where Joe was to speak to director Richard Lester to discuss the filming of *Up Against It*. Halliwell was naked when he was found. Joe was now dead and it is not known whether he regretted having fun with his genital organs or not.

Chapter Fourteen

The Naked Civil Servant

Quentin Crisp became, to use his own words, one of the stately homos of England, before buggering off to the United States – I use the word advisedly – where he claimed to have rediscovered his virginity. It's a nice trick if you can do it.

Born Denis Pratt, he only changed his name to Quentin Crisp in his late 20s. The youngest of three, he was a sickly child and, for the first 12 years of his life, slept in a cot in his parents' bedroom from where he frequently overheard "the long despairing groan" that his father let out when he came.

Despite being frail and pale, with crooked teeth, he was, on his own admission, "a monstrous show-off".

"I had this terrible lust for attention," he said, "every hour of every day. I ought to have been an only child. I should have gone on the stage, but I was very plain."

He enjoyed his prep school, though the headmaster alternately browbeat the boys and kissed them. Both reduced him to tears. At boarding school he was "very unpopular indeed" and spent most of his time wishing he was dead. The headmaster, he said, was a "mixture of menace and flirtation". His only relief came from long walks with his English teacher Douglas Laughton, a cousin of Charles Laughton*.

At the age of 17, Quentin escaped to King's College, London. He was already uneasy about his sexuality. He felt no attraction to women or girls and believed that he was the only one of his ilk in the world. He soon sought out the Chat Noir café in Soho where gay prostitutes hung out.

"I took to them like ducks to ducks," he said. At last, he was not alone.

He began to wear make-up and spent much of his time in the Black Cat talking about which Hollywood goddess he would most like to be. He also fantasised about having a sex change operation and opening a knitting shop in a provincial town where "no one would have known my guilty secret".

When local hoodlums came into the café, he loved the way they chatted him up like they were chatting up a girl. He would flounce around the West End with his over-painted chums and, at the age of 20, he went on the game, charging as little as 7s 6d – 38p – for sex in an alleyway, doorway or the back of a taxi. Occasionally he gave blowjobs, but usually it was merely masturbation. And anal sex, though endured, was repellent – "like undergoing a colostomy operation without the anaesthetic," he said. However, Crisp soon became conscious that his clients' real thrill lay in degrading him.

"Of course, I was terribly bad at it," he said later. "I was so condescending."

He gave up prostitution after six months. Even so, the following Christmas, his father told him: "You look like a male whore."

That was it. He left home and moved in with a young admirer from the Black Cat he only ever referred to as "Thumbnails". A postal clerk, Thumbnails, was slightly in awe of the still-unnamed Quentin and treated him to tea at Lyons Corner House. They had no sexual relations, but Thumbnails somehow acquired a dinner jacket and took Quentin, in a borrowed black silk dress and velvet cape, for drinks at the Regent Palace Hotel. It was not an experiment Quentin was going to repeat. For him, drag was a drag and he never attended a drag ball. Also, thanks to Thumbnails, Quentin got the chance to partner a speciality dancer at a charity concert at the Scala Theatre in front of a cheering audience. It was his first experience of the stage.

Turned down by St Martin's School of Art, he took life classes at Regent Street Polytechnic. Meanwhile, his appearance progressed, he said, "from the effeminate to the bizarre". His approach was theatrical, though he was sometimes mistaken for a woman – on one notable occasion for the wife of the French ambassador. He moved out of Thumbnails' flat and began to call himself Denis Crisp then, at the suggestion of friends, Quentin Crisp was born.

By this time, his appearance had grown so outrageous that he was ejected from every Lyons Corner House in London. Even the Black Cat banned him. He was an embarrassment to other gays. When he went into a gay pub or club, he would be greeted with a stony silence. Gay men would cold shoulder him or condemn him for damaging their cause. However, Quentin gained friends on the margins of society, including a young male prostitute who called him Greta for his devotion to the great Garbo*.

Since his time on the game, he had given up sex which he referred to as "the last refuge of the miserable". At least with masturbation, "you know what you are doing and you know what you want." He had not done himself up the way he had to attract men. It was to fulfil a dream. It brought with it a nightmare, however – regular beatings in the street, to which he would famously respond:"I seem to have annoyed you gentlemen in some way."

He was not cowed by violence, though. He simply slapped on more make-up and dyed his hair "screaming red".

Quentin may have given up sex, but it had not given him up. When he was 30 he was picked up in Sloane Square by a 45-year-old man who he said was "rather highly placed in one of the ministries". They made love in Quentin's squalid and famously undusted room – he said that after four years the dust did not get any thicker. Their trysts attracted the attention of the police, who paid a visit after receiving complaints from the neighbours. After that the Man from the Ministry would telephone before he came round. He could not risk being caught and did not want to be seen with any of Quentin's gay friends.

When war broke out, Quentin stocked up on henna. The blackout brought furtive kisses outside Leicester Square underground station. London, he said, became a "paved double bed", but the darkness also brought more beatings as thugs took out their wrath on him with impunity.

He tried to join up out of poverty. He even attended the medical without make-up, though there was nothing he could do about his hair. After an intimate and invasive examination, he was rejected on the grounds of sexual perversion.

To make ends meet, he took to posing for life classes in art school. Here he found his true vocation. He loved to adopt dramatic poses – especially favouring the crucifixion – and the contrast of his red hair and pale skin gave him the look of a Mannerist martyr. Famously, when a bomb dropped near Goldsmith's College in Lewisham and blew the windows out of the life room, Quentin held the pose without batting an eyelid.

The war brought easy-going American servicemen to Britain. Some picked him up thinking he was a woman, but were not disappointed to find out that he was not. He indulged them orally and anally. For the first time in his life he enjoyed the pleasures of unrestrained promiscuity.

"Never in the history of sex was so much offered by so few," he said.

The GIs were not out to degrade or defile him and he loved the way their young muscles bulged in their uniforms. He had a prolonged affair with a "voluptuous" truck driver from Seattle. When he did not return, Quentin assumed that he had gone to heaven or New York – which, for Quentin, were much the same thing.

His activities attracted the attention of the police, who arrested him for soliciting and took him to West End Central police station where he was stripped – but only far enough to see if he was wearing women's underclothes.

The next day he appeared in the dock at Bow Street Magistrates Court. In his defence, Quentin simply offered himself. It was plain from his appearance that he was a flamboyant homosexual, he said. How could he possibly hope to solicit anyone in the street in broad daylight? He then called his numerous friends as character witnesses. The magistrate soon grew tired of this "recital of praise" and dismissed the case. The police took their revenge by getting him banned from the pubs he frequented in Fitzrovia.

At the end of the war, he met the tall, strong, working-class, ex-RAF man John Haggarty. He was everything that Crisp had long fantasised about – his fabled "Unavailable Great Dark Man".

Haggarty had never seen anything like Quentin.

"I never imagined that such a person existed," he said. "He was a great original. He stood out instantly, advertising that he was a remarkable man … I didn't see him as a wee poofter."

They were like "a couple of birds in Trafalgar Square, strutting around together for a while and then flying off in different directions". They remained friends for years and Haggarty frequently helped Crisp out with money, giving him cash he "could not squeeze under the mattress".

In 1948, Quentin stopped dying his hair red and started dying it blue, making him "no longer conspicuously available for sex". Although some gay men admired him, especially for his wartime courage, he still caused disquiet in gay circles for being too *outré* and because he simply dismissed St Oscar* as "gross".

However, he came to the attention of Tom Maschler at Jonathan Cape, who encouraged him to write *The Naked Civil Servant*, which appeared in 1968. It was sold to Thames Television in 1975. His role was played by John Hurt and it made the original a star. And when it appeared on American TV, he was a star there, too. He seized his chance to move to New York, where he became a kind of elder statesman on the gay scene. In 1981, he wrote a second volume of autobiography called *How to Become a Virgin*. And it was a trick he pulled off. In his one-man shows and on TV chat shows, he came across as everyone's maiden aunt.

He died in 1999 still a "resident alien" in the New York he loved. It is a shame that he could not go to heaven, otherwise he would still be alive in New York.

Chapter Fifteen

Sex and the Single Samurai

In 1970, the Japanese author, lover of transvestite geishas and would-be samurai, Yukio Mishima led a raid on the offices of the self-defence forces in Tokyo, where he disembowelled himself. Friends said that, for Mishima, hara-kiri was the ultimate in masturbation. He had always been a strange fellow.

Born Hiraoka Kimitake, he came to fame in 1949, at the age of 24, with the autobiographical novel *Confessions of a Mask*. In it, he reveals that he is a man incapable of feeling passion, or even feeling alive, unless he is embroiled in a sado-masochistic fantasy, dripping with blood and death.

Mishima said that he had written the book to channel his own homicidal instincts. And at the age of 18, he had said, prophetically: "The murderer knows that only by being murdered can he be completely realised."

The first-person protagonist in the book says that he had his first ejaculation at the age of 12 – over a reproduction of the death of Saint Sebastian. The tense agony of the dying saint's arrow-torn body drove him to ecstasy. The protagonist then dons the mask of homosexuality to hide his own dark feelings. Toward the end of the novel, he takes himself to a brothel to demonstrate, with some satisfaction, that he cannot get it up with women.

Mishima had little trouble in that department, even as an adolescent.

"Having attained puberty, other boys seemed to do nothing but think immodestly about women," he said. "I, on the other hand, received no more sensual impression from 'woman' than from a 'pencil'."

Other boys' feelings were a closed book to him.

"I did not know that each night all boys but me had a dream in which women – women barely glimpsed yesterday on a street corner – were stripped of their clothes and set one by one parading before the dreamers' eyes," he said. "I did not know that in the boys' dreams the breasts of women would float up like beautiful jellyfish rising from the seas of the night."

Throughout his youth he was a passive homosexual, admiring other boys from afar, but too timid to do anything about it. However, the success of *Confessions of a Mask* allowed him to give up his job and, in the summer of 1950, Mishima began cruising the gay bars that had strung up in Tokyo after the war. He was a regular at the Brunswick, which was a favourite with GIs for its handsome young waiters who doubled up in the floor show at night. One of its stars was Akihiro Maruyama, a chanteuse in drag, who was called the Edith Piaf of Japan.

"He was as pale as death, so pale that he had a purplish tint," said Mishima. "And his body seemed to float in his clothes. Yet he was a narcissist and had a true eye for beauty. In those days, before he began the body building, when he looked at himself with those eyes that could really perceive beauty – and he looked at himself constantly – he was filled with disgust at what he saw."

Mishima was captivated and they were often seen dancing together. Maruyama, however, protested that they did not have an affair. Mishima was handsome enough he said, but "he was not my type".

However, Mishima immortalised him in print in the character Yuichi in *Forbidden Colours* who, when he first appears in the gay bar in Tokyo, "floated on desire – the look they gave him was like that a women feels when she passes among men and their eyes instantly undress her down to the last stitch."

Later, Maruyama played a leading role in Mishima's play *The Black Lizard*.

In 1951, he went to the US, then on to Rio for the carnival, where he threw himself into the action, dancing half-naked in the streets. His guide was the *Asahi* correspondent Mogi, who was shocked by Mishima's "unabashed homosexuality". He regularly brought boys of around 17 years of age to his hotel in the afternoon. They were "the sort that hung around in the parks". Mogi asked how, without a word of Portuguese, he had managed to pick them up. Mishima said that "in that world" there was an unspoken understanding.

Mogi also recalled getting a call one afternoon from Mishima, begging him to come and rescue him from the wife of a Japanese businessman who seemed determined to seduce him.

After carnival, Mishima headed for Paris, where he met the composer Toshiro Mayuzumi, who took him to a "bar for pederasts". Mishima was not best pleased, because all the boys went to Mayuzumi as he could speak French.

After a visit to London, he made the compulsory trip to Greece.

"Greece cured my self-loathing," he said, "and awoke in me a 'will to health' in the Nietzchean sense."

Back in Tokyo, he began to go out with a college girl. Her name was Eiko and she was the daughter of a wealthy industrialist. He met her at a posh party in Karuizawa, but they did not hit it off immediately. When she mentioned that she was a sophomore at the Peers' School, his own *alma mater*, Mishima said that he doubted whether the school's founder, General Nogi, would be pleased that they now admitted women. No small talk then, Yukio?

Eiko was offended by this tactless remark, but had plainly got over it when Mr Charm called her up a week later and asked her for a date. She was a bit of a playgirl and was surprised when he turned up with flowers and perfume. He refused even to come up to her room, insisting on the formality of waiting in the lobby until she was ready.

She never did get him up to her room. The relationship was purely platonic. Eiko thought that the shy samurai was too timid to make any advances. And just to make sure there was no hanky-panky when they went out on a date, Mishima would bring his mother along. The relationship largely consisted of dressing up. He would phone before a date and tell her what to wear and where to meet him, then he would appear in some matching male outfit. It was play acting. After she graduated from Peers', Eiko married and Mishima moved back into gay circles, ostensibly to finish his research on *Forbidden Colours*.

On the gay scene, it was said that he favoured two distinct types of lover. One was the slender, tender young intellectual with a taste for literature. The other was the swarthy, hirsute gangster type.

He also mixed with the theatrical crowd and began to write plays, often with disturbing and violent themes. Then he wrote his one and only straight love story, *The Sound of Waves*, though, admittedly, his lyrical descriptions linger longer over the body of the fine young fisherman than over that of the young woman he falls for. He later claimed that he had written it as a joke and was disappointed when it did so well, as this threw "icy water on my Greek fever".

On his 30th birthday, he invited two friends over for drinks and told them that he was now too old to kill himself as he could no longer be a beautiful corpse. He took up weight-lifting, swimming and boxing, though he was hopeless and was beaten senseless regularly. He went to the gym three times a week without fail, in an attempt to build himself the perfect body.

Photographs of the famous writer now appeared in magazines and newspapers naked from the waist up. At the same time he was taking pain-killing injections for the stomach cramps that plagued him all his life.

He tried to take a play to Broadway, and was delighted when more than a hundred young actors responded to his casting call, including "girls so beautiful they would have been instant stars in Japan and one young man in particular, who was the spitting image of James Dean"*.

Back in Japan, his father put pressure on him to marry, because his younger brother was already married and he had heard rumours, which he dismissed, that Yukio was gay. His mother almost certainly knew that Yukio was gay, but thought marriage might "cure" him.

When Mishima notified Peers' School alumni that he was looking for a wife, the response was overwhelming, but he dismissed most on the basis of their photographs. There was one woman who attracted him, though. She was a fan of Toshiro Mayuzumi, so Mishima got him to intercede. As was often the case, the girl's name had been put forward without consulting her and, when Mayuzumi contacted her, she said that she would rather kill herself than marry Mishima. Undeterred, Mishima got Mayuzumi to set up a "chance meeting" at a popular restaurant called Kettel's. The girl immediately spotted that it was a set-up. The evening was a disaster and Mishima got no further than driving the girl home in a hire car.

Of course, there were "literary virgins" who swooned over Mishima's beefcake shots in the papers. Mishima, however, told his mother that he wanted nothing to do with women who were interested in his work.

A friend then drew his attention to 19-year-old college student Yoko Sugiyama, the daughter of a famous traditionalist painter. Full-bodied and fleshy-faced, she was not the boyish type that most people thought he would have been attracted to. However, Mishima had an inferiority complex when it came to art and she was shorter than him – an important consideration when you are a short-arse. He also thought that she could carry off the public role of being the wife of a famous writer and, more importantly, would guard his privacy.

It is unlikely that he told her about his homosexuality and he burned all his diaries the day before the wedding. However, she soon found out. A blackmailer threatened Mishima, but he refused to pay up so the blackmailer honoured his promise and told Yoko everything. Even so, they never discussed the matter. Yoko had geisha lineage and would have understood, and like a dutiful oriental wife, she went along with it.

Mishima and his wife got on well enough, though she objected to the body-building parties he held during the 1960s, when the lads from the gym would come round, strip off and oil their bodies. She was also annoyed when Mishima posed nude for the photographic study *Punishment by Roses*. However, they had two children, a daughter and a son, and Mishima set aside time to be with the family.

In his work, Mishima began to mix together erotic desire, patriotism and a quest for death as some sort of mystical cocktail. He began to wear uniforms and founded the Tate no Kai – Shield Society – a small private army of young men who he went to training camp with. Military and imperial fantasies blended with masochistic visions of a bloody death. He wrote a play called *My Friend Hitler* and posed by a swastika for the poster. Another play featured *seppuku* – ritual suicide by disembowelling. At the dress rehearsal, Mishima stopped the action and asked for more blood.

The members of the Shield Society were hand-picked from students who had done their compulsory one-month's military training. Mishima would take recruits out to get to know them better. One he took a particular shine to was Masakatsu Morita. They spent a lot of time together and a friend said that, in Mishima's company, Morita was "like a confident fiancée".

By the spring of 1970, Mishima and Morita had decided to die together in what was thought to be a "lovers' suicide". Mishima was certainly in love with the young man, though it is not known whether the relationship was physical. However, there is a tradition of homosexuality in the Japanese warrior code. One of Mishima's favourite books, which he always kept on his desk, was *Hagakure* – "Hidden Among the Leaves" – by the 17th-century samurai Jocho Yamamoto. In it, he says: "Homosexual love goes very well with the way of the warrior."

For a long time, Mishima had talked about *kirijini*, which is the samurai tradition of going down fighting, sword in hand. Now he began to talk of *seppuku*. His aim was to disembowel himself in the traditional manner with a short sword, then have Morita decapitate him with a long samurai sword.

In September, he posed for a series of photographs called "Death of a Man" by photographer Kishin Shinoyama. These showed Mishima as St Sebastian, tied to a tree and bristling with arrows, Mishima drowning in mud, Mishima crushed under the wheels of a cement lorry. Most disturbing of all, however, is a picture of Mishima squatting naked on the floor with a short sword buried in his belly, while behind him, a long sword held, in this case, by Shinoyama. Some of these were to be included in a photographic retrospective he planned meticulously. It was also to show a number of earlier nude studies.

Mishima said goodbye to his comrades and issued his last instructions at the Misty Sauna Baths. He told them that he had now thrown away the pen and had decided to die by the sword. His plan was to shame the Japanese Self-Defence Force, the only army the country was allowed under the peace accords ending the Second World War, with a true display of the samurai spirit.

On November 25, 1970, Mishima and his men headed for the headquarters of the Self-Defence Force. On the way, they drove past the elementary school that his daughter was attending. Mishima then said that they needed some music – such as the music they had in gangster movies – and started singing. They arrived at the headquarters at 10.50 a.m. and seized its commandant. Officers tried to storm the commandant's office, but Mishima and Morita drove them back with a display of swordsmanship.

Mishima then gave a short speech to members of the Self-Defence Force drawn up outside. Afterwards, he squatted down in front of the window and unbuttoned his uniform jacket. With Morita behind him, Mishima took the short sword and plunged it into his left side, then drew it across to his right. He had intended to write the character for "sword" in his own blood but the pain was too debilitating. He slumped forward and, without so much as a "how was it for you", Morita brought down the long sword on his neck. Unfortunately Morita was not a skilled partner and Himomasa "Furu" Koga, who was looking on, shouted: "Again!"

Morita, however, just could not get it off, so Koga grabbed the sword and despatched Mishima with a third blow. Then he swang around and beheaded Morita with a single stroke. I think I'm beginning to prefer Proust's rats.

Chapter Sixteen

Action!

Film-maker Derek Jarman claimed he had his first homosexual experience when he was nine. He was at a boarding school in Hampshire overlooking the Solent at the time. A compulsive and – it has to be said – unreliable autobiographer, he has, thoughtfully, left us several conflicting versions of the event.

In the *Dancing Ledge*, he said he found out that sleeping with someone was more fun that sleeping alone, so he innocently slipped into his mate Gavin's bed for a bit of a cuddle. But a jealous dormitory captain sneaked out to inform the headmaster's wife. She descended on them like a harpy and tipped them out of bed. The headmaster then beat them savagely, denounced them in front of the whole school and threatened to tell their parents. Jarman said that from then on, he mistrusted the adult world which had sought so brutally to suppress his sexuality and sow the seeds of self-doubt and self-loathing.

In *The Last of England*, published three years later, none of this seems to have happened. The result of his "first confrontation with oppression" was to become "detached and dreamy". The only thing that seems to have happened at school was that he "spent hours alone painting or watching the flowers grow". He also developed a "physical aversion to chumminess and sexual innuendo, organised games, and school showers.

"I was set apart," he said.

Then, in his book *Modern Nature*, he recalled lyrically how, as skinny nine-year-olds, he and his friends would "explore the contours of forgotten landscapes" – these included "big foot, tight arse and stiff cock". This time, apparently, it went unpunished. While in *At Your Own Risk* he said: "I was unsuccessfully trying to fuck the boy in the bed next to mine – quite unaware that I was doing anything out of the ordinary – when the sky fell in as we were ripped apart like two dogs."

Take your pick.

However, there was one even more disturbing incident he told friends about that does not appear in any of his diverse autobiographical writings. Again, it comes in several versions. In one, he was grabbed by a bunch of boys, stripped and had his penis stroked with a feather duster until he came. In another, he was raped.

He seems to have got over it well enough though. When he was 11, Lord Montagu of Beaulieu was accused of indecently assaulting two boy scouts in a beach hut on his New Forest estate. Jarman had a friend who lived nearby and paid a visit, rather wishing that he had been one of the scouts in the hut with the peer.

When Derek graduated to the senior dorm, he indulged himself in wanking competitions. Jarman had already spotted a political dimension to his sexual orientation. He noted that the boys in the dorm could be divided into three groups. There were those like him who enjoyed themselves. There were the future moral guardians of society who reported their behaviour to the staff and there were the rest, who were "frightened by their own come and probably destined for the cloth".

Although wanking was all right, the adolescent Jarman liked to do it with someone else if he could. Behind a hedgerow leading down to the cliffs, he discovered a secret bower of purple violets. He swore another boy to secrecy and took him down there. In the spring sunshine, the boy stripped off. Jarman pulled down his own trousers and lay down beside him. The boy turned onto his belly and Jarman caressed his back. He simply laughed when the hand disappeared between his thighs. It was, he said, "a lovely feeling". That night he invited Jarman into his bed.

Though Jarman manfully pretended to be aroused by Marilyn Monroe* or Brigitte Bardot*, he found no pleasure in the well-thumbed copy of *Lady Chatterley's Lover* that was doing the rounds. He thought that the sexual manual full of colour photographs his parents had left on his bed one holiday had been put there by one of his friends and he guiltily burnt it on a bonfire.

The school doctor's sex lessons, complete with working models, did not help either. Nor did he take up the kind doctor's offer of a private consultation for anyone who had "problems".

Jarman was pleased to leave school and go to King's College, London, where he had some desultory fumblings with girls. One night at a party, everyone paired off. Jarman was with Caroline Green who, when the lights went off, was less than impressed with his enthusiasm. But then, at that time, he was not very good at being gay either. On one occasion, he spotted a "handsome young man" in the refectory at King's and hung around endlessly, hoping to engage him in conversation. Nothing came of it. Then one night on the train, a businessman exposed himself to Jarman in his compartment, but he did not really know how to handle the situation.

On vacation he headed for Crete and, like everyone else in this goddamn book, went crazy about everything Greek. Hitch-hiking home, he was picked up by a tough-looking man in Switzerland who, without warning, drove off the road into a stand of trees.

"Without a moment's hesitation, he grasped me around the shoulders and tried to kiss me, while with the other hand he unzipped his flies," Jarman said. "Before I took in what was happening, he had my hand in an arm lock and was trying to make me suck his cock."

Jarman reckoned this experience set his sexual clock back several years. However, back in London, he was a regular visitor to the flat in Gloucester Crescent that Roger Ford, a contemporary at boarding school, shared with his older lover, a teacher called Michael Harth. Jarman and Ford enjoyed talking and wrestling on the sofa, while Harth would sit at his piano singing the "songs he had composed for unperformable musicals about buggery". These would make Jarman blush.

He also developed a crush on a theology student called Roger Jones. One evening, he told Jones that he thought he was homosexual and related his experience in Switzerland. He was relieved to have got it off his chest, but it got him nowhere with Jones.

One night Jarman stayed over at Gloucester Crescent. By this time Harth was sharing his bed with a Canadian student called

Ron Wright. Harth was away that night and Jarman got into his bed, only to be followed by Wright. He said that he was rather startled and just lay in his arms. When he awoke the next morning, Wright was gone.

Something had certainly happened during the night, as Jarman could not face work that day and wandered around in a daze. He hoped that he would bump into Wright again that night at a party, but Wright never showed up. Distraught, Jarman consumed an entire bottle of whisky and had to be carried home. The next day, Wright was still missing and Jarman threatened to commit suicide with a pair of dress-making scissors. While Jarman was slashing his paintings, friends tracked Wright down. He came over and stayed the night.

Jarman fell deeply in love with Wright and took him to meet his parents. On Wright's side, things were less satisfactory. He said he found Jarman physically remote and "very rigid" in bed. Well, you need a bit of rigid, I would have thought.

Now that Jarman was a bona fide member of the brotherhood, Harth insisted on taking him to the "Willy" – the William IV pub – in Hampstead. Jarman said he was horrified by the idea of going to a gay pub, but thought there was "safety in numbers". It is not known how much of an initiation Harth, a devotee of a quick one in the bushes behind Jack Straw's Castle, gave the young Jarman that night, but he was soon a regular at the "Willy", befriending Stanley Spencer's* mistress who held court there and deftly avoiding invitations from middle-age men to have coffee back that their place.

When Wright set off back to Canada, Jarman was determined to pursue him across the Atlantic. North America attracted him. He liked the sexual openness of the poetry of Alan Ginsberg and Walt Whitman* – and everything was "bigger and better" over there. As, indeed, it was.

He first flew to New York, where Wright had given him the name of a priest who would put him up. Once Jarman had located him, they piled into a cab together.

"We had hardly gone a block before his hand was on my crotch," said Jarman. "I decided that the best course was to pretend it wasn't happening… hoping the taxi driver wouldn't notice."

The gay father took Jarman to the mission on Henry Street where "I found all the priests were after me, all of them unbelievably forward. I felt as though I were a lottery ticket". They all wore tight jeans and T-shirts, and were a very liberal brotherhood.

The next day, Jarman went to a service at the church they called "Mary on the Verge", where the handsome altar boys cruised the all-male congregation, "winking at them through clouds of incense and lace." This was all too much for the young Jarman, who was not ready for a "priestly gang bang" and he jumped on a Greyhound for Calgary and Roger Wright. They both got jobs and spent their free time hanging out at a swimming pool or taking trips to the Rockies.

On one memorable occasion, they stripped off to do some nude sunbathing near a railway cutting when the Canadian-Pacific Railroad train came hurtling by. Instead of covering up, they threw their arms around each other in an unambiguous embrace.

"It was a moment of naked triumph," exalted Jarman.

This may have been memorable for Dirty Derek, but Roger Wright did not remember it at all and said that, if anything like it did happen, Jarman was exaggerating. Even Jarman was not sure whether they had sex on his Canadian visit. Wright even had a girlfriend at the time. Sorry Derek, your pants are on fire.

Soon, Jarman was on the bus for San Francisco. After a Californian experience mellowed by marijuana, he headed back to New York. Again he got in touch with the gay mission and one of the priests, called Tom, agreed to put him up. When Jarman arrived at his apartment, Tom whisked him off to a party at "a small flat which was so packed that people were hanging out the window".

"In the centre of the room a gang of black drag queens were swishing around announcing they were the most 'glamorous', and when some weedy-looking white drag queen took them on in the beauty stakes, the room divided," said Jarman. "It nearly started a fight in which someone pulled a knife. I took refuge in a bedroom with a black boy, Marshall Hill, who was at art college – painting. We curled up on the floor and made love."

Tom had disappeared, so Marshall gave Jarman a lift back to the priest's apartment. Tom had not arrived back home, though, so the two of them settled down on the carpet in the hall in front of his front door and fell asleep in each other's arms. When Tom finally arrived home, Jarman asked whether Marshall could stay. Tom immediately had a hissy fit and threw him out – "so much for Christian charity," said Jarman.

When Jarman arrived home in England, he found that crabs had taken up residence in his pubic hair. Innocently, he told his parents about it. The family doctor asked disapprovingly: "Have you been sleeping with prostitutes, Derek?"

Unprepared for the question, Jarman blurted out: "Yes."

Despite this setback, Jarman began cruising gay London with fellow Slade student Peter Docherty. He began to frequent a dive in Chelsea called the Gigolo. It had a raised area at the back where "everyone had their flies undone … and you might find yourself blown in a dark corner".

Jarman did not like cottaging, but was happy to have sex in a nearby graveyard on a warm night. He found casual pick-ups in the street with "the long journey to his place or yours; cocks throbbing and minds racing", the most exhilarating of all.

Then would come the moment of bliss, "slipping him out of his jeans and sucking his cock, the ecstatic kiss, the discovered tattoo. Wild as a boy can be, sparkling eyes, laughter, the taste of him, the sudden mad rush to orgasm after hours on a tightrope of sensation."

Even the fashions were a turn on. He sand-papered the crotch of his Levis to buff up his package and sat in a bath of lukewarm water to shrink-wrap them around his arse – not too tight though "or your partner couldn't get his hand down the back and dance with his fingers, stroking your arse when no one was looking".

After a night in Le Duce on D'arblay Street or at Yours or Mine on High Street Kensington, he would have breakfast in a greasy spoon, then move on to the Biograph, a fleapit in Victoria, which showed dodgy German films featuring topless girls in leather shorts, documentaries on the body and the odd Pasolini. Straight men went there for the girlie pix, so you had to be careful whose crotch you groped. You could easily grab a tramp just in for a sleep who would start cursing "fucking queers" while the ushers' torches raked the seats like searchlights in an air-raid. Then it would be up to Islington in the hope of catching a glimpse of Joe Orton.

Until 1967, homosexuality was still illegal, which led to "fumbling, furtive sex" but did not make it easy to form a relationship. There were tortuous conversations until the other guy got the point. Then the *Sexual Offences Act* legalised homosexual acts for consenting males over 21 in private, provided they were not members of the armed forces. The night the bill passed, Jarman did not go out, knowing that TV cameras would be in the gay clubs and he was frightened that his parents would see him. He wanted to celebrate, but was angry that there had been laws against homosexuality in the first place.

By the end of the decade, all shame had been swept away. American guys particularly just said: "Hi, let's fuck." Jarman had given up his search for a "regular lad" to lay, went wild and paid his first visit to the clap clinic, at University College Hospital. By then it had struck him that: "Heterosexuality isn't normal, it's just common."

He began to believe that heterosexuality was "an abnormal psychopathic state composed of unhappy men and women with arrested emotions". As they can find no natural outlet, they are condemned to be bound to each other in "lives lacking warmth and human compassion". Way to go, Derek.

Jarman grew a little attached to Keith Milow from the Camberwell School of Art, but he had a passion for bankers. There were plenty of other willing partners though and, when he grew tired of his current companion, he simply palmed them off on someone else.

He had a particular passion for American boys. One of them was Keith Bowen, who had "jet-black curls, grey-blue eyes and a Texan slouch". A wealthy member of the Kellogg family, his room was full of pornographic magazines with a "tideline of KY round the wall". He dreamt of bedding the entire Italian football team and collected cards of them which he wanked over "so his spunk splashed across them".

Jarman and Bowen went to Amsterdam, then on to Venice, where they were befriended by a priest who offered them a bed, but was disappointed when they did not strip off for their siesta. Back in England, Jarman was working for film director Ken

Russell and would sneak boys into the studio at night for sex among the sets.

When Robert Mapplethorpe, then a jewellery-maker, came over from New York, he and Jarman had a torrid affair. Next, he had 20-year-old waiter Alasdair McGraw, who found him cold and only ever willing to hug during the sexual act itself.

Despite his brave words, Jarman was still not very comfortable with his sexuality. He made regular visits to Amsterdam, but always pretended to browse the heterosexual shelves in the pornographic bookshops before stumbling, as if by accident, into the gay section. He was nervous in saunas and once asked a friend if people in the street could tell he was gay.

In Rome, the 30-year-old Jarman met Tunis-born Gerald Incandela, ten years his junior. When the film project he was working on there collapsed, he brought Incandela back to London with him. They took a flat in Butler's Wharf and, for the first time, Jarman had a live-in lover. Jarman himself had entered the first Alternative Miss World contest, now he filmed Incandela in a see-through plastic frock at the second. They broke up soon after. Incandela had been seeing a young art dealer behind Jarman's back. Mind you, during the cohabitation, Jarman had had numerous one-night stands, lashings of casual sex and a number of prolonged affairs. Even so there were plenty of tears. Who was shedding them, depends on whose side of the story you hear.

Away from his professional work, Jarman experimented with a Super-8 and particularly enjoyed shooting groups of naked men. He thought he would have a try at making it in the United States, so he headed for New York. This time, he stayed with his friend Anthony Harwood in a house Harwood rented on Fire Island with his boyfriend Robert Darling. They played host to all-male parties and Jarman spent time filming more male nudes. One day, Jarman picked up a boy on the beach and was horsing around with him, when the boy's mother showed up. It was said that she was so horrified by Jarman's poolside gymnastics that his hosts had to ask him to leave. Jarman, as ever, told a different story. He was innocently swimming, he said. Besides, that morning, the woman had watched a movie in which her son was engaged in activities a good deal more vigorous then the backstroke, he claimed.

Exiled from Fire Island, Jarman sought solace in the bath-house scene. In the Continental, the Everard and the St Marks, handsome young men would lounge around with the door to their cubicle slightly ajar, gently masturbating in the hope that someone would blunder in and lend them a hand. For the more uninhibited, it was an opportunity to make love in a swimming pool full of naked bodies. Then there were the derelict piers on the West Side, where you would see guys in boxer shorts getting blown while they leant against bikes or the flash of naked young men caught in the shaft of light from a window. It was all too much for Jarman. He went back to England.

Jarman got to work on *Sebastiane*, a ground-breaking portrait of the early Christian martyr, replete with homoerotic themes, male nudity and, as Jarman proudly boasted, the first erection on the big screen. Most of the parts went to friends, but Jarman could not resist the lure of the casting couch. He got actor Ken Hicks around to Anthony Harwood's Sloane Square flat, where he gave him a screen test. He got Hicks stripped down to the briefest of denim shorts and boots, stood him in front of a mirrored wall, then got him to scrap a strigil across his well-oiled torso, the way a Roman soldier would clean himself. His use of the tool so excited Jarman that he bundled him into the bedroom. Hicks then produced a number of old-fashioned glass poppers, said Jarman, "and had me fuck him on Anthony's enormous and ruined bed in the bright sunlight, lithe and glistening with sweat and his come all over the sheets and walls." I hope they cleaned up afterwards and did not just leave it for the char.

Later, Jarman compared the moment with "the day I pushed my cock in Ron [Wright]'s arse ten years before when neither knew where we were going and the few feeble strokes were stymied with guilt". Now fucking Ken, Jarman felt he was riding back into history. They were Alexander the Great, Hadrian*, Caravaggio*, Edward II*, every gay man in history.

"Power, conquest, surrender," mused Jarman. "My paradise was whole, balanced as the rhythm of the pendulum, back forth, pleasure pain, but none of the guilt."

To that, one can only add: "Ooh, err, get her."

By the 1980s, London's gay scene was catching up with New

York's. There were clubs, Jarman boasted, where two or three thousand people were all having sex. This time, by his own account, Jarman took full advantage of it. By then he had lost his earring and cut his hair short. Clad in a leather jacket, he would stick some poppers and KY in the pocket of his jeans and go out on the hunt for fun. This could be found at the Catacombs, Bang, Traffic, the Sanctuary, Flamingo, Pink Panther, Heaven – and the dive behind it where you could be pissed on by rough boys, if that took your fancy. There were gay pubs, like the Salisbury, Brief Encounter, Global Village and the Bell near King's Cross, where he went to pursue "psychobillies", the amphetamine-driven neo-Teddy boys that Jarman particularly fancied. He loved the backroom at the Subway in Leicester Square and was seen at a party in a ground-floor council flat in Vauxhall, sticking his dick out of the window so that a man outside could give him a blowjob across the sill.

He was quite happy to have sex in public. He liked putting on a display, especially when fuelled with vodka, ecstasy, acid, opium and nicotine. And it was in the backroom of the Subway that he first enjoyed being the recipient of anal sex. He had met a young Adonis with a hard body who put his beer on the pin-ball machine and pulled out "the biggest, thickest cock I have ever seen". Jarman was instantly infatuated.

The guy entered him carefully, knowing that he was tearing him apart. However, the pleasure was so intense that Jarman came with tears of relief after a handful of thrusts. It was an epiphany. Now he had experienced both sides of love and felt infinitely superior to heterosexuals who, at best, get only half the experience.

He had a series of younger lovers who often became collaborators and long-term friends – Shaun Allen, Ken Butler, John-Marc Prouveur and Keith Collins – who stayed with him to the end. Then there was "Spring" – Rupert Adley, the son of an MP – who disliked Jarman's film *Caravaggio** and thought his movies "pointless". So Jarman got the version of the painting *Profane Love* that had been used in the movie and filmed Spring masturbating over it with "his finger stuck up his arse".

AIDS soon became an issue, though. Jarman stopped kissing people and began to worry about sharing cups or glasses and touching the children of friends. When he was diagnosed HIV positive, he said he rather enjoyed regaining his status as an outsider. Even so, his condition robbed him of the carefree sex that had energised his work and brought him friends.

While becoming a prominent AIDS campaigner, he slept with other men rarely and safely. He would still visit Hampstead Heath and watch other men at it, but he did not join in because he could not be bothered with condoms. He went there mainly to stay in touch with the gay world and to free himself from the straight world in which he was now largely confined.

He took to writing homoerotic poetry, enjoyed listening to the gay experiences of others and took a big party to see the Chippendales. They were the only men in the audience.

He died after a series of wracking spasms on February 19, 1994.

To the end he maintained that "a boy's arse is the hole to heaven". But curiously his last words were: "I want the world to be full of fluffy little ducks." Or should that have been, "ducky little fucks"?

Chapter Seventeen

Mad About the Boy

I know that in the eyes of gay men, St Oscar* can do no wrong. However, although I still love his writing, personally I like him a lot less now, than I did when I started this book. I agree with Quentin Crisp*. He is gross. It seems to me that if he was around now he would go to jail for a lot longer than two years. Some of his lovers were 14, 13 or younger. Uranism was all about doing it with young boys. Noticeably, many of his heterosexual friends had a similar taste for young girls. Today, they would all be considered paedophiles and the law would throw the book at them. Even as a celebrity, Wilde would not get the relatively easy ride he got in prison. He would be segregated for his own protection. Even then he would probably be beaten up as a nonce and would spend the rest of his life on the Sex Offenders Register as an unrepentant child-molester.

Compare him to my favourite gay, Nöel Coward*. At a time when being gay was against the law on both sides of the Atlantic, he made a virtue out of his proclivities, even writing the song "Mad About the Boy", which has now become a gay anthem. Although his name was Coward, he certainly was not one. He never hid his sexuality and was tangibly camp. He was also a lot more talented than Oscar* – he could act, sing and play the piano, as well as write plays, books, songs and movies – which he directed and acted in, too. From Coward, we get none of Wilde's brutal bluster about women. Instead, he was clever and kind, even putting Winston Churchill* straight on the abdication crisis.

"Why shouldn't the King marry his cutie?" blustered Churchill.

"Because England does not want a Queen Cutie," said Noël.

And he was always at Vivien Leigh's* bedside with flowers and perfume when she was going crazy and Larry* could no longer cope. He makes more appearances in my *Sex Lives*... books than anyone else. So welcome Sir Nöel, come on in – or rather, out.

In his plays, of course, Coward played a homosexual masquerading as an unscrupulous womaniser. But then he also played the sophisticate on and off stage, though he came from a down-at-heel background and was born in the anonymous London suburb of Teddington.

At the age of 12, Nöel tried to kiss fellow child actor, 13-year-old Esme Wynne. However, neither of them took it seriously. There was no physical attraction between them, but Esme and Nöel liked to get naked together and often bathed together in the all-together. She even took some nude photographs of the youthful Nöel.

A handsome young actor called John Elkins turned the couple into a trio. He may have been interested, romantically, in Esme, but Nöel was smitten. He died suddenly at a young age and Nöel never really got over him. He lost Esme too, when she quit the theatre, married and joined the Christian Scientists, who are very sad on all things gay.

At the age of 15, Nöel grew enamoured of the 30-year-old painter Philip Streatfield. In the spring of 1914, when Streatfield headed off to the West Country to paint landscapes, Nöel went with him. His letters home to his mother revealed that he spent much of his time indulging his life-long love of sunbathing. Nöel soon lost Streatfield, too. When the First World War broke out that summer Streatfield joined up. He died in the trenches in 1916.

Nöel became an actor and tried his hand at writing light comedies between engagements. He met the young actress Gertrude Lawrence*, who preached free love. Nöel was not excluded. One evening at a party, she took him into a private room and gave him a practical, hands-on demonstration of the facts of life – or, at least, the heterosexual version. Nöel was inordinately proud of having Gertie – or rather, of her having him – and bragged about it far and wide.

Despite this feast at the straight table, Nöel already knew where his true inclinations lay, but Gertie would remain a friend – and even a procurer – throughout his life. When he was a famous playwright, she would turn up to tea with a job lot of Coldstream guards, so that he could take his pick. He always liked an erect man in uniform

There seems to have been only one other piece of heterosexual fumbling in Noël's life. One night in Scotland in 1942, he was playing opposite Judy Campbell, who thought she could persuade him to give heterosexuality another go.

"Shivering our way through the love scene in *Present Laughter*, he folded me in his arms," she said, "then slid his hand under my dress and over my naked breast. I thought, 'Ah, at last!' But afterwards he said, 'Thank you, Judy dear, that's the first time my hands have been warm all evening.'"

In 1917, Coward was called up.

"At the end of several hours of beastliness, during which I stood about naked on cold floors and was pinched and prodded by brusque doctors, I was told to dress," he recalled, "and line up with a group of about five men in various stages of physical and mental decay."

Coward had suffered a bout of tuberculosis as a child and was unfit for combat or officer training, so he was posted to the Labour Corps. This was not to his taste and he was determined to get out of it. He had met a number of senior officers at West End parties and began to lobby them. One gave him a note to take to Lieutenant Boughey at the War Office. When Noël arrived in his office, Boughey immediately offered him a drink.

"After this we had another drink and discussed Lord Kitchener, the war, the theatre and my immediate future in the army," wrote Noël. Lord Kitchener has come up a couple of times in this book already and it is clear that the words here are gay code.

Boughey offered Noël a place in a special unit and sent him on two-weeks' leave. However, Noël tripped over a plank and knocked himself out. He was in a coma for three days and saw out the war convalescing in hospital with his new-found friend Geoffrey Holdsworth.

Generally, Noël's taste was for anything but rough trade. He liked his lovers to be well turned out and from the upper classes. This is what gave him his taste for the Coldstream Guards. He first dip in the stream seems to have been with Lieutenant Stewart Forster, who invited the 19-year-old Noël to dine in the mess.

"The traditional pomp of the atmosphere felt chill at first, but there was an underlying glamour in it which thawed me presently," he said. The sherry might have had something to do with warming his cockles too.

Noël was thrilled to the core when Forster suddenly buckled on his sword, donned an enormous bearskin and marched out to change the guards. Afterwards they got into the port.

One night in the mess swept away all Noël's previous experience of the army, an institution that he now eagerly embraced. Noël remained firm friends with Forster for the next 20 years, though Noël noted, with some regret, that over the years Forster's "timid butter-coloured moustache … became large and quite red".

Noël also became friendly with a captain in the Coldstreams, Jeffery Holmsdale, later Lord Amherst. He was small and fair, and, in Noël's words, "gay and a trifle strained, and there was a certain quality of secrecy about him." Gay men at that time would have needed all the secrecy they could get.

"I dined with him several times," said Noël, "'on guard' and at home with his family. I watched him twinkling and giggling through several noisy theatrical parties, but it took a long while for me to get to know him."

And know him he did. Amherst was Noël's travelling companion throughout the 1920s and '30s, when the two of them were regularly in foreign parts.

Noël also used his homosexuality to further his career. He was young and attractive, and in a series of one-night stands he made his way around the gay Mafia that ran a theatre in the West End. Soon he was out on Broadway, but in New York, his habit of throwing off all his clothes and walking around his apartment naked got him into trouble. Seeing the nude Noël through a window, a cop beat on his door. Noël slipped on one of his trademark silk dressing gowns and invited the cop in for a glass of wine. Noël's manner was so winning, that instead of carting him off to the precinct on a charge of indecent exposure, the cop lent him a gun as his apartment was in a "dangerous neighbourhood".

Back in London, Noël, Gertrude Lawrence* and Beatrice Lillie put on a review called *London Calling*. It was backed by Lord Ned Lathom, one of Noël's gay friends, who liked to hang around with theatre folk. During the run, Noël had a brief fling with Prince George, the Duke of Kent*. It is said that they even went out in drag together and once had to flee down the street in high heels after a police raid. The royal family were not amused, but then the Duke of Kent also took drugs and slept with black people of either sex – which was consider really rather racy back then. To clean up his act, Prince George married Princess Marina, but Noël remained a friend and was a regular guest at their country home, Coppins.

Particularly resentful of this liaison was Edward, the Prince of Wales*, perhaps because Noël was received at Buckingham Palace, while he and Wallis Simpson* were not. Noël had his own theory, though: "He pretends not to hate me, but he does, and it's because I'm queer and he's queer, but unlike him I don't pretend not to be."

When the Duke of Kent died in a plane crash in 1941, Noël rued in his diary that the "young and charming" had died, while the Duke of Windsor lived on.

Coward achieved fame in 1924 with a serious play called *The Vortex*, which is about homosexuality and drug addiction. It attracted the attention of the Wall Street broker Jack Wilson, who saw it on a visit to London.

According to John Gielgud*, Coward's understudy, Wilson was "strikingly good looking, in a beautifully cut dinner jacket with a carnation in his button hole". Noël spotted him sitting in the stalls. So did his co-star Lillian Braithwaite and both of them began playing to him.

When *The Vortex* transferred to New York, Wilson arrived at the stage door of the Henry Miller theatre "drunk enough" to make an advance, but too drunk to remember Noël's name. Noël received an invitation to lunch, but when he turned up at the appointed time and place, he found that he had been stood up. When Wilson appeared at the stage door again, Noël asked why he had not shown up. He said that Noël had not replied to his invitation. It seems there had been a postal mix-up. After a couple more false starts, Wilson came to dinner at Noël's digs, where they became lovers. Then Wilson quit Wall Street and established himself as Noël's business manager. It is thought that Wilson was the inspiration for the song

"Mad About the Boy" – though they were, in fact, the same age. However, there is another theory that Noël had Douglas Fairbanks Jr* in mind when he wrote it. At the time he was a lover of Gertrude Lawrence's*, so maybe she was procuring again.

Coward and Wilson were seen out together in Paris, on the Riviera and at the Lido in Venice, but Jack continued to base himself in New York. It was a long distance affair. In 1926, Noël and Jack were in Venice where they met up with Cole Porter. A rivalry began to see who could put on the most extravagant party. This came to a premature end when the police raided a bash at Cole's house – though it is said that Porter was delighted to see a squad of swarthy Italian policemen forcing entry. The raid would have turned into a full-blown scandal were it not for the fact that the police chief's gay son was among the guests.

Back in New York, Wilson and Porter became friends. Together they would visit the black gay brothels in Harlem, where naked African-American men mixed with well-dressed white men and guests could watch the older prostitutes showing the younger ones the ropes through peepholes. Jack's constant infidelity and compulsive kleptomania took a toll on Noël personally, but he used these emotions to fire his work. It also left him free to have a brief dalliance with Laurence Olivier*.

In 1937, Wilson married French-born Natasha Paley, a Russian princess no less, the daughter of the Grand Duke Paul. It is thought that she was a lesbian and she had previously been married to dress designer Lucian Lelong. Noël attended the wedding, calling it "Jack's 21st fine, careless rapture of youth". He consoled himself by composing a filthy song in French with Baron Nicolas de Gunzburg. The *chanson* described the use of petroleum jelly to make one's machinery suitably slippery for the wedding night and speculated which of them would be on the receiving end. As most of the guests were Wilson's family, only the bride would have understood. Naughty, naughty, Noël.

By this time, Coward was rich and famous, but he was also middle-aged and could no longer go around the gay clubs picking up guardsmen. In 1931, he had auditioned 13-year-old Graham Payn for his revue *Words and Music* and was so taken with the boy that he gave him two small parts. The story goes that they met up again years later and became lovers. He was so much in love with Payn, however, that Coward might have given him one big part there and then.

In 1945, Noël wrote special songs for him in *Sigh No More*, his first post-war revue. One of them, "Matelot", does not exactly hide its light under a bushel.

> Matelot, Matelot
> Where do you go
> My thoughts go with you…
> Though you may find
> Womenkind
> To be frail,
> One love cannot fail, my son,
> Till our days are done.

He might as well have written "Hello Sailor". In fact, Payn often played a sailor on stage for Noël, who wrote "Something about a Sailor", "Sail Away" and "My Kind of Man" for him.

Even though Wilson had been married for eight years by then, he was fiercely jealous when Noël and Payn got together. Noël remained committed to Payn for the rest of his life and tried to make him a star, but he eventually concluded that Payn did not have the ambition to make it. No joke about being a Payn in the arse here.

Although Noël and Graham Payn were an item, it did not mean that Noël could not have a bit on the side – especially as his post-war productions lent him a convenient casting couch. One potential victim was the handsome young actor Kenneth More. Noël had seen him in *Power Without Glory*, a critically acclaimed play that was doing badly at the box office.

Noël was casting *Peace in Our Time*, his play about what life in England would have been like if the Nazis had won the war. He invited More to the Haymarket, where he was packing them in with *Present Laughter*, saying that he had "something that will interest you". Noël greeted More in his silk dressing gown and organised tea. He gave More a copy of the script and invited him to come and discuss the play over dinner at his home in Barnes.

After dinner, Noël turned the lights down low and lulled More with a medley of his songs. Then he got up from the piano and advanced on the nervous young actor, who leapt from his chair in terror.

"Oh, Mr Coward," he blurted, "I could never have an affair with you, because… because… you remind me of my father."

"Hello, son," purred Coward.

More starred in the show and the two men remained friends, but it was actor Louis Hayward that Noël took cruising around the Mediterranean. After visiting Lord and Lady Mountbatten* in Malta, Noël grew ill and had to have his appendix removed. The sailing was pretty disastrous, too. They were wrecked off Corsica, after a "terrible night in the storm with a fainting French Captain and me at the wheel held up by gin and my ex-appendicitis truss".

Noël began a long series of cabaret appearances in Las Vegas, where he met up with Cole Porter again. He partied with Frank Sinatra* and the Bogarts*, and had dinner *à deux* with the gay movie start Tom Tryon.

In the United States, his plays began to appear on television and he found that, on that side of the Atlantic, his fame continued to grow. This brought him to the attention of the scandal sheets and *Rave* magazine rehashed a lot of old rumours about him. Noël complained: "There was an article in *Rave* which, complete with photographs, stated that I was the biggest tulip (better than a pansy) who had ever been imported into America; that during the war I sang 'Mad About the Boy' to an RAF officer and was ducked in a pond by his incensed comrades; that I had set up a young man in Jamaica in a travel agency … It doesn't upset me but it does lead me to think … if I had been seen naked in an opium den with several Negroes stripped for action and the story appeared, I should be in exactly the same position I am in now … I must gird my loins and be prepared for a fresh onslaught."

However, this did not stop him going after whatever he wanted. And girding his loins meant taking an injection of whatever was fashionable at Swiss clinics at the time. He also had a face-lift, though he publicly teased Marlene Dietrich* for doing the same thing.

In New York, he met Ambrose de Bek, who was famous for his all-male parties where all clothing had to be left in the hallway. Noël joined in enthusiastically. One young actor came screeching out of a bedroom: "I've just had sex with Noël Coward."

"Well, do shut up about it," said de Bek. He was an executive at CBS and insisted there was some discretion about what went on in his apartment.

While producing *Nude with Violin* on Broadway, Noël fell for 27-year-old actor William Traylor. He was straight and Catholic, but what actor would give up the chance to appear on Broadway? The affair was fraught. According to the producer Charles Russell, Traylor could not deal with Coward's attentions and tried to commit suicide.

Things were no better on Noël's side. He never knew whether Traylor would turn up for their dates. He even bought a toupee in a pathetic attempt to look younger and more desirable. It was heart-rending and the last time that Noël would fall in love.

"I wish to God I could handle it," he wrote. "But I never have and know I never will. Let's hope that it will ultimately rejuvenate my ageing spirits. Let's hope I get something out of it at least."

Realising that the affair would only bring more heartache and pain, Noël cut short the Broadway run of *Nude with Violin* and took it to California, where Eva Gabor* was cast as the female lead. She claimed to have pimped for Noël during the play's runs in Los Angeles and San Francisco. Afterwards Noël went to Jamaica, where he had just bought a house to lick his wounds. It was there that he sunbathed and held all-male parties where Laurence Olivier* and his lover Danny Kaye* cavorted together, dressed as bride and groom. Then he went back to Graham Payn in London.

And Noël did get something out of the affair with William Traylor – *Cheap Excursion*, where an ageing star gets turned on by a younger actor.

"I'm in love and I'm desperately unhappy," says the star. "I know there's no reason to be unhappy, no cause for jealousy and that I should be ashamed of myself at my age."

Although Graham Payn was shaken by the Traylor affair, he remained a permanent fixture in Noël's life. Noël continued to have casual sex when the fancy took him. Toward the end, when he was no longer capable, he indulged himself, hiring a giant, blond, blue-eyed Swiss masseur called Jean-Rene Huber. Noël found that he could take all his frustrations out on this vision of loveliness. If he called Huber a "stupid cunt" the blond giant just laughed.

Noël Coward died in 1973. He had been a new kind of homosexual. He was not tormented about his sexual identity. Nor did he believe that homosexual love was higher than heterosexual love. He did not try to hide his sexuality, nor did he need to make a song and dance about it. For him, your sexual nature was just something to be accepted, both by yourself and by others.

The greatest tribute to Coward's personal conduct came from his life-long friend Rebecca West, who wrote: "There was an impeccable dignity in his sexual life, which was reticent but untainted by pretence."

We need more like you, Sir Noël.

*The Daisy Chain

Asterisks in the text indicate that the person has appeared in another book in the *Sex Lives...* series. Starred figures, plus those who appear for the first time in this volume, appear in alphabetic order below. Now you too can start to play Truman Capote's* game, "International Daisy Chain" at home – or, better, in bed. You could even play it for a forfeit, Strip Daisy Chain, perhaps. Pick any two people from this list and see how many lovers you need to make a daisy chain between them. The player who can make the chain with the least lovers wins. According to Capote*, Mercedes De Acosta* is the wild card. With Mercedes, he said: "You could get to anyone – from Pope John XXIII* to John F. Kennedy* – in one move." Remember, though, that there are plenty more links in the chain out there in the rest of my *Sex Lives...* series.

Acosta, Mercedes De – *Sex Lives of the Hollywood Goddesses*, *Sex Lives of the Famous Lesbians*, *Sex Lives of the Hollywood Idols*
Auden, W.H. – *Sex Lives of the Famous Gays* (Chapter 4)
Bacall, Lauren – *Sex Lives of the Hollywood Goddesses 2*
Bacon, Francis – *Sex Lives of the Great Artists*
Bankhead, Tallulah – *Sex Lives of the Hollywood Goddesses*, *Sex Lives of the Hollywood Idols*, *Sex Lives of the Hollywood Goddesses 2*
Bardot, Brigitte – *Sex Lives of the Hollywood Idols*
Beaton, Cecil – *Sex Lives of the Hollywood Goddesses*
Benny, Jack – *Sex Lives of the Hollywood Goddesses*
Bernhardt, Sarah – *Sex Lives of the Hollywood Goddesses 2*, *Sex Lives of the Kings and Queens of England*
Bertie, Prince of Wales – *Sex Lives of the Kings and Queens of England*, *Sex Lives of the US Presidents*
Bogart, Humphrey – *Sex Lives of the Hollywood Goddesses 2*
Bonaparte, Napoleon – *Sex Lives of the Great Dictators*, *Sex Lives of the Kings and Queens of England*, *Sex Lives of the Popes*
Britten, Benjamin – *Sex Lives of the Great Composers*

Buchanan, James – *Sex Lives of the US Presidents*

Capote, Truman – *Sex Lives of the Hollywood Goddesses, Sex Lives of the Hollywood Goddesses 2*

Caravaggio – *Sex Lives of the Great Artists, Sex Lives of the Popes*

Caesar, Augustus – *Sex Lives of the Roman Emperors, Sex Lives of the Popes*

Caesar, Julius – *Sex Lives of the Roman Emperors*

Chaplin, Charlie – *Sex Lives of the Hollywood Goddesses, Sex Lives of the Hollywood Idols, Sex Lives of the Hollywood Goddesses 2*

Chapman, Dwight – *Sex Lives of the US Presidents*

Christ, Jesus – *Sex Lives of the Popes*

Churchill, Winston – *Sex Lives of the Hollywood Goddesses, Sex Lives of the Hollywood Goddesses 2*

Cocteau, Jean – *Sex Lives of the Great Artists*

Colbert, Claudette – *Sex Lives of the Hollywood Goddesses*

Coward, Nöel – *Sex Lives of the Hollywood Idols, Sex Lives of the Hollywood Goddesses, Sex Lives of the Hollywood Goddesses 2, Sex Lives of the Kings and Queens of England, Sex Lives of the Great Artists, Sex Lives of the Famous Gays* (Chapter 17)

Crisp, Quentin – *Sex Lives of the Famous Gays* (Chapters 11, 12 and 15)

Dali, Salvador – *Sex Lives of the Hollywood Goddesses 2, Sex Lives of the Great Artists*

D'Annuzio, Gabriele – *Sex Lives of the Famous Lesbians, Sex Lives of the Great Dictators, Sex Lives of the Great Artists*

Dean, James – *Sex Lives of the Hollywood Idols*

Debussy, Claude – *Sex Lives of the Great Composers*

DeMille, Cecil B. – *Sex Lives of the Hollywood Idols*

Diaghilev, Sergei – *Sex Lives of the Hollywood Goddesses*

Dietrich, Marlene – *Sex Lives of the Hollywood Goddesses, Sex Lives of the Hollywood Goddesses 2*

Dillinger, John – *Sex Lives of the Hollywood Goddesses 2*

DiMaggio, Joe – *Sex Lives of the Hollywood Goddesses*

Douglas, Kirk – *Sex Lives of the Hollywood Goddesses, Sex Lives of the Hollywood Goddesses 2*

Duncan, Isadore – *Sex Lives of the Great Artists, Sex Lives of the Famous Lesbians*

Eddy, Prince – *Sex Lives of the Kings and Queens of England*

Edward II – *Sex Lives of the Kings and Queens of England*

Edward VIII (here as Prince of Wales) – *Sex Lives of the Kings and Queens of England*

Ehrlichman – *Sex Lives of the US Presidents*

Eisenhower, Dwight D. – *Sex Lives of the US Presidents, Sex Lives of the Hollywood Goddesses 2*

Elagabalus – *Sex Lives of the Roman Emperors, Sex Lives of the Popes*

Fairbanks, Douglas, Jr – *Sex Lives of the Hollywood Idols, Sex Lives of the Hollywood Goddesses 2*

Forster, E.M. – *Sex Lives of the Famous Gays* (Chapters 2 and 12), *Sex Lives of the Famous Lesbians*

The Daisy Chain

Selected Bibliography

André and Oscar – Gide, Wilde and the Gay Art of Living by Jonathan Fryer, Constable, London, 1997

Arthur Rimbaud by Benjamin Ivry, Absolute Press, Bath, Somerset, 1998

At Your Own Risk – A Saint's Testament by Derek Jarman, Vantage, London, 1992

Auden by Richard Davenport-Hines, Heinemann, London, 1995

Auden and Isherwood: The Berlin Years by Norman Page, Macmillan, London, 1998

Auden in Love by Dorothy J. Farnan, Simon and Schuster, New York, 1984

The Boss – J. Edgar Hoover and the Great American Inquisition by Athan G. Theoharis and John Stuart Cox, Temple University Press, Philadelphia, 1988

Backing into the Limelight – A Biography of T.E. Lawrence by Michael Yardley, Harrap, London, 1985

Because We're Queers – The Life and Crimes of Kenneth Halliwell and Joe Orton by Simon Shepherd, The Gay Men's Press, London, 1989

Charles Laughton – A Difficult Actor by Simon Callow, Methuen, London, 1987

Charles Laughton – An Intimate Biography by Charles Higham, W.H. Allen, London, 1979

Christopher Isherwood by Jonathan Fryer, New English Library, London, 1977

Christopher Isherwood – The Diaries, Vantage, London, 1997

Christopher Isherwood – His Era, His Gang, and the Legacy of a Truly Strong Man by David Garrett Izzo, University of South Carolina Press, Columbia, South Carolina, 2001

Christopher Isherwood and His Kind, 1929-39 by Christopher Isherwood, Eyre Methuen, London, 1976

Derek Jarman by Tony Peake, Little, Brown and Company, London, 1999

Diaghilev by Richard Buckle, Weidenfeld and Nicolson, London, 1979

Diaghilev's Ballet Russes by Lynn Garafola, Oxford University Press, Oxford, 1989

The Diary of Vaslav Nijinsky (Unexpurgated Edition), translated by Kyril Fitzlyon, Allen Lane, London, 1999

The Director – An Oral Biography of J. Edgar Hoover by Ovid Demaris, Harper's Magazine Press, New York, 1975

The Essential T.E. Lawrence – A Selection of his Finest Writing, edited by David Garnett, Oxford University Press, Oxford, 1992

Eye of the Camera – A Life of Christopher Isherwood by Jonathan Fryer, Allison and Busby, London, 1993

From the Secret Files of J. Edgar Hoover by Athan Theoharis, Ivan R. Dee, Chicago, 1991

The Gay 100 by Paul Russell, Kensington Books, New York, 1995

Genet by Edmund White, Chatto and Windus, London, 1993

Genius and Lust by Joseph Morella and George Mazzei, Robson Books, London, 1995

The Golden Warrior – The Life and Legend of Lawrence of Arabia by Lawrence James, Weidenfeld and Nicolson, London, 1990

Hoover's FBI – The Inside Story by Hoover's Trusted Lieutenant by Cartha "Deke" Deloach, Regnery Publishing Inc, Washington, DC, 1995

How to Become a Virgin by Quentin Crisp, Fontana, London, 1981

Jean Genet by Jeanette L Savona, Macmillan Press, London, 1983

Jean Genet in Tangiers by Mohamed Choukri, The Ecco Press, New York. 1973

J. Edgar Hoover – As They Knew Him by Ovid Demaris, Carroll and Graf Publishers/Richard Gellen, New York, 1975

J. Edgar Hoover – The Man and the Secrets by Curt Gentry, W. W. Norton and Co., New York, 1991

Joe Orton by Maurice Charney, Macmillan Press, London, 1984

Kicking the Pricks by Derek Jarman, Vintage, London, 1996

Lawrence – The Uncrowned King of Arabia by Michael Asher, Viking, London, 1998

The Last Years of Nijinsky by Romola De Pulszky, Victor Gollancz, London, 1980

Liberace by Bob Thomas, Weidenfeld and Nicolson, London, 1987

Liberace – An American Boy by Darden Asburty Pyron, The University of Chicago Press, Chicago, 2000

Liberace – An Autobiography, W.H. Allen, London, 1973

Liberace – A Bio-Bibliography by Jocelyn Faris, Greenwood Press, Westport, Connecticut, 1995

The Life and Death of Yukio Mishima by Henry Scott Stokes, The Noonday Press, New York, 1995

The Life of Noël Coward by Cole Lesley, Penguin, London, 1976

The Man Who Was Dorian Gray by Jerusha Hull McCormack, Palgrave, New York, 2000

Marcel Proust by Jean-Yves Tadié, Viking, London, 2000

Marcel Proust – A Biography by George D. Painter, Penguin Books, London, 1990

Marcel Proust – A Life by William C. Carter, Yale University Press, New Haven, 2000

Mishima – A Biography by John Nathan, Da Capo Press, New York, 2000

Morgan – A Biography of E.M. Fortster by Nicola Beauman, Hodder and Stoughton, London, 1993

The Naked Civil Servant by Quentin Crisp, Duckworth, London, 1977

Nijinsky by Richard Buckle, Weidenfled and Nicholson, London, 1980

Selected Bibliography

Nijinsky and Romola by Tamara Nijinsky, Bachman & Turner, London, 1991

Noël and Cole – The Sophisticates by Stephen Citron, Sinclair-Stevenson, London, 1992

Noël Coward by Cliver Fisher, Weidenfeld & Nicolson, London, 1992

Noël Coward – Autobiography, Methuen, London, 1986

Official and Confidential – The Secret Life of J. Edgar Hoover by Anthony Summers, Victor Gollancz, London, 1993

The Orton Diaries, edited by John Lahr, Methuen, London, 1986

Oscar and Bosie by Trevor Fisher, Sutton Publishing, Stroud, Gloucestershire, 2002

Oscar Wilde by David Pritchard, Geddes & Grosset, New Lanark, 2001

Oscar Wilde – A Biography by H Montgomery Hyde, Penguin, London, 2001

Oscar Wilde – A Certain Genius by Barbara Belford, Bloomsbury, London, 2000

Oscar Wilde – His Life and Confessions by Frank Harris, Constable, London, 1938

Oscar Wilde – A Long and Lovely Suicide by Melissa Knox, Yale University Press, New Haven, 1994

The Oscar Wilde File, compiled by Jonathan Goodman, Allison & Busby, London, 1988

Oscar Wilde: Myths, Miracles, and Imitations by John Stokes, Cambridge University Press, Cambridge, 1996

Prick Up Your Ears – The Biography of Joe Orton by John Lahr, Bloomsbury, London, 2000

A Prince of Disorder – The Life of T.E. Lawrence by John E Mack, Harvard University Press, Cambridge, Massachusetts, 1998

Prisoner of Love by Jean Genet, New York Review Books, New York, 1986

A Quest for Proust by André Maurois, Constable, London, 1984

Remembering the Earlier Auden by Edward Upward, Enitharmon Press, London, 1998

Quentin and Philip – A Double Portrait by Andrew Barrow, Pan Books, London 2002

Rimbaud by Graham Robb, Picador, London, 2000

Robbie Ross – Oscar Wilde's True Love by Jonathan Fryer, Constable, London, 2000

Secrecy and Power – The Secret Life of J Edgar Hoover by Richard Gid Powers, Hutchinson, London, 1987

The Secret Life of Oscar Wilde by Neil McKenna, Century, London, 2003

Social Life in Greece by J.P. Mahaffy, Macmillan, London, 1874

Solitary in the Ranks – Lawrence of Arabia as Airman and Private Soldier by H Montgomery Hyde, Constable, London, 1977

Somebody Else – Arthur Rimbaud in Africa 1880–91 by Charles Nicholl, Jonathan Cape, London, 1997

Sun and Steel by Yukio Mishima, Kodanska, Tokyo, 1970

T.E. Lawrence by Desmond Stewart, Hamish Hamilton, London, 1977

T.E. Lawrence – Biography of a Broken Hero by Harold Orlans, McFarland & Company, Inc, Jefferson, North Carolina, 2002

Selected Bibliography

T.E. Lawrence – Unravelling the Engima by Dr Andrew Norman, Central Publishing, Huddersfield, West Yorkshire, 2001

A Touch of Genius – The Life of T.E. Lawrence by Malcolm Brown and Julia Cave, J.M. Dent and Sons, London, 1988

The Trials of Oscar Wilde – Deviance, Morality, and Late-Victorian Society by Michael S. Foldy, Yale University Press, New Haven, 1997

The Unmasking of Oscar Wilde by Joseph Pearce, HarperCollins, London, 2000

W.H. Auden: A Biography by Humphrey Carpenter, Allen and Unwin, London, 1981

W.H. Auden – The Life of a Poet by Charles Osborne, Eyre Methuen, London, 1980

Who's Who in Gay and *Lesbian History*, edited by Robert Aldrich and Gary Witherspoon, Routledge, London, 2001

The Wilde Century by Alan Sinfield, Cassell, London, 1994

Index

Index